*To those who follow as Michael's proudest living legacy;
Jennifer, Regan, Jim and Olivia.*

NO MAN'S SON

A FLIGHT FROM OBSCURITY TO FAME

LINDA CHOWDRY

Copyright © 2020 by Linda Chowdry.

All rights reserved. No part of this book may be reproduced in any written, electronic, recording, or photocopying without written permission of the publisher or author. The exception would be in the case of brief quotations embodied in articles or reviews and pages where permission is specifically granted by the publisher or author.

Linda Chowdry/No Man's Son
Printed in the United States of America

Although every precaution has been taken to verify the accuracy of the information contained herein, the author and publisher assume no responsibility for any errors or omissions. No liability is assumed for damages that may result from the use of information contained within.

No Man's Son/ Linda Chowdry -- 1st ed.

ISBN 9798691623431 Print Edition

Contents

Introduction	1
Author Note	5
PART I	9
Chapter One	11
Chapter Two	35
Chapter Three	41
PART II	57
Chapter Four	59
Chapter Five	63
Chapter Six	69
Chapter Seven	79
Chapter Eight	83
Chapter Nine	87
Chapter Ten	89
PART III	97
Chapter Eleven	99
Chapter Twelve	111
Chapter Thirteen	117
PART IV	129
Chapter Fourteen	131
Chapter Fifteen	137
Chapter Sixteen	147
Chapter Seventeen	155
Chapter Eighteen	173
Chapter Nineteen	177
PART V	181
Chapter Twenty	183
Chapter Twenty-one	189

Chapter Twenty-Two 199
Chapter Twenty-Three 203
Chapter Twenty-Four 215
Chapter Twenty-Five 225
Chapter Twenty-Six 229
Chapter Twenty-Seven 235
Chapter Twenty-Eight 241
PART VI 247
Chapter Twenty-Nine 249
Chapter Thirty 253
Chapter Thirty-One 263
Chapter Thirty-Two 273
Chapter Thirty-Three 285
Chapter Thirty-Four 293
Chapter Thirty-Five 297
Part VII 299
Chapter Thirty-Six 301
Chapter Thirty-Seven 303
Chapter Thirty-Eight 309
Chapter Thirty-Nine 319
Chapter Forty 321
PART VIII 347
Chapter Forty-One 349
Chapter Forty-Two 353
In Their Own Words 363

Introduction

By Greg Anderson
Former Executive Vice President of the Experimental Aircraft Association, Former CEO, Wings Over the Rockies Air & Space Museum, Denver, Colorado

Aviators are calculated risk takers. Even more, they are people who love to see the world from a different vantage point and look at things in their own unique way. They are the kind of people who are compelled to push toward the next horizon. Aviation is the modern-day equivalent of the American Frontier. Instead of people coming to this country and sweeping across the continent settling uncharted lands, aviators seek to explore the frontier above our heads.

Aviation is a demanding industry. Whether it's flying across the ocean, setting a record, building a new airplane, or just going higher, farther, or faster than somebody else, there's a desire to do so with the highest standards. There are a lot of talented, capable people in the aviation community, but few in my personal estimation, rise as high in their significance as Michael Chowdry.

INTRODUCTION

I believe Michael Chowdry has been in my heart all these years because he not only lived an amazing life but became one of those iconic leaders of the aviation community.

Born in Pakistan, Michael spent his youth dreaming about the bigger, wider world and a life that wasn't restrictive in its expectations for him. He wanted to go wherever he wanted, be his own boss, and make his own way. Most important, he longed to appreciate his world from above. Despite a difficult childhood, and a challenging young adulthood in England, aviation-- both literally and figuratively--brought him to the United States where he built a hugely successful business from the ground up. Michael Chowdry saw things he was moved to do in the industry and used his myriad skills and acumen to accomplish far more than most people would ever dare to dream.

In recent years, there's been a rise in paranoia over immigrants, yet so many people owe their livelihood to this particular Pakistani, Muslim-born man. He not only developed a freight airline that crosses the sky we all share no matter our origins but was responsible for creating hundreds of jobs which enabled his American employees to provide wonderful lives for their families.

As a pilot, businessman, father, husband, and a man of faith, Michael embodied the highest and best attributes of aviation and lived a truly American story. Michael was a man formed by his faith as well as aviation. His conversion to Christianity was an important part of his life and relationships. He had a strong sense of his own purpose and destiny. It was often as though he was guided by a providential force outside of himself that enabled him to bring so many people—friends, family, business associates, and employees alike into his fold and thus brought the world closer together.

Michael Chowdry was, and continues to be, a true inspiration to immigrants, entrepreneurs, and anyone who has ever looked up into the sky, dared to dream, and then set about making that dream soar.

Author Note

In April 1981, I was thirty-two years old, newly divorced and working as a sales rep for a small, post-Ma Bell break-up interconnect phone company in Fort Collins, Colorado. One morning, while scanning the local paper for prospects, I spotted an ad for Airlink, a brand new commuter airline that had just opened an office at the Fort Collins Airport. I called and made an appointment with the owner, Ejaz Akbar.

The next afternoon, I showed up to a small office filled with unopened boxes and a young, handsome, sharply dressed business owner with a warm smile.

"You must be Linda," he said offering a firm handshake. "I'm Jazi."

"Where are you from?" I asked, intrigued by his exotic accent.

"Minnesota," he said, with a sparkle in his eye, "via London and Pakistan."

"That's quite a journey. How in the world did you land in in Fort Collins?"

"All I've ever wanted to do was fly," Jazi said glancing out the window at the airfield behind us. "Opportunity brought me here."

Still in sales mode, but definitely intrigued by Jazi and his infectious enthusiasm, I asked, "What are your long-term goals and plans?"

AUTHOR NOTE

"I'm going to make a difference in the aviation industry," he said, without a second's hesitation.

I had met a variety of business people, but none with such a clear vision for their future. Saving more questions for later, I slid into my initial sales presentation. Jazi showed a keen interest and had plenty of questions of his own as I made the case for how the new phone system would save money over his current equipment.

The meeting went so well, I was back a few days later to finalize the details and formally close the deal.

"You should take a flight with me down to Denver sometime," Jazi said after reviewing and signing the contract.

"Sounds fun," I said, always up for an adventure.

"Conditions are supposed to be ideal on Thursday afternoon. Want to be my co-pilot?"

Two days later, I was curious and nervous as I showed up for my first flight in a small airplane. I noted that Jazi loaded the bags, personally greeted the paid passengers, and then piloted the Cessna 172. It was clear he was willing to do whatever it took to make his fledgling company succeed.

Forty-five minutes later, we'd landed at Stapleton airport in Denver with time to kill before the return flight. While we waited, we strolled the airport sharing easy conversation and ice cream cones. I noticed and appreciated Jazi's intelligence and wit. While we weren't on a date, and, in fact, I was involved with someone else, I did note the way the sun shone on his thick, blue-black, wavy hair as we boarded the plane for our return flight. Because there were no passengers scheduled for the return trip to Fort Collins, we were poised to enjoy a peaceful trip for two.

As we took off, the rear suicide cargo doors, closed by a careless ground crew member, flew open.

"We have a big problem," Jazi said with measured calm.

As he contacted the flight tower and requested an emergency landing, my mind raced. I had two young daughters who needed a mother at home. What was I doing circling a major airport with a Pakistani pilot about whom I knew next to nothing in a tiny plane with open rear cargo doors?

All I could think to say was, "Should I close the doors?"

Jazi answered with an emphatic, "NO!"

Thankfully, it was a calm day and I remember a beautiful view of Denver as we circled back and Jazi set the plane down smoothly. We taxied to a safe stop and the doors were secured by Jazi himself instead of the deeply apologetic "ramp rats" who'd failed to do their job properly prior to take-off.

I learned a lot that afternoon about the skill, confidence, and steely nerve of the young Pakistani pilot and businessman—enough to know he was one of the most intriguing people I'd ever met. Little did I know, I'd boarded a flight that would define the next twenty years of my life.

PART I
AN AMERICAN ABROAD
1954-1981

Chapter One

As a young boy, Ejaz Akbar gazed up at the jets streaking across the Pakistani sky and the seeds of a dream were planted. How could he have known he would someday rise to the greatest heights of the American aviation industry. Reaching his destiny, however, would prove to be a turbulent journey composed of will, desire, and an all-consuming need to chart whatever lay over the next horizon.

His story, that of a little boy who just wanted to fly, but was bound to be so much more, is the embodiment of the American Dream. While Ejaz Akbar belonged to America and America belonged to him, his story, like many of the greatest success stories, starts impossibly far away from the United States.

***

The story of Ejaz Akbar began before his birth at the end of World War II. India, a British colony, had helped England win the war with the promise that after the fighting ended and peace prevailed, they would be granted independence.

India had existed for thousands of years as a vast region comprised of small independent princely states. It was only during the

PART I

Moguls and later under the British that it existed as a united subcontinent made up of India (Bharat), Pakistan, and Bangladesh. The subcontinent population was 70 percent Hindu and 30 percent minorities (Muslim, Christian, Sikh, and Buddhist). The movement of Indian Independence had started in the 1920s with the vision of creating a secular independent country. But, as the prospect of attaining independence approached, the minority population realized that under dominant Hindu population they might not enjoy equal rights. Therefore, just a few years before independence it was decided to split the subcontinent into Hindu and Muslim countries.

The consequence was a hurried partition of India into two countries, Hindu India and Muslim Pakistan. Although migration was a choice, the result was a difficult, oftentimes bloody movement of people crossing the newly drawn borders in both directions. Before the subcontinent was divided by religion, people of different faiths lived in general harmony. Afterward, and as a result of the difficulties inherent in having to pick up, leave everything, and move arbitrarily across borders that were once open, there was extreme unrest and an underlying threat of violence that could and did break out at any time.

Ejaz's mother's family were Muslims who lived in a hot, arid border town on the Muslim side of India so they never had to move. Ejaz's mother, Hameeda Begum, was from an influential family. One of her brothers was the only licensed medical doctor, and her father was the one-time mayor of their town. Hameeda lived through the influx of Muslim refugees migrating from India while Hindu friends and neighbors migrated in the other direction. Hameeda and her family helped to organize refugee camps for those Muslims who'd come into Pakistan with only what they could carry.

Hameeda's family were Janjua Rajputs. Most Rajputs used the "Rana" surname. Their ancestor, Raja (king) Mull established a vast kingdom in AD 980 in northwest India. According to the genealogy chart, they converted to Islam in AD 1398. During the Mughal Emperors, they served in commanding positions in the army and king's court. During the nineteenth century, the British rulers of India acknowledged that the Junjua they were held in high-esteem and gave them the caste distinction Martial Race. As a Janjua Rajput, it was natural for this family to assume a leadership role during the post-partition unrest.

Despite the high born stature of the family, Hameeda was destined to live a difficult and turbulent life marked by one tragedy after another. When she was only a teenager, she was coming home on the train from a nearby town where she was training in the medical field when a deadly skirmish broke out between Hindus and Muslims. Startled and afraid, she hid in the train bathroom under the sink, which likely saved her life.

Hameeda was married at very young age to a distant cousin, who was a well-educated school teacher. They were happily married and had a son, who, devastatingly, died suddenly. Soon after, Hameeda's husband also died. She was so grief stricken, she refused to recognize the sudden loss of her son, and then husband. Hameeda couldn't fathom how God could be so cruel to her and abandoned her religion and joined various cults in search of peace. She became a follower of a Hindu Yogi who practiced in spirits and

PART I

magic--so much so that she wanted to perform a ritual on her dead son's grave, believing she could resurrect him. As a result, her family was obliged to exhume the body to convince her that her son was indeed dead.

Several years later, as her grief subsided, she went to school and received a diploma in midwifery. While it was rare for women to work due to the scarcity of jobs and the fact there was only one university in Pakistan, Hameeda accomplished both, finding employment in military hospitals.

During this period, her younger brother Salim, introduced her to Chaudry Mohammed Akbar, a handsome captain in the Air Force.

Hameeda and Mohammed fell in love and married in a Muslim ceremony. As a couple, their observation of the high holidays such as Eid was the extent of their religious practice. Otherwise, they were secular in their approach. They began their life together in a town known as Daska.

With their union came the large parcel of land Mohammed inherited from his father as the first-born son. The land had been given to his father as a reward for his years of service as a high-ranking officer in the Air Force. The tradition of bequeathing land had come from the British occupation and was common practice at the time to curry favor, thank, and sometimes, bribe those in important positions.

The land he'd inherited was in the Punjab, the breadbasket of both India and Pakistan where most of the cotton, wheat, and vegetables, in the country were grown and farmed. Some would say the best mangoes in the world were grown there as well. This land, which was located in a distant sector of the province, was not only valuable but profitable. Local farmers were granted permission to construct small huts or houses on the property, plant crops, and sell the agriculture they harvested, sending the larger percentage of earnings to the owner. The steady stream of farming income ensured that Hameeda and her husband would live comfortably and prosperously in poverty-stricken Pakistan.

Both Hameeda and Mohammed continued to work, however. When she became pregnant, the couple settled in Gujranwala, building a nice house in a new settlement near much of her family. At that time, most babies were typically born at home with a midwife, but Hameeda, who'd begun to work as a public health nurse, was well-educated in modern medicine and wanted to have her baby in the hospital. At the first signs of labor, they drove to nearby Lahore, the capital of the Punjab province, to ensure she could deliver at the Mayo Hospital, the oldest, largest, and best in Pakistan.

Ejaz (Jazi) Akbar was born on October 20, 1954. His parents were elated at the birth of their first son.

Pragmatic and career-oriented, Hameeda left her infant son in the capable and loving hands of a wet nurse named Bundi during the day while she and her husband pursued their careers and otherwise enjoyed their lives as a young, upper-class couple.

Tragically, just as young Jazi turned two, and before they could have any other children together, Mohammed died suddenly of a brain aneurism. Hameeda was left a young, grieving, vulnerable widow yet again, this time with a fatherless toddler. To add to her immeasurable grief, she soon found herself embroiled in a legal battle over the claim to various portions of the land. As Mohammed's son, she assumed the land was Jazi's rightful inheritance. The land, however, had been awarded by the British to Mohammed's father for his service in the Pakistani military as was their custom, but with little regard for the people who'd been living and working there, sometimes for generations.

While technically squatters, the people who lived and farmed there believed they were more entitled to the land than a widow and her young son who'd never even seen the property itself. Ejaz's uncles on his father's side felt they were even more entitled to the land and brought a lawsuit claiming he was illegitimate.

The legal system in Pakistan is complicated and burdened with endless bureaucracy. Legal disputes of any kind quickly become a full-time job that stretches for an indeterminate span of years. In addition, women in Pakistan did not engage in legal matters. Hameeda found it hard to be a working widow with a young child, but impossible to effectively conduct the court case without a man by her side. Needing a remedy for her legal battle, she found herself a suitor in Chaudry Buthar a quiet, yet cunning, man who worked for the government recording land deeds in small villages. A man of the land, but not a land owner himself, he was only too happy to step in to become her third husband and add Sahib (a title similar to Mister) to his name.

While other people would now refer to him as Chaudry Sahib, Buthar would never be considered a Sahib by Hameeda's relatives. Everybody understood that Hameeda married him when Jazi was almost four, not because she loved, or even liked him, but for his current position as a government employee.

Although legal battles could drag on for years, Chaudry Sahib knew how to work through the system and was well-equipped to handle what she needed to have done. In addition, he was tall so Hameeda, who'd lost two husbands and a child and was constantly afraid she would also lose Jazi, imagined he could physically protect her and her young son from anyone who might wish them harm.

Hameeda was Chaudry Sahib's second wife, which was common practice at the time in Pakistan. He split his time between families, and Jazi gained stepsisters in the union, although those children lived with their mother and he wasn't even told about them until his teens. While Chaudry Sahib lived with Hameeda intermittently, his loyalties were likely with his first family.

Loveless by all accounts, their marital/business arrangement suited Hameeda well. She was a widow and a working professional woman in a male-dominated country. She was also determined that her son Jazi be the only inheritor of the land, and she didn't want to cloud the picture in any way. She dangled potential money in front of Chaudry Sahib, who'd been motivated to marry her for primarily that reason. In turn, he helped her with the official matters that needed handling.

Her sheer pragmatism spoke to her survival skills. She always worked and provided for Jazi, but she wasn't wealthy aside from the land. Chaudry Sahib supported himself and his first family on his meager government salary. In essence, he was little more than a hired servant as he took on this second job.

Hameeda and Chaudry Sahib had no children together, and most people assumed he was Jazi's real father, including Jazi who had no memory of his biological father. Although Chaudry Sahib was a quiet and seemingly kind man, he didn't treat his stepson as his own. Jazi was never told otherwise, but all Hameeda's relatives knew and conspired to keep the information from him. In her cunning way, his mother went about poisoning her son's opinion of the man by filling his mind with negative lies and misconceptions of the only father Jazi had ever known.

Their life as a family, though financially stable, was far from happy, and while Jazi's existence was that of a typical Pakistani boy, he was anything but carefree. Hameeda was good to her son in that she saw to it that he has all the necessities and she continued to battle in court for the land to which he was entitled, yet her heart had hardened. She wasn't warm, loving, or nurturing by nature. After all the loss she'd endured, she'd closed off emotionally, but remained extremely possessive and protective of her son. As for Chaudry Sahib, he barely spoke, and was often found in a quiet place with his prayer beads in hand. If he espoused an opinion, Jazi listened respectfully, but their interaction was limited. His mother had seen to it that Chaudry Sahib had little opportunity to be any kind of father to his stepson. Jazi was mindful of all the negative impressions Hameeda had given him of this man he called Father.

Because Hameeda was, or had become, a sour, unhappy woman, and complained about Chaudry Sahib more than anything else, Jazi grew to hate his stepfather almost as much as she did.

For the first six years of his life, he was primarily raised by Bundi who was warm, loving, and nurturing, while Hameeda worked and dealt with details associated with the land dispute.

Understandably confused, he sometimes called Bundi, "Mother."

Hameeda overheard one such incident and fired Bundi on the spot.

Tragically, six-year-old Jazi never saw nor heard from the beloved nanny he thought of as his true mother ever again. A depth of loneliness he'd never experienced settled over him. It was an early, stark, painful lesson in how his mother operated.

He would continue to suffer injustices at her hand.

It was Hameeda's belief that the world was rough and it was her obligation to toughen her son in preparation. She saw to it that he had food and clothing, but she didn't believe in nurturing or coddling. In addition, she was difficult and punitive. In fact, she thought nothing of perfecting her medical technique by doing practice polio immunizations on her young son's back. As a result, permanent circular scars dotted his torso. And, although Pakistani boys are typically circumcised in a ceremony that takes place soon after they are born, Hameeda didn't get around to getting the procedure done for Jazi until he was eight years old. He never forgot the excruciating pain and embarrassment he suffered in the aftermath. As an adult, he grew a mustache to cover a scar from a hard slap Hameeda gave him that had split his lip.

Over the years, Hameeda continued to grow increasingly bitter and abrasive.

As her career evolved, she became a public health nurse and did field work. Moving around was part of her job. Due to her difficult personality, she was sent to the least desirable posts in one rural town after another.

Every time Hameeda moved to another small town, quiet, reserved Jazi moved to a different school. Because she was a proud woman who was acutely aware of her upper class heritage, she would make him dress like a little gentleman. The rural kids resented the medical worker's son wearing a fancier version of the knee-length, cotton, salwar kameez and pants that the rest of the boys wore. Jazi was shy and didn't blend in or make friends very easily and ate school yard dust more than once. It was hard for him to be set apart like that, but Hameeda wouldn't let him mix in, leading to growing feelings of anger and a need to rebel.

Eventually, Hameeda quit working entirely and the family settled in Gujrat, one of the larger cities in Pakistan. They moved into a roomy home complete with an extra bedroom for guests and a large courtyard that featured a shade tree and a fully functional outside kitchen—a common household feature in the warmer regions of Pakistan.

Once they were permanently settled, Hameeda assumed Jazi would comply with her overall plan for him which included following the examples of his uncles and cousins by gaining admission to, and graduating from, a prestigious university. Her oldest brother was a well-known physician, her other brother and his children, and two of her sister's children were all physicians as well. She wanted her son to follow in their highly respected footsteps, marry a well-born Pakistani woman, and Jazi would take over the land once she prevailed in the courts. He would be set for life, practicing medicine and living off the income like a landed gentleman. In her dreams, Hameeda would also be cared for in the Pakistani tradition and criticize and demean her daughter-in-law at will.

Unfortunately for her, academics were not of great interest to Jazi. He did go to school, and he learned to speak English, but even if he initially had an interest in academic pursuits, all the moving around had dulled his desire to be a top student. Plus, he continued to fantasize about being a pilot which was not part of Hameeda's plan. She was not at all pleased by any ambitions that strayed from her carefully drawn path for his life.

Her attitude was no surprise given she was a critical person who constantly poked at those around her, scared away any household help, and made negative comments to the people she supposedly cared for most—namely Jazi.

As a result, there was always a great deal of tension; drama and rebellion became part and parcel of their contentious relationship.

As he got older, Jazi would disappear with his friends—many of whom had no interest in going to school and no particular plans for the future. He lived for outdoor adventure and Hameeda would worry until Jazi returned from wherever he'd gone at whatever time he pleased. She would berate him for leaving without telling her where he was going, or what he did, and staying out too late.

Jazi learned to be submissive in front of his mother because she was always commanding, overpowering and overprotective. In truth, he wasn't usually getting into any particular trouble. He didn't drink alcohol and he didn't smoke cigarettes. Mainly, he and his friends spent their days trying to chase girls, going to the movies, and, often hunting for small game with his air rifle. When he shot something—be it dove, quail, or rabbit—he would always bring it home to cook and eat.

During that time, he and his friend took off on borrowed motor bikes to northern Pakistan without Hameeda's knowledge or permission. On what they considered an adventure to observe a border dispute, Jazi sustained an injury to his leg that had to be treated for days by his aunt and uncle, both of whom were doctors. The

PART I

stories vary as to how he got hurt, including the unlikely theory of getting shot at or having been hit with a bullet that ricocheted, but he was left with a big, permanent scar.

From that moment on, Hameeda spent an inordinate amount of time worrying about what she perceived to be her out-of-control, hapless son.

***

Jazi enjoyed hanging out with his friends, but he spoke with true joy and happiness about the time he spent with his cousins at his beloved Uncle Salim's house in the mountainous region of Abbottabad. This area, north of Islamabad, gained notoriety as the final hideout of Osama bin Laden. In Jazi's youth, however, it was actually a quaint, beautiful region known for fine schools, tight-knit communities, and all-around peaceful living.

Hameeda had grown up with multiple siblings, but was very close with her brother Salim, who was the youngest in the family. When Hameeda married, she remained in the Midlands where they'd grown up. Salim, married Khurshid, the love of his life, and settled in the small, pleasant, family-oriented town in a valley surrounded by mountains where his wife had been born and raised. Although her family didn't initially accept him because he'd dropped out of medical school in his second year, they started a family and happily raised four sons and a daughter.

Abbottabad, which was named after the commissioner who built the first drainage system in the valley, was a famous apple and apricot growing region and a onetime popular recreation and relaxation spot for the British Army. The mountains were cool in summers, but cold and snowy in the winter. The schools in the area were set up to accommodate the seasons: three months of vacation in winter, and only a month off in the summertime.

Once a year, Uncle Salim, who valued having a close-knit family, made a point of loading Khurshid and their large brood into their too-small car (usually an Opal) and went on an annual trip to see family in the Midlands during winter break. At that time of year, the weather was like December in Arizona.

They'd set off with the younger kids up front on his wife's lap, and the older three kids jostling for space in the back. First, he would stop at the Haripur movie theater, one of three theaters he owned, to catch the 9:00 p.m. showing of whatever film was being screened. They'd drive on from there, Khurshid dozing and Salim singing, well into the night. Despite his predilection for getting into fender benders and hitting the occasional stray sheep, they would eventually arrive in Gujrat where they would spend a night or two with Hameeda and Jazi.

Typically, they'd arrive at the concrete and wood house around one in the morning. When they knocked at the door, Hameeda would greet them complaining of a headache and with a wrap tied tightly around her head. In a scene that played out year after year, the kids were hungry and Hameeda hadn't prepared anything ahead of time. She'd start cooking on the wood-burning clay stove only after they'd arrived, and she'd make a small amount of food that they were expected to share.

Due to the heat in Punjab, kitchens were typically outdoors. She'd set up beds for the kids in the outside courtyard as well. While they slept, Salim and Hameeda would catch up, the conversation turning quickly and inevitably to Jazi—specifically Hameeda's concerns about her son and his future. She worried he wasn't interested in getting a formal education like she felt he should be. She worried he didn't listen to her advice. She worried he wasn't cut out to be much of anything.

Salim was more concerned about his nephew's lack of appropriate guidance from his sister and Chaudry Sahib, although he'd never voice such an opinion outright. Instead, Salim stepped in as best he could, serving as a father figure to Jazi. He wanted to mentor him and do anything to help him become the successful young man Salim knew he could be.

Jazi's cousins would wake up to a breakfast of chapati or fried bread, tea, a refreshing yogurt drink known as mango lassi, and their father quietly speaking with Jazi.

Jazi's head would be down as Salim asked him, "Why aren't you studying harder? Your mother is very concerned."

Salim would take into consideration whatever Hameeda had said about her son and what Jazi said in response. As a result, Salim developed a plan of action for molding his nephew into the man he was destined to become. He implemented his plan when Jazi and Hameeda came to visit them, which they did, for a month every summer.

Jazi, an only child who was no stranger to intense loneliness, couldn't wait for this month every year to be carefree and fun with his cousins, particularly his favorite cousin, Shazad.

Back home in Abbottabad, Salim's wife, Khurshid also worked in healthcare, treating patients at the Red Cross civil hospital for women. As the only female in the town with medical training, she basically served as a doctor. She not only worked at the walled compound, but was so valuable an employee, they gave the family a huge house surrounded by fruit trees on the expansive property.

Because she was an educated woman working long hours, the family didn't operate in traditional Pakistani fashion. Whatever male dominance prevailed in the rural areas and was part of Pakistani culture didn't much exist in their liberal household. Salim prepared meals when he wasn't off working. Since the kids participated as well, Jazi developed a lifelong love of cooking and Pakistani cuisine while at his cousins' home.

Due to Khurshid's position, they enjoyed a very comfortable lifestyle. They had servants to do the domestic work. Because they lived in the mountains, they never used fans. Food was kept in a mesh cabinet outside to stay cool. There was no central heating, and the nights were chilly. The servant would light a fire in the bedroom fireplaces and put a hot water bottle in the beds before they retired for the evening.

By the time they got up in the morning, the sun was out, and there was a warm fire going in the indoor kitchen. It was far too cold to have an outdoor set up like Hameeda had in the Punjab, but they did have an outdoor dining table in summer, complete with pots where they'd pour hot water to keep the food warm. On summer mornings, they would have tea outside.

It was a different life than the one Jazi lived in Gujrat. Jazi and his cousins spent their days running along the barrier walls of the property, eating apricots and plums off the trees, taking wood off a nearby fence to play swords, and spending endless hours playing

PART I

soccer on the broad expanses of lawn. They never watched television. There were no coffee shops or tea houses, much less bars or pubs. Home was the hub of their life and they shared most activities together.

One evening, Jazi, Shazad, and one of the older brothers decided to sneak out. They jumped the wall and went to see the nine p.m. movie.

In those days, the women and kids sat together in a different section, separate from the men. The movies were projected from two large film reels. There was a twenty minute intermission where people ate, drank, and socialized.

When the lights came on halfway through, there were friends of the boys' mom in the audience. Shazad, his brothers, and cousin, Jazi, were treated to a chorus of, "Oh my God, those are Khurshid's kids!"

They bought snacks, chatted with them, and of course, told Salim and his wife that the boys had been there.

It was just too 'dangerous' to do anything wrong in such a small town where everyone knew the family. Jazi, who was used to roaming around as he saw fit, learned that his behavior wasn't acceptable when he was staying with his cousins.

From then on, when Jazi and Shazad went into town, it was mostly to shop at the local open air markets. Since they had no refrigeration, they'd go daily to pick up fresh ingredients for meals.

Salim had a bias that lamb or chicken should only be eaten once a day, at lunch, and beef was never eaten. Dinner was meatless and usually consisted of vegetables or lentils. He would rotate certain foods into the menu, pronouncing them good for your liver, good for your heart, etc. Even though they went from having a wood-burning to a kerosene oil stove, Salim stuck to the wood and a clay pot. He never would eat anything made in a stainless steel, silver, or aluminum.

"Why won't you eat beef?" Jazi would ask him.

"There's a lot of tuberculosis and these animals don't get treated for that."

In the evenings, as soon as they were finished eating and all homework was done, all the boys would race outside to play and roughhouse. Jazi enjoyed being in the mix and they made the most of their simple fun when their cousin came to visit. Jazi made the most of it as well. He was never rebellious, nor caused any trouble. He did go hunting, but only with permission. He'd bring back the ducks he'd shot and look to his aunt and uncle for affirmation. He saw his Uncle Salim as a father figure and treated his aunt with great respect. Jazi loved being there so much he didn't even complain about his aunt's insistence that they shower in cold spring water from the spigot in the front yard.

Hameeda, however, brought her bitter, critical, dramatic personality. The household help couldn't stand her and seemed to quit regularly when she was in town.

One summer, she announced to Khurshid, "This kitchen is a mess. While you're off at work, I am going to help you by cleaning everything."

As soon as Khurshid left for the day, Hameeda took the contents of the kitchen outside and spent the next few hours ordering the servant around while she scrubbed every surface herself. By afternoon, the servant was gone for good.

PART I

The kids, including Jazi, were forcefully recruited to put the entire kitchen back together in time for the evening meal.

***

Salim and Khurshid lived in an area that was renowned for its schools. People from all over the country sent their kids to the region to get an education. The Rana children were sent to an Irish Catholic elementary school across from the hospital where some of the teachers were British ex-pats who had chosen to stay after Pakistan became a country. For their first three or four grades, the school did not have a Pakistani-based curriculum. Everything was in English.

While the early grades are similar, the educational system in Pakistan differs from the United States model as the student advances. After 10th grade, there are tracks a student must choose between, all of which branch off into specialties. One is pre-medical, one is pre-engineering, and a third is pre-art. The 11th and 12th grade are known as college. By the time a Pakistani student is done, they have applied for university and enter upon graduation. The system for admissions is merit based, with some allowances for specific quotas. If forty students were accepted in a specific track, the top forty in the province where the schools were located got the spots.

Salim and Khurshid sent three of their four children to a highly prestigious boarding school in eighth grade that required a multi-day testing process and took only ninety students from 5,000 candidates. Students who got into the school, which was modeled after a military academy, were considered top in the nation and could go anywhere or do almost anything they desired professionally upon graduation.

In the years before they started, Salim would take each of them to tag along with him during their three months of winter vacation so they could learn to understand the business world. When Jazi came into town, he came along too.

Salim used to tell all of them, "I want you to know how to live like a poor person and a rich person so you can sleep on the floor as well as the bed. Neither should worry you."

There was plenty to learn from him and they all soaked in his wisdom and advice, particularly, Jazi.

When he was twelve, Hameeda's legal dispute grew more heated. She worried that Jazi could be in danger and decided he would be safer in the mountains with his uncle and cousins.

"Dad, is Jazi going to go to school with us?" The boys asked when they heard Jazi was coming to stay.

"No," he said, definitively.

"No?" they'd repeat, shocked because education was the highest of priorities in their home.

"Jazi needs his education, but not at the school you are attending," Salim would say. "He is going to be a businessman."

Instead, Jazi went to the local school and also worked as Salim's intern. He accompanied his uncle to his three movie theaters and even off to Lahore, where the movie studios were located. Like Mumbai, much of the movie wheeling and dealing happened there.

While all the children had 'interned' for him, Jazi soaked in business unlike any of the others. The experience of accompanying his uncle gave him a lifelong passion for movies and a not-so-secret

PART I

fantasy of someday becoming a Bollywood producer. After he'd become a successful pilot and businessman, that was.

Like his mother, Jazi was developing into a self-reliant, tenacious, and fearless person. While he'd definitely inherited some of the tougher aspects of Hameeda's personality, he saw that being dramatic, harsh, and angry didn't serve her well. Instead, he learned to master that aspect of their shared qualities. Jazi was a person who could have fired Bundi, the nanny, just as his mother had done, but he knew enough not to follow this instinct. He also learned some more refined, astute qualities during his time interning for his Uncle Salim. Jazi learned the art of being a very tough negotiator while observing Salim make business deals.

Salim not only nurtured and encouraged his nephew but even risked his life on his behalf during the court fight, taking his brothers as well as his older son, Yazi, to throw squatters off the land that was to become Jazi's. Hameeda also had reason to believe that Jazi's uncles had been behind the scenes encouraging the squatters to take hold of the land. A gunfight broke out and the squatters tried to shoot at Salim and the men, but luckily no one was hurt, or worse. The police were called, but to no avail, due to the lawlessness in that part of the country.

In the end, Salim had been right there, as always, looking out for his nephew's best interests.

***

Jazi finished tenth grade. Whether it was his long-standing dream to take to the skies, or sheer rebellion against the life Hameeda had mapped out for her son, Jazi wanted no part of her plan. He didn't care in the least that the land she was fighting for would be his by birthright. He didn't want to attend university, and he hated how she would scold and embarrass him in front of the family for his lack of interest in formal education. He was tired of his mother's protective, jealous behavior and their constant bickering. Above all, he was furious when his maternal grandmother told Jazi that his mother had misled him about Chaudry Sahib, the man he believed to be his biological father, leaving him feeling he had no father at all.

At that moment, Jazi decided that he wanted to leave Pakistan entirely. He'd had enough of seeing scenes like vendors weighing out rice for sale with a brick hidden at the bottom of the scale in order to cheat the shoppers. In his mind, this was indicative of how everything worked in Pakistan. His home country was poor, corrupt, and politically fraught. During this time, Zulfakar Ali Bhutto gained power and nationalized all industries, banks, and other institutions. The result was massive unemployment, lack of opportunities, and prospects for young ambitious youth like Jazi. Young people started to migrate en masse to the Middle East and Europe.

He was convinced he needed to seek his own fortunes elsewhere.

His friend Naseem had already immigrated to England. In those days, there were ways to get a visa by being admitted to a school there, but attending after you arrived was entirely optional.

Exotic and fascinating London, he decided, was where he was headed as well.

Hameeda did everything she could to change his mind. She couldn't believe he had decided not to go to university and refused

PART I

to accept that he was planning to leave Pakistan entirely. Maybe he had, as people said, inherited her tenacity, work ethic, and drive, but he had no job and no plan other than to leave the country. Hameeda had spent her entire adult life making sure he inherited land that was rightfully his. She'd sacrificed her own happiness to ensure his life would be comfortable and easy. Worse, she couldn't conceive of the fact that her only child would abandon her so thoughtlessly. The whole idea was, in her mind, senseless. Jazi could stay, never work, and still live a very good life as a landlord.

Terrified of losing her son, Hameeda insisted Jazi accompany her to see all the relatives in the hopes that they would talk him out of his plan.

Unfortunately for her, the outcome was very different than she hoped. She always feared, rational or not, that Jazi was in danger because of the land dispute. Everyone felt that Jazi would actually be safer in London, at least in the short run. After all, he would be a continent away from squatters or the relatives they long suspected had funded the squatters from coming after him.

Uncle Salim, the most powerful voice in the family, took a different tack. He believed his nephew was going to be a very successful businessman and felt it necessary that Jazi leave the country to learn about business and other cultures. He felt that his nephew not only should go to London, but needed to leave Pakistan, in order to be successful.

Because Salim was her favorite brother and she knew he had Jazi's best interests at heart, she reluctantly agreed to allow her son to move, temporarily, to London. It also helped that Salim gave Jazi the money for the flight.

Despite being a frightened teenager, Jazi boarded an airplane for the first time. The plane took off and he looked out into the clouds at the landscape he was leaving behind. He had no idea where this path would take him, but he was excited to begin the journey.

Chapter Two

In the aftermath of World War II, England was short nearly a generation's worth of working-class young men. In order to resolve labor shortages in steel, textile, and engineering industries, the British government instituted a policy of open immigration from both India and Pakistan. Doctors from Pakistan were recruited by the National Health Service. Other highly skilled workers were encouraged as well. A huge migration followed and Pakistani communities sprung up in London and took root in various boroughs throughout the city.

When the UK experienced deindustrialization in the 1970s, many British Pakistanis lost their factory jobs and turned to self-employment, opening businesses like the ubiquitous halal butchers and grocers that now line the streets of London's ethnic neighborhoods. One in seven British Pakistani men worked as a taxi driver, cab driver, or chauffeur.

Sixteen-year-old Ejaz Akbar landed at London's Heathrow airport in 1970. While the move was somewhat natural given the large, established Pakistani community, the hustle and bustle of Lahore, Pakistan was nothing compared to the overwhelming, multi-cultural, metropolis that was London, England. He was on his own and would remain that way for the duration of his years in Great Britain.

PART I

Then again, Jazi was nothing if not a survivor.

His friend Naseem, who had immigrated earlier, helped him find room and board with a Pakistani family in their modest home in the township of Slough. Unlike homes in Pakistan, there was only one bathroom for the whole family. During cold nights, Jazi had to put a pence in the heater to turn it on and then feed it periodic coins to keep it going. To earn change for his heater, as well as pay for his accommodations, Jazi worked in the owner's grocery store delivering food and doing whatever needed to be done at the store, dusting and stocking shelves, and waiting on customers. As soon as he was able to get his driver's license, Jazi also drove a cab and worked as a blood courier, transporting blood from one hospital to another. To appear older, he grew a mustache and took up smoking. He drove at night until the bars closed, dealing with drunks throwing up in his cab and being cheated out of fares.

Jazi quickly knew his way all around London, but England never felt like home. He'd left Pakistan as rebellion against his upbringing and a future in which he had no freedom to be a pilot, or really anything beyond that which Hameeda planned for him. Unfortunately, life in London wasn't altogether different. He was lonely, had transitory friendships, and he spoke little of this time period in his life beyond how difficult life was. Unwelcome to become part of British culture, working-class Pakistani men fraternized amongst each other. Work was endured, not enjoyed. Despite strong Indian and Pakistani communities, London didn't provide an easy experience for an immigrant. Over the seven years he would spend in the United Kingdom, Jazi experienced racism and saw that roads toward education and careers were closed, not because of his mother, but because he was brown-skinned and considered working-class.

Instead of succumbing to prejudice or limitations, Jazi grew that much more determined to make his way in the world. He'd come from a very well-educated, accomplished family and though he had no interest in being a doctor or lawyer, he intended to prove his worth and realize his dream of becoming a pilot.

He was grounded in England due to a variety of factors outside of his control, but he wasn't one to accept limitations, so he looked to the United States. To him America was the land of opportunity and the place where he could pursue his passion for flight and the reality of success in aviation. The sky was literally the limit.

The clearest path for entering the United States and staying there was as a student. To that end, Jazi researched gaining admission to a school and getting a degree in aviation. He found two programs that offered business aviation: Embry Riddle Aeronautical University in Florida, and the University of Minnesota at Crookston.

While there are always a variety of obstacles a prospective student must overcome to obtain admission from overseas—everything from finances and dealing with mountains of foreign paperwork to adjusting to a completely unknown culture, Jazi had an even bigger hurdle than most: Hameeda.

Back in Pakistan, his mother was nearing the end of her decades-long court battle against Jazi's uncles for the land. Assuming a favorable outcome, she continued to dream of welcoming back her one and only son who would take residence on the land to which he was rightfully entitled. From there, he would get married to a nice Pakistani girl from a good family—a girl who understood her place, especially in regard to being subservient to her mother-in-law. Jazi and his bride would have children and they would all live together in comfort until the end of her days.

When it was time to call Hameeda about money for school in America, Jazi's fingers trembled. He dialed the series of numbers connecting him to the operator in Pakistan who would connect him with his cold, obstinate mother. Because calls to Pakistan had to be booked ahead of time, he spent three days practicing what he'd say.

With the sound of her hello he feared he wouldn't be able to speak at all, but despite his trepidation and a staticky connection, he didn't waver as he laid out his plans for the future.

"I've always wanted to be a pilot. It's the only thing I've ever really wanted," he told Hameeda. "It's time for me to go about the business of getting my education so I can achieve my goal."

"Acha," she said, letting him know he had her attention.

Jazi took a deep, silent breath for courage. "In order to get the finest education possible, I need to go to the United States where they have the best aviation programs in the world."

There was silence on the other end of the line.

When he was sure she hadn't hung up, Jazi went on to explain that by getting his pilot's training in the United States, he was setting himself up for a career that could take him worldwide. He omitted, of course, that despite the training he would receive, he never intended to return to Pakistan.

Jazi knew Hameeda's continued silence didn't indicate agreement, but she hadn't hung up either. Certain it was just a matter of time until she did, he rushed to lay out the steps he'd taken, including applying to and having been accepted at aviation business programs at both Embry Riddle in Florida and the University of Minnesota at Crookston.

Hameeda asked him about the locations, reputations, and offerings of the two schools. He explained that both were top notch, outlined the differences between the two, and reiterated that he didn't care where he went, just that he intended to enroll in one or the other.

When he was finished making his case, Hameeda, shrewd businesswoman that she was, delayed giving him an immediate answer. "I need time to obtain a map and familiarize myself with the geography of the United States."

"Okay," he said, wanting to feel relieved that she hadn't said no, but knowing he couldn't celebrate yet.

"Call me back and I will have a decision for you," she said.

The line went dead.

Jazi scheduled a follow-up call immediately after they hung up.

The soonest appointment he could make was in another three days, but it might as well have been three months. He vacillated between hope and despair, the suspense nearly killing him. He needed the funds from home. He couldn't afford to go to school, much less an aviation program in the United States which required additional fees beyond tuition to get his pilot's license. He spent sleepless nights thinking about his future and how it hinged on his mother's decision, one way or the other.

Finally, it was time to make the call.

Jazi struggled to control the quaver in his voice as Hameeda answered.

PART I

"Have you made your decision?" he asked.

"I have," she said.

"I will only pay if you attend the University of Minnesota, Crookston," she said, to Jazi's surprise and disbelief. "Minnesota offers an equal program for a more reasonable price."

"Wonderful!" Jazi said, readily and joyfully.

As he thanked her over and over for allowing his dream to become a reality, he should have known that her motives for having him go to Minnesota were not simply fiscal.

In fact, her decision didn't involve tuition expenses at all.

Hameeda knew her son well. He wasn't going to take no for an answer. She also knew from the research she'd done that Daytona Beach, Florida was sunny and warm. Crookston, Minnesota, on the other hand, was just ninety miles south of the Canadian border and would be utterly freezing from early fall through late spring. She knew Jazi was anything but enamored with cold, drizzly, overcast London. Hameeda was convinced the frigid temperatures would drive him back to Pakistan, where he belonged.

More determined than ever, Jazi filed all the necessary paperwork, was granted a student visa, and booked his flight.

Chapter Three

Twenty-two-year-old Jazi Akbar arrived in the United States in July of 1976. Waiting for him at Newark airport were Hameeda's sister's children—his cousins Maqbool, Masood, and Masood's wife, Sultana. All three had been part of Hameeda's failed campaign to talk her son out of leaving Pakistan. Now in their early thirties, they too had emigrated from Pakistan and were permanently and happily settled in the United States.

Jazi spent his first few days in America at Masood's comfortable home in picturesque and aptly named Bethlehem, Pennsylvania. While visiting with his cousins, Jazi got his first taste of American life, the highlight of which was a barbecue in Masood's backyard. Jazi was struck by the fact that Maqbool and Masood had a large, racially diverse group of friends. He loved everything about the party—the food, the mixed company, and the friendly atmosphere. He had such a good time that at some point during the evening, he turned to Masood and said, "America is home."

Masood, who felt exactly the same way, nodded and smiled.

A few days later and due to attend his first day of classes, he bid his cousins farewell, got on a plane, and headed into the heartland of his new country: the sugar beet farming community of Crookston, Minnesota, U.S.A.

PART I

Jazi arrived on the small, upper Midwestern campus, settled into his dorm room, enrolled in his first semester classes, and went to see *Star Wars* his first American movie on U.S. soil.

He went out of his way to introduce himself to everyone he encountered and attended the new student orientation. As part of the festivities, the kids took a bus tour of the town. Everyone was talking, laughing, and joking. Jazi, shy and reserved by nature, told a joke that was considered hilarious in England, not realizing it didn't quite translate in the U.S., particularly in rural Minnesota.

His inevitably corny joke flopped, but his warm nature and infectious laugh were a hit.

Becky Stolhammer, a fellow new student and soon-to-be friend, thought, "boy this guy isn't cut from the same cloth as the rest of us."

Becky's thoughts were prophetic, as Jazi would soon find himself faced with a challenge that would test anyone's mettle and determination. Classes hadn't even started when he got a call from his mother.

"We won!" Hameeda exclaimed. "The court ruled in our favor!"

"Congratulations!" Jazi said. He had never heard his mother sound happy and she was elated. "This is truly cause for celebration."

"We'll have a big party as soon as you get back home," she said. "I'm getting you a ticket."

"I can't come home right now," he said. "School is about to start."

"You don't need to go to school anymore. You are a land owner!"

Finally on the way to fulfilling his destiny, Jazi had no intention of returning to Pakistan, possibly ever, regardless of the circumstances.

"I need to start class," he told her. "I'm where I'm supposed to be."

Despite the contentious nature of the conversation, Jazi assumed they would put the celebration on hold... indefinitely, as far as he was concerned.

Hameeda was clearly disappointed, trying everything from guilt to anger but they eventually hung up agreeing, at least in Jazi's mind, to disagree. He put the uncomfortable thought that it wasn't finished out of his mind.

Jazi started classes at Crookston. He was excited to take everything from the required liberal education offerings to the one class that he'd come halfway across the globe to be able attend: Introduction to Aviation.

On the first day, the instructor began to review the syllabus, explaining that the class would prepare them for the FAA private pilot written exam and teach them everything from FAA regulations, weather, radio navigation, flight safety, to emergency procedures. He was halfway through the outline when the registrar walked into the lecture hall and said he was looking for Ejaz Akbar.

Jazi raised his hand.

"Please collect your things and come with me."

"Why?" Jazi asked, grabbing his books.

"Your tuition is unpaid, so you can no longer attend this class or any other," the registrar responded.

"What?" Jazi asked, stunned.

Mortified and upset, he rushed to the phone to schedule a call to Pakistan.

He spent another three agonizing days wondering and worrying about what had happened while he waited for the call to be connected to his mother.

"I told you," Hameeda said when he finally got through. "It's time to come home."

Hameeda, who had given him money to fly to the States, had never intended to pay for his tuition. Not only hadn't she paid anything toward his first semester, she informed him that she had no plans of doing so in the future.

Jazi was devastated, shocked, and deeply hurt that his mother was willing to go to such lengths to get him to come back to Pakistan. He wasn't entirely surprised, however. Years later, he'd recount the story with a kind of grudging admiration. After all, this was a woman who'd brilliantly strategized her way into winning a seemingly impossible, nearly twenty-year court battle, doing whatever it took--including marrying Chaudry Sahib to do her legal bidding.

"America is my home," he told her and hung up the phone.

Hurt, dead broke, and all but abandoned in a foreign country, Jazi spoke with the financial aid office about what he needed to do in order to remain in school. He followed their directions, applying for loans and financial aid. He procured a work study position which had him manning a campus information desk, finding it was an excellent way to meet people. He also got an additional job driving a van that took students without vehicles (or who were too hungover to drive) to the church of their choice on Sunday mornings. Because he was from a Muslim background and didn't drink, it was an ideal way to make some badly needed extra money.

Jazi had learned from Salim that if he wanted something in life, he had to be willing to work for it and to channel disappointment into determination. Despite his financial woes, Jazi immersed himself in school and campus life. He became a friendly, well-known fixture at the main information desk. He spent time with a group of international students. In addition, he attended a Christian campus ministries group—not because he was particularly interested in religion—but because they organized fun outings and retreats.

It was at one of these retreats that he and Becky Stolhammer, whom Jazi had met at orientation and spotted around the small campus, struck up what would become an enduring friendship. Fascinated about where he'd come from, who he was, and wondering how a Pakistani Muslim wound up in Crookston, Minnesota, she began to ask him questions.

Jazi told her he was an only child whose father died when he was a toddler. He told her about his mother, a public health worker who was overbearing, protective, and preoccupied with their family land dispute. He also shared the story of how he'd ended up in Minnesota at his mother's urging, only to have her pull the financial rug out from under him.

As for why he'd come to Crookston in the first place, he simply told her, "to fly."

When she asked him why he was at a Christian retreat, he told her he'd joined the group because he'd been welcomed and that he was only Muslim by culture. Jazi wanted to be around people who accepted him. With no family, and only newfound friendships in Crookston, he also spent far too much time alone. He'd spent his first Thanksgiving holiday at the campus infirmary where he'd slept on the exam table because the dorms were closed. He didn't have anywhere to go for Christmas that first year either, so he spent two weeks alone on campus, yet again in the infirmary.

"The highlight was Perkins," he later told Becky, "I discovered I can get two eggs and a piece of toast for ninety-nine cents."

Faced with deep loneliness after his holidays, he was determined to double his efforts to fit in, make friends, and build relationships. Luckily, Jazi's wealth in terms of his social circle and friendships constantly multiplied. As an international student, he stuck out at Crookston, but used the notoriety to his advantage, making an effort to get to know people, cooking Indian dishes for friends, and eventually running for and being elected to the Student Senate.

Still, Jazi's financial circumstances were a perpetual struggle. Embarrassed, he kept his dream of owning a Pinto station wagon (because he could fold the seats down and sleep in the back) to himself. While he was eventually able to buy an old, used hatchback and managed to pick up a black-and-white TV, his tight finances remained front and center throughout school.

Although he was in the aviation program and Becky Stolhammer was in a dietetic technician program in the school of hotel and restaurant management, the two continued to cross paths on campus and at the occasional retreat. It was clear that Jazi was flourishing academically at Crookston, but Becky sensed he still felt unsettled and lonely. As one of six children from a family that included foster kids, and was known for being warm, welcoming, and commonly had multiple foreign guests crowded around the dinner table, Becky accurately assessed that Jazi lacked the comfort of family. The Stolhammers were a mission-oriented clan and Becky had found a personal mission of her own on the college campus. It was only natural that she invite him to make the three-and-a-half hour trip east of Crookston to her hometown of Hibbing, Minnesota for a weekend visit.

***

Jazi was touched by Becky's invitation, but he was overjoyed when he arrived at the Stolhammer home. Knowing that Jazi and Becky had developed a brother/sister type relationship, Becky's father, Ken, and mother, Signora, welcomed him as though he were a long-lost son. It was certainly something he'd never before experienced.

Ken Stolhammer, a quiet, intelligent man, started his career as a math teacher, attained his masters, and became a full-time guidance counselor at the local high school. Signora was a homemaker who spent her days managing their brood of children. Married in 1954, the very year Jazi was born, they settled in Hibbing in 1963 and were an established family in the small community of 15,000.

To say Hibbing lacked diversity was the greatest of understatements. Other than a handful of residents and a sprinkling of foreign students at the local community college, the differences between people came down to the specific Scandinavian country from which their ancestors had hailed. The Stolhammers were church-going folk who attended a congregation where visitors from different cultures and countries were welcomed with open arms. Ken, who'd gone to school at the University of Minnesota in Minneapolis, taught his children to celebrate differences, and reach out to people from other places and cultures. His daughter

PART I

Becky clearly took his lesson to heart when she befriended Jazi and welcomed him to the fold.

Jazi was delighted by the warm chaos at the Stolhammers. He reveled in their hospitality and generosity. He particularly enjoyed their lively dinner conversations about politics, current events, religion, and his favorite topic: flying. Becky's older brother was also getting his private pilot's license, and the two had plenty to talk about.

All weekend long, Jazi took part in family activities. He ate whatever was served at meals. One morning he was still asleep when everyone else had breakfast. When he awoke, he was embarrassed to eat alone, preferring to wait until the next time they all sat down together. Life at the Stolhammers offered the perfect antidote to his lonely childhood with Hameeda and Chaudry Sahib.

Contrary to Hameeda's prediction, the cold of Minnesota didn't freeze her son's love of his new country, especially not after being welcomed into this family's warm embrace. As a result, Jazi started making the trip to Hibbing on a regular basis, visiting over long weekends, holidays, and spending extended time over the summers with his "American family." It was with the Stolhammers that he learned American customs and traditions, celebrating everything from the 4th of July to his first homemade birthday cake. In their Christian household, Jazi also experienced unconditional love and heard the story of the Gospel.

Before the end of his college career, he became a Christian. While he hadn't come from a strict nor overly observant Muslim family, the sheer act of renouncing his birth religion and converting made quite a statement of his newfound allegiance to family and faith.

Once Jazi left Pakistan, he never looked back, and his welcome to the Stolhammer family only confirmed his decision.

***

As part of the two-year degree, aviation students at the University of Minnesota, Crookston learned to fly via a joint program with the University of North Dakota Aerospace Foundation. Jazi was in his element around airplanes and talking with pilots. Consequently, it came as no surprise to anyone that he loved every moment of the process of learning to pilot an airplane.

He attended his regular classes on the UMC campus and drove in his newly acquired Pinto station wagon to learn to fly at the University of North Dakota Aerospace Foundation flight training center at the Crookston Municipal Airport, located three miles north of the University. There, he was provided the aircraft, flight instructors, and all the requisite materials needed to get his private pilot's license.

Jazi didn't waste any time putting his enduring passion-turned-newfound-skill to work. One cold winter weekend, as soon as he had his pilot's license, he rented a small plane and flew Becky back home. Jazi took great joy in every step of the process, from de-icing the plane to flying her into and out of the tiny Hibbing airport.

Jazi had gained his license to fly single engine propeller planes but had his sights set on getting instrument rated which would allow him to fly in weather, not rely on visual flight rules, and operate an aircraft in conditions where there wasn't a minimum of three miles visibility. Unfortunately, the cost was a prohibitive $800. By that point, he was close enough with the Stolhammers to ask Ken for a loan. Jazi had become such a part of the family that he would serve as an usher at Becky's upcoming wedding to her soon-to-be husband, Eldon. Ken didn't hesitate to front Jazi the funds. He knew this remarkable young man would be true to his word and pay him back soon after he graduated.

Ejaz Akbar graduated from the University of Minnesota, Crookston in May 1978, receiving a degree in Agricultural Aviation with an emphasis in Business Aviation.

Upon graduation, he paid back his loan to Ken Stolhammer by working at an ever-growing variety of aviation related jobs from selling Piper airplanes to giving flying lessons to farmers. Ever fascinated by his new profession, he learned how to work on airplanes and grew adept at the technical and mechanical aspects of airplane operation. In the process, he logged enough flight hours to test for his commercial pilot's license.

***

As an aviation student at Crookston, Jazi developed connections for a specific job opportunity that would not only pay the bills, but satisfy his adventurous spirit and need to take flight: crop dusting. Jazi gained his commercial pilot's license as well as a Class Two medical license and a permit from the Environmental Protection Agency. Once he'd met the many requirements and proved to be both insurable and capable, he applied and was hired. His new career would prove to be exhilarating, demanding, and develop his skills in one of the most rewarding and necessary, but dangerous areas of aviation.

While turbine, and even some rotary aircraft, are commonly in use today, Stearman aircraft were once the cornerstone of the crop dusting industry. In the 1970s, there were around 4,500 of these aircraft in use around the country, many of them converted from piston-driven, 220 horsepower World War II Air Force trainers to 450-horsepower engines for higher performance.

The Stearman was considered the Harley Davidson of the air. It was a smooth, colorful, fun-to-fly airplane that was beefy and noisy, requiring precise seat-of-the-pants flying skills as well as mental discipline. There was no getting lazy with any controls. It was the pilot and his skills against the situation, weather, and circumstances. Unlike today's crop duster pilots who utilize the benefits of advanced technology, Stearman pilots couldn't be reliant on warning lights, instruments, or avionics telling them they'd better check the compression on the number four cylinder.

The typical crop duster pilot climbed into the cockpit before dawn in the semi-dark, adjusted his goggles, and flew until just after dusk, sometimes up to seventeen hours per day. The goal was to try to get the most out of the season, which began around June 1 and concluded around September 30. Pilots flew seven days a week and as many as 800 hours in a four-month season, accruing flight time and a bond with the airplane and the sky.

The Stearman was an airplane that could kill people in service to a task and could make or break a farmer's crops and annual well-being. The pilot had to calculate how best to cover his assigned fields utilizing the least amount of time and fuel while simultaneously spraying the most amount of product. Flying was typically three to ten feet above the height of the crops. Farmers needed the pilot to get as close as possible, which concentrated the spray, making it much more effective in terms of crop yield. Pilots who were doing their job properly came back with leaves in their gear.

Along with flying height, pilots also had to figure in winds so the pesticide wasn't misdirected. If it was very windy, more than ten to twenty knots, the pilot didn't fly or only flew fields aligned into the wind. Flights were typically twenty to thirty minutes in length, depending on how far the strip and refill station was from the fields. The ground crew would be there waiting to stick the hose back in the tank, refill the plane, and then pull the hose. The pilot would fire up and race down the strip to finish the field and move on. Crop dusting was a thrilling profession, but one that required a balance of risk management, responsibility, and discipline. Accidents were fairly common, so the pilot had to be on his game every second of every minute of every hour of every flight.

Jazi Akbar was perfectly suited for this type of flying. He loved the immediate wind in your face rush and reveled in the freedom of flight. He also understood and took seriously the responsibilities inherent in such a high-risk profession. While most crop dusters were older pilots, many in their fifties, Jazi was not only well-liked, but quickly became a well-regarded pilot despite only being in his mid-twenties.

Once, while visiting the Stolhammers after a crop-dusting job in the Dakotas, he turned to Signora, and lifted his sleeve to reveal the dark skin of his shoulder and his darker "farmer's tan."

Despite the arduous work, long hours, and many a night sleeping in the barns of the farmers who hired him, his smile was broad and joyful.

Jazi's years as a crop duster not only provided the foundation for his abilities, but cemented his passion for flying.

***

Jazi piloted the Stearman, making the necessary adjustments and refinements to get every ounce of product, every minute of time, and every fraction of horsepower to do the job efficiently and effectively. He took his responsibilities seriously and handled the challenges and inherent hard work with grit. But, over the many hours he spent above countless fields, he realized this was only a fraction of what he wanted to do. The demands of working as a crop duster pilot had honed his skills and confidence. He was not only ready to fly different, more powerful, long-distance aircraft, but wanted to experience everything he could in the world of aviation.

Crop dusting had a starting pay of $0.50 an acre, but along with his non-seasonal work, Jazi managed to make enough money to put a down payment on a small propeller plane of his own. To keep up on the monthly payment of $2,800, he had to keep that plane working. To supplement his income and keep his new plane in the sky, Jazi parlayed his crop dusting experience into a job with the flying ambulance service for the Mayo Clinic in Rochester, Minnesota.

As a pilot in this government contracted program, he flew to Indian reservations scattered across Minnesota and the Dakotas to pick up Native Americans who needed transportation to the Mayo Clinic. Jazi reveled in the adventure and rugged glamour of flying

PART I

onto a remote Indian reservation, collecting his ailing patient, and flying him or her in for treatment at the world-renowned hospital.

His job included tricky take-offs and landings on gravel roads and inclement weather. He was on call at all times and had to carry a big radio backpack around with him. One evening, he was dispatched for the tribal chief who had fallen off a horse and broken his leg.

Jazi arrived at the reservation, landing at night on the bumpy gravel road that served as a landing strip. In addition to having a broken leg, the chief was also morbidly obese and dependent on oxygen. Jazi somehow managed to load the man in the back of the plane along with his oxygen tank. He did his safety check and they were ready to go. As they roared down the road to take off, the tank got loose and literally began to pound the man on his already broken leg. For years, Jazi retold and embellished the story.

It was one of many adventures. Jazi Akbar, the Pakistani emergency ambulance pilot, quickly became known around the Dakotas not only for his skill as a pilot but his energy, drive, and winning personality.

***

Jazi continued to crop dust in season, give flying lessons to local farmers, and flying under the government contract serving Indian reservations. He became known in the skies, by his radio transmissions. In the heavily homegrown aviation community of the upper Midwest, his distinctive accent was recognized by all.

It was during this time he met two gentlemen who owned a small, fixed-base commuter airline that flew out of Aberdeen,

South Dakota and Fort Collins, Colorado. They were interested in hiring a pilot/manager to run the operation.

Jazi, who was single, unencumbered by a set schedule, and had his own plane, perfectly fit the qualifications. In 1979, they convinced him to join their company, Fort Collins Flying Service. As the manager of their two locations, he would commute back and forth. Jazi was excited about the opportunity. As part of the deal, he negotiated to move to Fort Collins, Colorado, a place that reminded him of the mountainous region of Pakistan he'd so loved as a child. It was also the area in the United States where he'd plant permanent roots and come quickly to think of as his true and forever home. While the state of Alaska has the highest number of pilots, Colorado, which is in the heart of the Rocky Mountain region, has more pilots per capita than any other area in the country. Colorado, with its big skies and majestic mountains, was truly the place where his dreams could take flight.

PART II
AIRLINK
1981-1983

Chapter Four

Jazi moved to Fort Collins, purchased a modest house with his savings, and settled into his new job as manager of Fort Collins Flying Service only to make a sobering discovery: his new bosses had not been paying their payroll taxes. In fact, they were so in arrears, the government was on the verge of shutting them down and prosecuting.

While Jazi hadn't planned on crop dusting and flying for an emergency ambulance service forever, at least his previous jobs paid the bills. He had made what he assumed was a career leap only to find himself in a job that would most likely end before he ever got started.

Instead of panicking, and in what would become his trademark style, Jazi saw the demise of Fort Collins Flying Service as a potentially golden opportunity. FCFS had been badly mismanaged, but the business model itself was basically sound. At that time, the Carter administration was finalizing deregulation of the commercial aviation industry. This meant the government would no longer subsidize air transportation to remote areas, thereby opening the market for small and regional commercial airlines.

Jazi analyzed Fort Collins Flying Service from both a financial and business standpoint and knew he should take over the small airline. All he needed was a cash infusion.

PART II

Unlike the painful growth experience he had suffered at the hands of Hameeda, Jazi had reason to believe that this time, familial financial goodwill would be on his side. Since their arrival in America, Jazi's cousins, Masood and Maqbool Qurashi, the sons of Hameeda's sister, had flourished in Bethlehem, Pennsylvania. Mac, as he was called by family and friends, was an engineer by training. Masood had a financial background. They had left their jobs, entered the fledgling cable TV business, and started a venture called AM Cable. They quickly became known as pioneers in the industry, had grown wealthy, and would become the first Pakistani Americans to take a company public on the New York Stock Exchange.

Jazi was close with Masood who was thirteen years his senior. Mac, who was a few years older than Masood and more circumspect by nature, had a soft spot for his young cousin. He also admired his ambition and confidence. They both recognized and celebrated the entrepreneurial drive that ran in their family bloodline. As a result, Jazi was confident they would listen to his plan and, at the very least, advise him on how best to obtain the money he needed.

Jazi flew to Pennsylvania, met with his cousins, and laid out his plan to buy the business from the current owners of Fort Collins Flying Service by paying off their IRS debt and assuming the payments on the small planes the business owned. Having analyzed their current business model, he knew the airline had a built-in base revenue from the cluster of United pilots who lived in affordable Fort Collins and commuted to and from Stapleton airport in Denver. Once he was the owner, he would build upon the base by advertising to residents of Fort Collins, expanding routes, and acquiring more planes.

As Jazi had hoped, Masood was warm and receptive to his business plan, encouraging him in his ideas. Mac seemed to appreciate Jazi's ingenuity.

"How much do you need?" Masood asked.

"$100,000," Jazi responded, his heart pounding, but not allowing himself to so much as blink. "At least."

"Excuse us for a minute," Mac said.

He and his brother went into another room leaving Jazi alone, his heart still thumping and wondering what his next step would be when they turned him down. What Jazi couldn't know was that Mac and Masood were looking for a tax write-off, and he had come to them at the perfect time. It didn't particularly matter whether the business was profitable. They had the money and they needed to spend it quickly.

They were both smiling when they returned to the room.

"We agree this business has potential," Maqbool said.

Still, Jazi held his breath until Masood said, "We will loan you the money you need."

"Let's celebrate over dinner," Maqbool added. "We'll invite the family."

That evening, Jazi enjoyed a festive meal with the family and was surprised to meet Mac and Masood's lovely, smart, niece who happened to be a very suitable young Pakistani woman.

Though the meeting was clearly arranged, Jazi wasn't involved with me or anyone else, so he didn't see a problem courting a perfectly pleasant young lady.

PART II

Jazi returned to Fort Collins with cash in hand and a plan to see the young woman again. He made a deal to pay off the back taxes in exchange for the company and a scattering of four or five small planes; everything from Cessna 172s to a larger and slower Islander. This random collection of aircraft comprised the real value in the business.

In January 1981, he renamed the company Airlink, and kicked-off his very first airline business. Twenty-seven year old Jazi Akbar had landed in the right country and at the right time to fulfill his childhood dream of being in the aviation business.

He would soon learn on the job, how to own and operate a small airline.

Chapter Five

Airlink had just opened its doors when I walked into his office, still filled with boxes, sold him a phone system, and ended up beside him in the passenger seat on a commuter flight to Denver.

As fate would have it, there were difficulties installing the new eight-line phone system I sold to Airlink and I found myself fielding a steady stream of complaints from my client, Jazi Akbar. Once the system was installed and working smoothly, I immediately began to receive more calls saying he didn't have enough capacity.

I wondered how a very small commuter airline could need more than eight lines?

Little did I know, it was to be my first glance into Jazi's twenty-four hour a day phone habit. I also suspected the reason he was calling me so often had less to do with the phone system and more to do with his repeated requests to have dinner with him.

After literally daily attempts, I agreed to a meal. We made plans for the Thursday evening before Easter, when my daughters, six and seven, would be with their dad in Cheyenne.

Sensing I wouldn't appreciate the bright blue Trans Am, complete with the eagle on the front hood, he usually drove, Jazi picked

PART II

me up in a more sedate sports car he'd borrowed from an Airlink employee. He took me to a small, well-known French restaurant in the tiny town of Berthoud, Colorado. Over dinner, after he shared more about himself and his childhood and he encouraged me to tell him everything about my life.

Jazi already knew that I'd moved to Fort Collins with my two young daughters via Cheyenne, Wyoming where I'd spent nine long years with a nice man with whom I had little in common.

He also knew our upbringings couldn't have been more different. Born in the dusty west Texas farm town of Lubbock, I was raised in a Levittown model house purchased for $7000 with the help of the GI Bill by my dad, a WWII veteran who sold insurance. He made a salary generous enough for my mom to stay home and raise me and my two younger brothers. In other words, I was the quintessential American girl.

We enjoyed a safe and relatively carefree childhood in Lubbock. I was successful in school and had many friends but chaffed under my parents' strict discipline. I lived at home while attending Texas Tech and began dreaming about escaping Lubbock.

During my junior year, I met Stephen, a kind, funny, unassuming boy at a fraternity party. As our dating relationship grew, I began to realize marrying someone from outside Lubbock was my ticket out of small town life. Stephen's best quality, at least in my mind, was that he was from Dallas. My parents recognized that we weren't a good match and disapproved which made Stephen that much more appealing. We planned our wedding, but as I walked down the aisle on the arm of my disappointed father, I feared I was making a mistake. Foolish pride won out.

Only twenty-one on my wedding day, I didn't plan much beyond escaping Lubbock. I definitely didn't factor in the Vietnam War, and the impact it would have on our new marriage. Nearing graduation, Stephen drew a low lottery number in the draft, guaranteeing he would be infantry in the Army. He managed to enlist in the Air Force to avoid the draft. After basic training in cold and windy Wichita Falls, Texas, he was assigned a desk job at F. E. Warren Air Force Base in colder and windier Cheyenne, Wyoming.

I couldn't imagine a place worse than Lubbock, but, for me, Cheyenne was that place. On Stephen's $5000 annual salary, we found a miserable little apartment in town, and began to build a life. We moved to Wyoming in January 1971, and as I would lay awake at night listening to the howling winter wind that seemingly never stopped blowing, I knew I had truly made the biggest mistake of my young life.

The one saving grace of Wyoming was that I was reunited with my best childhood friend, Lindi Kirkbride. Lindi had gone to school at the University of Wyoming where she met her husband who was from a prominent ranching family. They lived thirty miles outside Cheyenne. We'd both married between our junior and senior years, so we set off together on ice-rutted Highway 80 to finish our degrees at the university in Laramie. I went to school two days a week, and I worked in accounts receivable at a local car dealership the other three weekdays. In the midst of working and finishing my degree, I gave birth to my daughters, Jennifer and Regan, fifteen months apart.

As soon as I graduated, I got a commission sales position selling airtime at a radio station. I was soon promoted to sales manager.

PART II

Stephen was discharged from the Air Force and was hired at a bank. Despite careers that made ends meet and the birth of two daughters, we realized we weren't any more suited for each other than I was for living in Cheyenne. The marriage lasted nine years and ended in a painful divorce.

I was thirty years old when I packed up, took the girls, and moved to the nearby and vibrant college town of Fort Collins. I parlayed my job in Cheyenne to a radio advertising position in Fort Collins where I again moved into the sales manager position. I splurged on a posh condo and leased a small BMW.

Soon after, I left radio sales for work at Rocky Mountain Telephone, a step-up in my mind.

The job led to my first meeting with Jazi.

***

"Would you like to go away somewhere together?" Jazi asked at the end of our first dinner date.

"Yes," I said, just as interested in him as he was in me.

"How about tomorrow?"

"You're not serious," I said.

"I'm thinking Hawaii," he responded.

For a girl who had never been outside the continental United States, this was exciting stuff, but I only had four days until the girls came home from being with their father. Hawaii was just too far to go on such a tight timetable. Instead, we settled on Phoenix, a place I'd never been before, either.

Jazi had tickets in hand the next day. We boarded a Frontier jet and set off for Arizona. Masterful at coming on strong, but maintaining proper boundaries, Jazi proved himself to be a gentleman by reserving separate hotel rooms at the Double Tree in Scottsdale.

Over the next three days, we talked nonstop, took long walks, ate wonderful meals, and indulged in a trip to Neiman Marcus where he told me to buy whatever I wanted. I was just getting by on enough to support myself and the girls and was already completely overwhelmed not only by the dinner we'd shared in Berthoud, but the whirlwind trip to Phoenix as well. His offer to pick out something for myself with no price limit was just too much, too soon. Instead of allowing him to buy me a gift, I simply thanked him and refused.

Jazi was pleased by my response. By not taking him up on his offer, he knew for sure I was interested in him, not what he could buy me.

I wasn't just interested. I was completely taken with Jazi Akbar. As soon as I got back home, I ended my relationship with the other gentleman I was seeing. I wanted to spend as much time with Jazi as possible.

Chapter Six

Whenever Jazi called the house, my young daughters, Jennifer and Regan, would jump to answer the phone.

"Who has a name like Jazi?" they both wondered.

When Jennifer, nearly seven, first met the man with the unusual name, he gave her the exotic gift of a conch shell. Regan, six, hadn't met him yet herself, but was impressed by the gesture and took note. One evening, Regan was in the bedroom she shared with Jennifer. She heard a warm, happy laugh coming from downstairs and crept to the top of the steps to investigate. In the living room was a man who looked different than anyone she'd ever seen before. He had dark skin, a distinctive nose, and then there was that laugh…

I invited her to come downstairs.

Regan had met Native Americans and Hispanic people, but Jazi was completely foreign to her in every way—from his strange accent to the way he smelled of good cologne. When he shook her hand, his palm was very soft. There was also the conch shell he'd given Jennifer which showed that he was, quite possibly, a little more special than any of the other men I had dated.

It quickly became obvious that Jazi was a lot more special. He was always taking me somewhere interesting that made the most

PART II

of our lives at that time. On the weekends, we would get in one of his airplanes and fly to places like the original Cabela's in Nebraska where they had a shuttle bus that made regular trips between the airport and the store to carry the many customers who flew in for the afternoon to shop. The girls came along and had a thrill they'd never experienced before. Another time, we flew to California on a commercial flight to pick up a plane for one of Jazi's clients. As we took off for Fort Collins and flew into thick clouds, I was a little frightened, but up for the adventure—especially when I looked over at handsome, confident Jazi.

I fell hard for the spontaneous, energetic pilot who took me to do everything from a day of romantic leaf collecting to dinners at great restaurants. Since he lived for flying, weekends were usually filled with adventure that involved an airplane.

The girls grew to like having Jazi around because of how happy he made me. Jennifer and Jazi generally got along, while Regan and Jazi were destined to clash, but both girls immediately recognized and accepted his significance in their world.

***

Not long after we began to date, I admitted that I could no longer afford the posh condo I was renting. I took the girls and moved into a smaller walk-up style, six-unit apartment building which we called 1212 B. Another casualty of the tight budget was my leased BMW 320i. I simply couldn't make the payments and would have to get along without a car. I talked Jazi into driving to Denver with me to leave the BMW and keys in the lot of the leasing company and followed up the next day with a phone call telling them where they could find the car.

The new apartment suited everyone. It was close to the girl's school so they could ride their bikes, and the rent was significantly less. However, the phone sales business ultimately produced more stress than commission and I quit. I was burned out on sales but had to do something to support my kids. With growing desperation, I picked up another job that July of 1981 through the county employment agency signing up households for home milk delivery from a local dairy.

Jazi later told me he'd really admired that I'd never asked him for any money, but simply went to work for Poudre Valley Dairy. Honestly, it never dawned on me to ask. I'd set out in the morning with two other people in an old, beat-up milk truck. We would drive to a cluster of neighborhoods, get out, walk the blocks, and sign people up for milk delivery. The pay was hourly, so my coworkers who didn't need the income as much as I did would start around 10:00 a.m., take a long lunch, and quit by 4:00 p.m. Because I didn't have a car, I was tethered to them and the rusty milk truck. Thinking I could make more money for myself and the company, I went to the owner and asked if I could go on straight commission. He liked the idea, but wondered how I was going to get to the various neighborhoods in town without a car.

"My bike," I said.

He laughed, but agreed to let me try it.

I hopped onto my ten-speed and started riding all through Fort Collins selling home milk delivery. As I'd hoped, by going on commission, I soon began to make enough money to pay our bills. An added benefit was how fit I became. My legs never looked so good in shorts as they did during that summer.

Jazi was impressed with my self-sufficiency; I'd left my upscale condo and luxury car for a modest apartment and a bike to do what it took to sustain my family. So much so, apparently, that he decided he was going to marry me. He kept that thought to himself.

Exactly when it would happen was an entirely different question.

***

By October the weather was changing and it was getting cold. I had been to every neighborhood in Fort Collins. While riding my bike, I would pray and ask God what came next—especially when I would ride by my old radio buddies in their fancy cars. One day, I came into the dairy to learn I'd been receiving calls all day from a man I'd known from radio sales back in Cheyenne. He offered me the position of sales manager at the local country western station two blocks from my apartment. Perhaps the most amazing part of the offer was that it came with a company car. The car, a white Chevy Chevette with KIIX, the call letters of the radio station, plastered all over it, might has well have been another BMW. I couldn't wait to surprise the girls and Jazi with my great news.

They were all delighted to find out that I was getting a new job *and* a car. A vehicle with radio station call letters all over it fit right in to our array of unorthodox vehicles including the Airlink Volkswagen van and Jazi's vintage (but mechanically unsound) Mercedes which required a very dangerous starting procedure. Jazi would sit in the driver's seat and turn the key in the engine while I squirted ether under the hood. Fearing an explosion, but believing the Lord watched over me and the girls, I would call on Him for protection every time we attempted to start the ancient car.

In addition to my new job at the radio station, I also began to sell Mary Kay Cosmetics out of my apartment. The unlikely combination of jobs proved unsuccessful. One day, as I met with a client, Regan came flying through the door.

"There's a garage sale down the street and they're selling Mary Kay and it's a great bargain!"

Jazi shot Regan a stern look but not quickly enough to save the sale.

As the customer wandered down the street toward new product for pennies on the dollar, he patiently explained to Regan that telling a potential customer she could buy the same thing for less had ruined my opportunity. He didn't blame her, just kindly helped her understand what she'd done wrong.

Regan, who was an inquisitive, bright little girl, appreciated Jazi's insight and willingness to relate to her on that level.

***

Jazi and I had fallen into an immediate, intense relationship, but one major problem threatened to ground us. He went back to Pennsylvania every month to attend meetings with airplane financing and leasing companies and have long talks with his cousins about the business and his desire to succeed. While there, he diplomatically took out his uncles' niece, but swore there was no

PART II

romantic entanglement. I didn't realize what a fine balancing act Jazi was managing and I wasn't comfortable with the arrangement.

I pressed him for months as to when he the arrangement would end.

"I'm working on it," Jazi would say.

I tried to understand that there were cultural expectations and accepted the unusual arrangement but wasn't happy in the least.

Jazi didn't mention to anyone in his family that he was also seeing me. He feared they wouldn't see an older, white, Christian divorcee from Texas with two kids as a suitable match.

Not a ladies' man by nature, Jazi continued to juggle my strong, independent personality with family approval. He and I grew more and more serious about each other, but Jazi still made trips to Pennsylvania.

I grew to resent any time he spent on the East Coast and finally decided I needed to protect my own interests and shield myself from potential heartbreak. The next time he left for Pennsylvania, I met and began to see another man with a career in advertising and a charming farm.

Regan and Jennifer met and liked the new fellow but wondered what had happened to Jazi. In their hearts, they hoped the new guy would disappear and that Jazi and I would stay together.

I felt the same way.

When Jazi returned, I gave him an ultimatum. "Do you want to be with me or keep making trips to the East Coast? It's time to decide."

I didn't realize that the young lady back east had lost patience with Jazi's indecisiveness as well.

"I want to marry you," Jazi said.

To confirm his intentions, he brought me to Bethlehem to meet Masood and Maqbool when AM Cable officially went public. From the very first, they proved to be the sweetest, dearest people. Maqbool had a large party at his new, palatial house. We stayed at Masood and Sultana's home where the cousins welcomed me with open arms.

***

From then on, Jazi spent the bulk of his time with me either at 1212B or having us over to his house at 3400 Stover. There, we entertained employees and friends, had barbecues, and went swimming. It was a time of laughter, great food, and cheap, abundant champagne.

I was in awe of Jazi—his intelligence in business, the fact that he could tell jokes in his second tongue, and that he could take apart and put together a washing machine. Equally amazing was that despite his technical skills, he wouldn't do his own laundry! Jazi was serious about his cooking and introduced me and the girls to Basmati rice, ginger potatoes, and other staples of Indian cuisine.

Jennifer liked Jazi, but she couldn't get used to their new diet—in particular, rice.

"How can you not like rice?" Jazi used to ask.

Regan liked rice, but she hated ginger and any type of meat, which left Jazi aghast. Jennifer was a diplomat but Regan was a rebel and a believer in causes. An animal advocate, she hated that Jazi was an avid hunter. She hated the thought of killing animals

PART II

and would speak up against how mean and wrong it was. She simply couldn't understand how anyone could shoot a defenseless deer and maintained her steadfast determination to get him to stop hunting, which, to Jazi, felt like disobedience.

He was even more shocked to discover Regan's aversion to flying. For her birthday that year, he and I decided to take Regan and a group of her friends up in the ten-seat Islander.

Regan remembers thinking, "Why would they make me do that for my birthday?"

She also knew Jazi would get very offended if she said anything, so she never said a word beforehand, or as kids arrived at the airport for the party, or when everyone excitedly boarded the plane. She said nothing as we took off. She simply grew more and more nauseous from the motion, the fumes, and the stress of having a birthday celebration in the sky. As I served cake to her amazed and delighted friends, Regan couldn't stand it any longer and threw up everywhere.

Other than the dietary and aeronautical differences, life proceeded otherwise smoothly. While Regan had the lingering sense that Jazi preferred her more diplomatic sister, they still shared their tender moments. Regan suffered from asthma and bad allergies. When she was seven, I took her to an allergist to get skin testing, which involved a series of uncomfortable pokes across her back. Jazi knew the test would be both painful, traumatizing, and a big deal for a little girl, so he insisted he drive her home.

"Are you okay?" he asked after the procedure.

She tried not to cry as she showed him the pinpricks all over her back.

"You know, I got these when I was a kid," he said, showing her the series of round, indented, polio vaccine scars along his upper arms and across his back. He shared that he'd gotten the scars from his mother who practiced giving polio shots on him while she was in training to become a public health worker.

"Don't worry," he told her. "Yours won't be permanent."

Regan appreciated Jazi's kindness and realized he'd had a childhood that was clearly much more difficult than anything she'd experienced. From that point on, she felt a kinship and wanted to know and have a closer relationship with the man who would soon be her stepfather. She asked him endless questions:

"Do you miss Pakistan?"

"What was it like?"

"Do you want to go back there?"

At dinner, she would beg him to tell her stories.

Jazi told her his childhood had been extremely hard and that he'd been very lonely with few friends. He said he hated Pakistan because it was poor and very corrupt.

Regan was inquisitive and intelligent but was also prone to getting in trouble. Whenever the school would call about something she did or refused to do—not an infrequent occurrence—I would deal with the situation. One time, however, Jazi did the honors.

"You're a smart person," he said to her after meeting with the teacher and the principal after Regan refused to turn in an assignment. "Save your rebelliousness for when there's a good reason. Otherwise, this trait of yours is going to cause you trouble."

Regan appreciated that instead of imposing punishment, he talked with her and tried to relate to her instead.

PART II

"Do you want a ride home?" he asked when they were finished.

While it was her immediate impulse to say no because she liked to meet up with friends after school to go to the park or jump on someone's trampoline, she chose the ride home with him. On the way, she remembers thinking, "I'm going to try harder."

That night, I thanked him for dealing with Regan.

"I knew you were a package deal," Jazi told her. "The girls are part of that."

I began to feel it was time to take Jazi to Lubbock to meet my parents.

While Jazi's family had made me feel welcome, our visit home was one of the most uncomfortable weekends I'd ever experienced. Mother and Daddy knew I had met someone who was very important to me. They were also aware he was Pakistani. Mom had a fairly open mind, but I'm sorry to say my dad was quite racially prejudiced and was not accepting of Jazi at all. He made a horrible slur about him that doesn't bear repeating but was truly awful. Although Mother was more welcoming, she was worried what some of her more bigoted friends would say. I was never more relieved to say goodbye and see Lubbock in the rear view mirror (as the song goes).

Chapter Seven

In the beginning, Airlink carried everything from crates of baby chicks to passengers. Jazi and I literally left the Thanksgiving table during our first year of operation to carry a rowdy group of holiday revelers from Denver to Vail in the Islander. There was no job too big or too small. It had to be that way in order for Airlink to stay aloft.

Over time, Jazi's thinking evolved. He realized the real future of Airlink lay in increasing his relationship with United Airlines into a formal arrangement. He negotiated for Airlink to become an official feeder airline, a new, promising concept at the time. Airlink would now carry both passengers and pilots as part of United from Fort Collins to the carrier's regional hub at Stapleton Airport.

Jazi also began to increase the number of routes Airlink flew. Along with flying pilots and other passengers to and from Denver, he added destinations like Rock Springs, Wyoming where they brought oil field workers to and from work. At the same time, he consolidated his smaller aircraft into fewer but larger planes. He would sell two of the small ones and get a slightly bigger plane to replace them. As a result, he was able to acquire faster planes, increase routes, and became a true commuter airline. Eventually, he got rid of all the small planes and replaced them with one nineteen-passenger Sweringen prop jet that was fast enough so all routes could be flown via a single aircraft.

By 1983, Airlink had grown into a costlier and more complex operation. There were employees in two offices--Fort Collins and Stapleton Airport in Denver. The business itself was doing well, but cash flow was a constant issue.

During a particularly difficult pay period, Jazi sold his home at 3400 Stover to ensure everyone was paid. After selling his residence, he lived primarily with me, but rented an apartment in the Crestmoor neighborhood in Denver. During that time, he and I were constantly on I-25 traveling the eighty miles between 1212B in Fort Collins and the apartment near Stapleton.

Despite our efforts, the business was losing altitude and the employees became aware of the precarious nature of meeting payroll. In a sudden and somewhat delusional move, and with no apparent foresight, the pilots revolted and went to Swearingen, where Jazi was behind on his payments and reported the scrambling going on back in Colorado.

In response, the manufacturer repossessed Airlink's airplane.

While Jazi didn't declare bankruptcy as a result, the repossession put him out of business.

It also put the rebellious pilots out of jobs.

One day in mid-July 1983 I got a call from Jazi at the radio station. It was the middle of the day.

"What's going on?" I asked him, knowing he never called during the workday.

Strangely his response was, "Nothing."

"Nothing?" I asked.

"Swearingen just repossessed the plane. Airlink is finished."

The second I got off work, I went rushing down to Denver to support Jazi in light of such a devastating blow. When I arrived at the apartment complex, I spotted Jazi waiting for me in the parking lot. We went on a walk, circling the complex. Jazi fumed, vented, and finally said, "We might as well get married."

Despite our cultural differences and divergent upbringings, Jazi and I shared similar values. Jazi grew to depend on my judgement, input, instincts, and our shared, common-sense approach to problem solving. Jazi also knew that I was 100 percent loyal and that he could count not only on my advice, but that I would have his back, something he hadn't had for much of his life.

Although I hadn't received the most romantic offer of marriage, and never mind he was broke and out of a job, my trust in our relationship carried the day. I had complete faith in his ability to take care of me, Jennifer, and Regan. I knew he had vision and a bright future and I wanted to be part of it, so I decided to hitch my wagon to his star.

Above all, I loved him deeply and knew he felt the same way about me.

Chapter Eight

I called my parents, BJ and Jim, back in Lubbock to tell them Jazi and I were getting married.

"We don't attend second weddings," my mom said coldly.

I was hurt that my parents had reacted negatively, but I was not surprised given our disastrous weekend in Lubbock. A Pakistani businessman was something of a novelty in a place like open-minded Fort Collins, but unacceptable in the conservative Bible Belt. I knew it was going to take time for my small-town parents to accept Jazi, but I hoped that when they came around they would love him as much as I did.

"You will be missed," I simply said, so in love that their rejection felt more like a momentary sting.

More pressing, in my mind, was planning a wedding on a shoestring budget of only $500.

Generously, some close friends offered their scenic lakeside backyard for the occasion. We chose a minister who was also a friend to conduct a Christian ceremony. A party would follow. Jazi and I planned a meal that would include roasted goat prepared by a local Chinese restaurant, rice pilaf, and a beautiful pear wedding cake from a French bakery. Regan was particularly taken with the

PART II

cake, which was decorated with sugared alstroemeria. A five dollar a bottle sparkling wine (known to cause wicked hangovers) would be served without embarrassment or apology.

I went to the local fabric store, and after spending a total of twelve dollars, walked out with blue cotton fabric to make matching flower girl dresses for Jennifer and Regan, and six yards of gray polyester for myself. Instead of wearing a traditional wedding gown, I planned to surprise Jazi by wearing a sari and setting it off with some exotic Pakistani silver jewelry he had given me as a gift.

We woke up on Saturday, August 15, 1983 to blue skies and the dawn of a stunning summer day in Colorado. There was no room left in the budget to rent anything, so the yard was set up with an odd assortment of leftover chairs and tables from Airlink. I decorated with borrowed tablecloths and simple silk flower centerpieces I'd created myself.

When everyone had gathered, I took a quick peek out the master bedroom window where the girls and I had been getting ready. Jazi, always a dapper dresser, stood by the minister looking incredibly handsome in a new navy suit with pale gray pinstripes (which had been charged on the already strained MasterCard).

Excited, I scanned the audience.

Along with our close friends, and a black lab named Max who was sporting a red bowtie, I was thrilled and grateful to spot two very special guests. Seated in the front row were my parents. They had made the ten hour drive that day out of love for me and a gesture of acceptance to the handsome Pakistani who would so profoundly impact all their lives.

Heart soaring, I smiled at my daughters who were utterly adorable in their blue dresses and matching French braids. I grasped their hands and we started for the doors.

Jazi was moved to tears when I entered the backyard wearing a gray sari created from the fabric I'd purchased. He was surprised and delighted by my love and respect for him and the way in which I'd chosen to honor his background.

The sunset ceremony was short, authentic, and, as we'd hoped, transcended any differences between us. We traded plain white gold bands, all we could afford at the time, and became husband and wife.

The small, intimate group of guests celebrated our union with toasts courtesy of my parents, who'd replaced the cheap sparkling wine with a chilled case of Moyer Champagne donated by my wine making cousin, Ken Moyer from New Braunsfels, Texas. We feasted on the delicious goat and good champagne flowed.

Regan and Jennifer remember the celebration, which lasted late into the evening, as happy, joyous, and the coolest wedding they ever attended. They felt blissfully happy.

My parents began to see in their new son-in-law everything that had attracted me to him and more.

As for Jazi and I, we were madly in love, newly married, and had managed to throw the perfect wedding on our very modest budget of $500.

***

Shortly after we were married, we embarked on the first of two honeymoon trips. We dropped the girls off with their dad in

PART II

Cheyenne and headed for a weekend away in Avon, Colorado, the poor neighbor of Beaver Creek. I had made reservations at a time-share. All that was required was a two-hour, verbal bludgeoning from a sales rep to earn two nights in the resort. After enduring the pitch, we got a free black-and-white TV and a toaster oven. I also managed to secured filet mignon steaks at a reduced price from a radio station client which we enjoyed with the leftover Moyer Champagne. All in all, it was a romantic, if economical, adventure.

Our second, more official, honeymoon was in late October. Jazi had finagled two first-class tickets to Hawaii on United. We rode up top in the 747 and sipped champagne all the way to Honolulu. When we arrived on Kauai, I (the girl from Lubbock, Cheyenne, and Fort Collins) was more than a little overwhelmed by my exotic surroundings. I turned to the car rental attendant and said, "We're from the United States."

"So am I, lady," the attendant replied.

Jazi roared with laughter

We went on to Princeville where we stayed for a wonderful week in a modest condo. How Jazi paid for the honeymoon was something of a mystery to me, but was definitely a harbinger of the rollercoaster I'd willingly boarded. We were on our way, rolling toward the next set of twists, dips, and turns.

Chapter Nine

Jazi had lost Airlink, and we were theoretically broke, but he hadn't declared bankruptcy. As fate (and his preternatural foresight) would have it, he didn't come out of the business entirely without resources either. While Airlink was operational, the airline industry was in the process of deregulation. Airlines owned the rights to take off and land at certain airports at certain times. The time slots were a commodity that could be bought, sold, and in some cases distributed through lottery. The lottery had been instituted to enable smaller airlines to own slots that would otherwise be purchased by the large carriers. Airlines with operating certificates could get into a lottery and be awarded slots without any particular capability of flying into or out of the airport where they were located. The better the location and time of day, the more valuable the slot.

Through the lottery system, Airlink had been awarded six slots, some of which were valuable because they enabled the airline who owned them landing times at Newark International Airport, regardless of where the flight originated. One of these landing slots was at 7:59 a.m., a premium time.

When Jazi lost the business, the time slots no longer had value for Airlink, but he still owned them and could sell them to another

PART II

operational airline. Due to Airlink's status as a feeder for United Airlines, Jazi knew and had developed good working relationships with various executives in the company. As soon as his business was officially shuttered, he negotiated a deal and sold all six landing slots to United.

They paid him a million dollars.

In a few short years, Jazi Akbar had managed to immigrate to the United States, graduate from college, attain his pilot's license, buy a business, marry an American woman, and become an instant family man. At twenty-eight years old, he was nowhere close to reaching his goals but, as a result of his deal with United, he now had a substantial sum of money in his pocket.

Chapter Ten

A month after returning from Hawaii, Jazi informed us that the apartment at 1212B no longer suited him. A search through the classified section ensued and we settled on 1301 Rollingwood, a house in the same elementary school boundary, but in a much more desirable neighborhood.

We moved into a three-bedroom ranch on a cul-de-sac in an upper middle-class development. Having gone from paying $235 a month to $1000 per month, the girls suddenly lived in what felt like a palace, in a real neighborhood, with a lake, lots of kids to play with, and friendly neighbors.

Here, Jazi set the stage for the family life that had eluded him as a child. He bought a trampoline and installed it in the backyard. Bicycles with banana seats and sparkly handles appeared in the garage. The basement, filled with leftover Airlink office furniture, became the ultimate play space where the girls spent hours creating make-believe stores, offices, and games with their friends. Jazi had attained the stable, secure home life he'd longed for, and made sure the dream included all the trimmings, complete with a labrador retriever named Lily and a stray cat the girls found on one of their nightly family walks.

PART II

I left the radio station and began life as a stay-at-home mom, tending to the house and cooking nightly meals while Jazi worked on his next steps in business. To me, it was wonderful and I relished every day.

We were on a trip in the California wine country when he decided to trade cars with a prospective business partner: Jazi's Mercedes for the man's Porsche. He was refining his knack for trading up and the car deal was no exception. Never mind that the Porsche had no title—that was a problem for another day...

Even from the vantage point of a 4th and 5th grader, the girls couldn't help but notice how much things had changed for the better. Their new much, more affluent lifestyle did not come without life lessons though. One afternoon as Regan came out of school, one of her friends noticed the Porsche 928 sitting in the carpool line.

"What a cool car!" the boy exclaimed.

"That's ours," Regan said proudly.

The boy punched her for being a rich kid.

Regan, who didn't suffer fools, fought back, got in trouble, and had to sit on the wall during the next day's recess. For her, it was well worth the fight. Their life had become the picture of stability. She was ready to defend it at all costs.

***

Jazi was proud of his new life, and his spirited stepdaughters. He told the family in Pennsylvania and back in Pakistan all about Jennifer and Regan, filling them in about their school, accomplishments, and life in Fort Collins.

One day, a massive box arrived in the mail from Pakistan. Inside were fifty Colorado-style ski caps complete with pom-poms on top. Sultana's aunt had made the hats on her knitting machine in the girls' school colors of yellow and red, and embroidered the name of their school, *Riffenburgh*, on each one. Although some of the hats had spelling mistakes, she sent everything she'd made. The girls were thrilled and had a great time doling out the caps to their friends at school. More important, they knew Jazi was bragging about them to his relatives, which made them very happy.

***

One afternoon, Jazi came out of his home office and announced it was time to change his name.

Always flexible and ready for the next (inevitable) development, I simply asked "Why?"

"I need a name that will be more palatable in the American business world," he said.

"What will your new name be?" I asked even though I had just completed filing the marriage certificate at the county courthouse that had changed my last name to Akbar.

"Our last name will be Chaudhury," he said.

"Which sounds just as foreign as Akbar."

"It's a prestigious name and I like the sound of it," he said.

"Then how about we Americanize the spelling?" I suggested. "To Chowdry."

"I like it," he said.

"What about your first name?" I wondered aloud.

PART II

"I don't know," Jazi said, genuinely stumped.

I thought for a moment. "Michael."

"Why Michael?" Jazi asked.

Always a student of the Bible, I'd actually said the first name that came into my head. "He was the archangel. One of God's most favored."

Jazi smiled. "Perfect."

At that moment, Jazi Akbar became Michael Chowdry.

We made another trip to the courthouse to file the necessary documents and fill out the paperwork.

No one, including me or the girls, ever referred to Michael as Jazi again.

***

The girls were thriving in our spacious, suburban house. Their father, Stephen, lived in nearby Cheyenne and was content to leave the day-to-day parenting to me and Michael. He drove back and forth to fetch the kids every other weekend and traded off holidays.

The divorce had never been an issue for Michael, nor was the fact that I had kids. There was never a conflict or any particular problem with nonthreatening, easygoing Stephen while Jazi and I were dating.

Post-marriage however, Michael began to struggle with what he saw as Stephen's influence over the girls and his involvement in their family dynamic. Specifically, Michael relished his role as the head of his family. The idea of co-fathering with another man clashed with some of his preconceived ideas and background—particularly given that he was taking care of the girls financially.

Michael unilaterally decided he was going to remedy the situation by adopting Jennifer and Regan. He stated many reasons, not the least of which was that he cared for his stepdaughters. Ultimately though, his rationale had a cultural element. He'd already made an unconventional choice by marrying an older, American divorcee. He didn't want to appear weak or as though he wasn't in control in front of his skeptical Pakistani relatives.

I was given no say in the decision and I knew my ex-husband wasn't going to agree to give up custody of his daughters. I also knew there was no stopping Michael when he set his mind to something. There was little I could do but allow Michael to approach Stephen.

As expected, Stephen refused and wouldn't budge.

I rarely questioned Michael on his motives or methods, but on this matter, I sided with my ex-husband. I felt that the girls had weathered the divorce as well as they had because of their father's established presence in their lives. Besides, he was their father, and there was nothing to be done as far as the law was concerned. Standing up to Michael took strength, but I held my own.

Michael, who was accustomed to figuring out a way to get whatever it was he wanted, had no choice but to back off.

The adoption failure, at least that was how he saw it, led to ramifications which played out in minor, and not so minor, ways for years to come.

***

PART II

Michael continued to simmer over his defeat in attempting to adopt the girls. Because he was providing a lovely home for them, as well as supporting them financially, he decided they should be calling him Dad.

I had already sided with Stephen on the more important issue of adopting the girls, so I realized that indulging Michael would, in small measure, placate him and his hurt feelings. I understood that he could be hard and unrelenting and that this was his way of dealing with disappointment. I also knew that the failed adoption was emblematic of Michael's frustrations. He had most all of the trappings of the American Dream, including a financial cushion, but was struggling to get his next business idea up and off the ground. I assumed his need to be called Dad was simply a way of taking out his frustrations on the family and asserting his authority.

In what would reveal itself as textbook Michael Chowdry management style, both personally and professionally, he insisted that I inform Jennifer and Regan of his new policy. Effective immediately.

Each of the girls handled the situation differently. Jennifer was behaved and compliant by nature. She'd already learned an early lesson with Michael by leaving her bedroom lights on one too many times, only to come home one day to find that all the light bulbs had been removed from her room. She would do as she was told, but resented Michael for imposing this edict so arbitrarily. Close with her father, she felt like she was betraying Stephen every time she called Michael, *Dad*. However, she towed the line to maintain peace in her world.

Regan, on the other hand, surprised both of us by taking the directive somewhat in stride. She saw herself as busy with a big life outside of the home. She figured Michael wanted to be called "Dad," so that's what she would do.

It was, however, a defining moment.

The girls' relationship with Michael changed when he was not able to adopt them. Regan felt that he considered them "Linda's children" from that point forward. She personally never felt warmth and closeness with him again. In her opinion, he not only distanced himself, but took out his anger on them from being denied adoption for the rest of the time that she would know him.

Already critical of his passion for hunting and flying, Regan, in an act of rebellion, challenged his cigar habit. Regan hated cigar smoke because it made her sick, so she found where he kept his stash, cut them into little pieces, and left them for him to find.

She was one of the few people that dared to cross Michael and speak her mind without concern for the consequences. Michael felt he should assert himself over her rebellious nature, and as the years went by their interactions grew increasingly strained and adversarial.

A knot of tension formed a permanent home in my gut as I watched the relationship between Michael and the girls go slowly but steadily downhill. There were fun times and joy but the path was set. The truth was, I feared it would not end well between my daughters and the man I had chosen as my life partner.

PART III
LEVERAGED BUYOUT
1984-1986

Chapter Eleven

Michael had floundered, trying to figure out what to do next through most of 1983 and 1984. He was not easy to live with as he toyed with several ideas, trying to come up with the concept that would lead to his big thing. I spent lots of time in the bathroom crying and hoping he would find his way quickly.

One day, Regan came in from riding her bike and discovered Michael and me sitting at the kitchen table with colored pencils and paper. We were hand drawing what turned out to be a logo for a business idea Michael had.

She asked what we were doing.

"We're making a new business," I said.

In her mind, ten-year-old Regan assumed that when you wanted to start a new business, all you had to do was get out your colored pencils, draw the thing you imagined, and it turned into what you wanted to it to be. In truth, that's exactly how handmade and down-to-earth the roots of Michael's business empire actually was.

Michael spent most of his time doing one of the things he did best, networking. He was constantly on the phone, a habit that would bring him success throughout his career. During that period, he made the most of his contacts at United while developing new relationships with Denver-based Frontier Airlines.

PART III

Thankfully, he also made time for recreation. If we weren't off on a weekend jaunt in a plane, we would go on drives to see the aspen trees in all their fall glory and for picnics in the mountains. We would take a bottle of wine, some cheese and bread, and set off on a beautiful Colorado day. Because Jennifer and Regan spent every other weekend with Stephen, we had the freedom to spend time together without the tensions that hovered around his relationship with the girls.

During that time, Michael determined that he couldn't make it, whatever it was, happen in Fort Collins. He needed to be in Denver where both United and Frontier maintained hubs. And while he enjoyed living with the mountains as a backdrop, he longed for just the opposite view. He wanted a home nestled in the hills that overlooked the plains, much like his cousins' home where he'd spent his summers back in Pakistan.

Michael and I made several trips to Denver locations, timing the drive to Stapleton Airport. Beautiful, scenic Genesee, situated in the foothills, and only thirty minutes away from the airport, fit Michael's criteria perfectly.

Jennifer and Regan had gone almost all the way through Riffenburgh Elementary when, in November 1984, I told them they were moving from Fort Collins to Denver. The girls were crushed. Not only were they going to be uprooted from their school and friends, but they would be living another hour away from their father.

I explained that Michael needed to be in Denver to grow his business.

The girls tried to make the case that they loved the neighborhood, their house, their many friends, and school. Regan was in fifth grade, played on various sports teams, and had friends all over their neighborhood. Jennifer was almost halfway through sixth grade and wanted more than anything to graduate from Riffenburgh.

Fortunately or unfortunately, and in a pattern that would play out repeatedly over the coming years, when personal matters and business were weighed against each other, business always won. Michael had become laser-focused and career achievements trumped family happiness.

The decision was final and the search for a new house began.

It was just past Thanksgiving and Jennifer had an extra layer of stress piled on with the wreath she was making for my Christmas gift. Secretly, she was going in after school to finish before we moved. In the end, I cherished that wreath because Jennifer had worked so hard on it for me. I pulled it out for years taking the hot glue gun and reassembling the pieces that needed repair. As I glued it together, I was reminded that all Jennifer wanted for that year for Christmas was to graduate from Riffenburgh.

Instead, the Rollingwood house was packed up and the movers unloaded their things into a large home in Genesee. The house was so big, I couldn't stretch the furniture far enough, so it felt cold, rambling, and empty. I did the best I could to talk up the house and describe how homey it would soon be, but both girls immediately thought of it as a cavernous, chilly place with a scary living room.

***

PART III

The very day of the move, Michael arrived at our new home from a week in Florida on business. He came straight from the airport that Friday afternoon to find me exhausted and wondering where to start.

"Sit down," he said, after kissing me hello.

"What is it?" I asked perching on a nearby box.

"The money is gone," he said.

"Gone?" I managed to utter.

Michael went on to explain the technical details of what had happened, a jumble of longs, shorts in American Airlines, and betting wrong on the advice of his broker.

I knew Michael had been making high risk buys in the stock market, but I also knew that was his nature. "All of it?"

"Pretty much," he said.

Michael's explanation was confusing, but one very important question emerged in my mind. "But you saved enough to pay capital gains taxes, right?"

"In Pakistan, the tax collector gets paid off, not the government," Michael joked. "Isn't the arrangement basically the same in the U.S.?"

I knew he was kidding, but the IRS didn't find the situation as funny. The IRS deems selling slots as income realized in the ordinary course of business. The losses associated with investing, such as option trading, are capital losses which you can only take $3,000 a year off against ordinary income. He made a million and lost the million, but because of the difference in the characterization of those gains and losses, he had a problem with the IRS.

As a result, we became the focus of a tax audit that would drag on for years. I would endure countless meetings in a small IRS auditor's cubicle where it was my job to convince the man that the padded budget I presented was accurate. The day Michael made the money to pay the tax bill and associated fines, which liberated me from the dreaded auditor and his stuffy little cubicle, was a joyous one.

In truth, I was shocked to hear Michael had lost such a substantial sum of money, more than I'd ever imagined having, really. However, I loved, trusted, and believed in him. We'd been married a little over a year and I was still astonished by how his mind worked. I knew Michael thought like a billionaire and was likely to instinctively make and lose money. I knew there would be setbacks and the ride would be wild, but I'd bet on him and would continue to do so. Luckily for Michael, on the night he broke the news, I was also exhausted from packing up and moving an entire household.

"Will we need to move the family out of the new house and back into somewhere like 1212 B in Ft. Collins?" I finally asked.

"No," he said. "We're staying put. I promise I'll make it work."

I knew he was as good as his word.

Instead of panicking about our reversal of fortune, we went to the local Charthouse restaurant for dinner that night, drank a bottle of wine, laughed together, and moved forward.

***

In 1983, Frontier Horizon, the low cost, non-union subsidiary of Frontier Airlines, operated seven 727-100 aircraft flying specific routes that fed passengers into the Frontier Airlines hub operation in Denver.

PART III

Just after losing his first fortune, Michael was contracted to do some freelance consulting for Frontier Horizon due to his knowledge of obtaining slots. It was during this time that he began pursuing a friendship with Hank Lund, then president of Frontier Airlines. Hank was a large man both in stature and demeanor. He was of Scandinavian descent and liked a good scotch and a steak. As a couple, Michael and I began spending more and more time with Hank and his wife, Bea.

John Blue was the president of Frontier Horizon at the time, serving under Hank. One of his coworkers came to him one day talking up a young, interesting go-getter in the airline business who'd been operating a shuttle for United Airlines and was currently doing consulting work for Frontier.

At that time, the executives at Frontier Airlines were considering the idea of liquidating Frontier Horizon due to disputes with the pilots' union. The union wanted current operations and all future growth to be with Frontier Airlines, not the non-union Frontier Horizon. The union was willing to negotiate wage- and work-rule concessions with management if Frontier Horizon was eliminated.

Michael was well aware of Frontier Airlines' issue with Frontier Horizon and recognized the dissension as his next big opportunity. He was introduced to John Blue and they started talking. At that point, Michael had lost Airlink and had sold the landing slots he'd purchased to United for a million dollars. It was an impressive and gutsy business maneuver that was not lost on John. Less impressive was that Michael had promptly invested the million he'd made into a failed stock market strategy and was in a difficult situation with the IRS.

John immediately saw Michael for who he was, both a good businessman and a gambler. But as they discussed Michael's vision and his plan, John Blue was also taken by Michael's belief in himself. John saw that Michael was a survivor and knew that he would be successful. Michael thought of his own financial situation as transitory and was much more focused on the issues at Frontier Airlines and how these problems could offer opportunities to Frontier Horizon and himself.

John left the meeting confident they would be talking more. Little did he realize how instrumental Michael would be to the future course of Frontier Horizon.

***

In the early 1980s, Gene Dessel was the manager of reliability and technical services at Frontier Airlines. He'd worked for a number of carriers and spent twelve and half years at Lockheed. He was involved in the startup of Frontier Horizon as part of a flight group that dealt with the regulations and requirements relating to the certification of the airline. He later became the manager of maintenance and engineering.

Gene had met Michael and was aware he was freelance consulting for Frontier to obtain landing and takeoff slots. He knew Michael had previously owned a small airline. Gene didn't know any more about Michael Chowdry until they had a chance meeting one evening at LaGuardia airport. This encounter became a turning point and the beginning of what would be a long, successful business relationship and friendship.

PART III

At La Guardia, Michael asked Gene about the values of the seven 727-100 aircraft in the Frontier Horizon fleet and his thoughts about the worth of the company. Gene was somewhat taken aback. He wasn't aware at the time that Frontier Horizon might be sold. He was surprised that a consultant like Michael understood that a good deal of the value in an airplane involved the residual times remaining on certain components, engines, and other parts. Most people in the industry had little or no idea how important this knowledge truly was.

While Gene was one of the very few people who understood technical crucial factors about the Frontier fleet and that these factors could add up to millions of dollars, he wasn't ready to divulge all the information. As Gene and Michael talked however, he realized that Michael was asking the right questions. Gene had found that it wasn't simple to explain things like oversight on the status of an aircraft, condition of an engine, or time remaining to major maintenance events, but Michael seemed to get all of it. Michael was not only interested in the real value, but also in Gene's expertise in determining the worth of each aircraft in relation to these technical factors.

Gene later found out that Michael was in discussions with Frontier Holdings and that he was looking into doing a leveraged buyout of Frontier Horizon. He needed to completely understand the full value of each aircraft in the fleet. Since doing a leveraged buyout meant acquiring all the equipment, he was doing his due diligence, not wanting to pay $10 for something that was worth only $4 because he didn't know what he had purchased.

Like John Blue, Gene Dessel was impressed. On the one hand, he recognized that Michael was a young guy with no real status in the company. On the other, Gene saw an intelligence and an eye for detail he couldn't help but admire and would soon come to respect.

***

During the early 1980s, there were a number of low cost, non-union startups like People Express and Value Jet. These airlines concentrated on reachable airports that were different from the hubs of the major carriers. Michael's plan was to transform Frontier Horizon into such a startup.

Having grown up under the constant scrutiny of his mother and perpetual harsh questioning about his manners and behavior, Michael had developed special senses. He was good at reading body language. He was always alert and on his toes. He was cautious of the words he uttered. He had mastered the art of imparting information on a strictly "need to know basis" and was always ready to take tough questions while keeping his cool. He did his homework before meeting somebody and had clarity of purpose. He had been trained and shaped to be a businessman by his circumstances and these skills served him well.

The vice president of finance at Frontier, who admired Michael told John Blue, "You know, Michael is the guy that if you have a dollar bill and he wants to buy it from you, it's worth $.50, but if he has a dollar bill and he wants to sell it to you, it's worth $1.50."

Michael did his due diligence, identifying the issues that needed to be addressed at Frontier, and determining the value of Frontier Horizon. Along the way, he continued to win friends and impress

PART III

people. By the time he was ready to present the plan he'd developed to Frontier Airlines, he had a support team that included John Blue, Gene Dessel, and others.

Meetings were set. Michael sat down with Hank Lund, executives at RKO General (who owned a controlling interest in Frontier Airlines at that time) and Frontier's general counsel, David Brictson, who, unbeknownst to either of them, would soon become an integral part of Michael's inner circle. Because Frontier Airlines needed to get rid of Frontier Horizon, they were willing to make a deal.

To finance the purchase, Michael negotiated a leveraged buyout. This method of financing, which rose to prominence in the 1980s, primarily utilized debt to finance the transaction. The company performing the takeover provided only a portion of the financing but was able to "leverage" a large purchase through the use of debt. During the 1980s and 1990s when leveraged buyouts were in vogue, debt could make up as much as 90 percent of the purchase of a business.

As part of the leveraged buyout of Frontier Horizon, Frontier would loan Michael the money and he would take over operations of the company. As part of the deal, he would assume the obligation of the existing office space at Stapleton, nearly 500 employees including John Blue and Gene Dessel, plus the seven 727-100s that made up Frontier Horizon's fleet. For a period of six months, Frontier Airlines would continue to subsidize Frontier Horizon on existing routes. After this transition period, Frontier Horizon needed to liquidate or find a different location in which to operate.

Michael assumed ownership of the airline as Frontier Horizon in late December 1984. Shortly thereafter, he was obligated to change the name due to a trademark issue relating to the name Frontier Horizon and a competing airline called Horizon Air. Horizon Air's parent company, Alaska Airlines had sued Frontier Holdings over the similarity of the names. This issue was ultimately resolved by changing the name of the company to SkyBus.

There was also another technicality that needed addressing: when Michael did the leveraged buyout of Horizon, a foreigner couldn't own an American airline.

On the day the paperwork for the leveraged buyout was finalized, I had a temp job sorting opinion letters in the mailroom of the Rocky Mountain News. It was totally mindless work I was doing strictly for the pocket money.

Michael called me the second the papers were signed.

"You have to leave your job right now," he said.

"Okay," I said. "But why?"

"The business section of *your* newspaper is about to run a headline that says I did the leveraged buyout for Horizon, but I can't own it, so I told the reporter that you, my unemployed housewife, owns the company."

I laughed and happily quit my job.

After that, I never worked anywhere except for Michael.

Chapter Twelve

Regan and Jennifer wondered how Michael lost money in the stock market when he worked in the airplane business? Why had they moved into such a big house if there was no money? They worried whether they would have to move again.

The question of whether Michael was making or losing money would continue to dominate our lives for the next few years, and we moved more than once. While I had blind faith in Michael, the girls weren't nearly as confident. The homes were not always bigger and better, and they were always rentals, which added to the feeling that our living situation could change at any time. Both girls thought they could end up back at 1212B at a moment's notice.

Because of the initial move, they were the new kids who had to come in midyear at a very different kind of school. Genesee and parts of Lookout Mountain were bona fide rich kid territory and it was a big adjustment. There was a definite division between the kids who lived at the affluent addresses and those who were considered "poor." Jennifer and Regan weren't sure where they fit in, especially given the financial uncertainty in their family.

Jennifer wasn't happy about the new dynamics but was always a good student and figured out how to fit in at the new school. Regan's adjustment was far less smooth. She felt unhappy, unstable,

PART III

and struggled to acclimate to their new world. Because their house was in one of the wealthier areas, she was pressured by the "rich" girls to be part of their clique. While we definitely lived on the "have" side of town, Michael had lost all of his money, then somehow bought an airline, but they still didn't even have "enough" furniture.

Wealth, at least in Regan's mind, had become all-important to her parents and a defining theme to everyone around her. The popular girls at school were unkind to the poorer and more down-to-earth kids in their class. As a result, she had altercations with mean girls who didn't approve of her being part of the in-group, while still being nice to everyone.

The kids in Genesee wore designer clothes and had rides to and from school and all of their activities. For Jennifer and Regan, who'd gone through elementary school wearing cute, homemade clothes their mother had sewn for them, they were never going to be indulged that way. Michael's uncle Salim had taught him *to be able to sleep on the floor as well as sleep on the bed* and he definitely raised the girls in the same manner. They walked, rode their bikes, or took the school bus every day. They literally walked uphill both ways to the bus because they were picked up at the top of the hill and then dropped off down below.

Jennifer and Regan saw that Michael was affected by his native culture in many ways. In Pakistan, families with means had servants. At home, the girls were taught to bring tea, carry bags, do dishes, clean the cars, and sweep the garage. While these were normal chores in a more average environment, they seemed excessive in relation to their new friends and classmates.

While he was a good man, Michael had a tendency to play favorites in business and at home. Jennifer was sometimes favored, but then he'd switch and prefer Regan. There seemed to be no rhyme or reason as to why one would be picked over the other. He made ultimatums that forced the girls to make choices, and sometimes brought more heartache than joy. He could be fiery, opinionated, and mired in his cultural biases.

I wasn't entirely immune either. Michael was hoping I would be more docile than I was and the cultural differences were easy to misread. The angriest Michael ever got at me happened one evening when we were having Shazad, who had also emigrated from Pakistan, for dinner. I had made lamb chops. Michael offered Shazad a third helping but I sheepishly admitted there were no more. Michael was furious. In Pakistani culture, it was a terrible reflection on the host to run out of food. Michael was embarrassed and we had a horrible scene over something as seemingly inconsequential as lamb chops.

As with all of our battles however, Michael soon realized he'd gone too far in the heat of the moment. He apologized, and I did too. This became a familiar pattern in our marriage. We would fight, cool down, overcome whatever issue had cropped up, and resume our loving relationship.

Some issues were, however, much more difficult than others to navigate…

***

I first met Michael's mother Hameeda and her husband, Chaudry Sahib, in the summer of 1984, four years into our relationship.

PART III

Hameeda and Chaudry Sahib flew from Pakistan to New York City. I recall spotting a tiny, dumbstruck woman being pushed in an airport wheelchair. She was completely out of her element in the hustle and bustle of Newark Airport. Chaudry Sahib stood beside her, looking just as overwhelmed by their foreign surroundings, but attempting to appear calm and in control. He was impossible to miss given his mustache which had been dyed a startling shade of orange. Chaudry Sahib didn't speak English at all, and Hameeda spoke very little, although she probably understood more than she could express.

I, who knew little about them and less about Pakistani culture, realized I was in for a crash course on all fronts.

We flew his parents from New York to Denver and then drove his mother and stepfather back to Genesee. Hameeda and Chaudry Sahib were duly impressed to see our large home. As soon as they got settled in, Michael took off for a business trip and I was left to care for and entertain my in-laws. To make matters worse, Jennifer and Regan were visiting their dad in Cheyenne for a month, so I was completely on my own. I had absolutely no idea what to do with the elderly couple. I lived in a state of panic, thanking God they went to bed early in the evenings.

With no common language and relying on rudimentary hand signals, I set about showing them the tourist sights of Colorado. I started with 14,000 foot Mount Evans, but quickly discovered that both of my passengers were utterly terrified of the winding mountain roads. On another outing, I took them to the Mother Cabrini shrine where Hameeda insisted on climbing the hundreds of steps past the Stations of the Cross to the base of the enormous statue.

Afterwards, her legs were so sore, she wasn't able to get out of bed for three days. Every time we drove past Target, I would suppress a laugh as Hameeda would say aloud, "O Target."

To compound the confusion, I hadn't yet learned how to cook Pakistani food. Both Hameeda and Chaudry Sahib were polite about eating whatever I prepared but seem to take no pleasure in the foreign dishes. That was, until they discovered Burger King. From that day on, there were many fast food meals, especially for Hameeda, who didn't eat beef, but craved French fries.

Every day was the same routine: they climbed into the car and I took them for an outing I hoped they would enjoy, but often turned out to be a disaster. They never seemed to enjoy where we went or what we did. I ended each day by escaping to the neighbor's house for afternoon gin and tonics, sometimes with multiple refills. I would return to Hameeda and Chaudry Sahib waiting on the front porch wondering when their dinner would be ready. It was a long, difficult, frustrating ordeal that left me wondering when Michael would come home.

Two endless weeks later, he finally returned.

I had never been so relieved when Michael entertained his mother and stepfather and took over the cooking. I didn't even mind being left out of their conversations as the three spoke in their native Urdu. Especially when they argued, which was often.

I learned that in Pakistani families, the husband's mother rules the household. In Michael's educated, higher class family, the older women were less subservient. I had no idea at first, but I was the embodiment of Hameeda's worst nightmare. In my mother-in-law's mind, her son had not only become westernized, but had a

PART III

feisty wife who was not Pakistani, and had no intention of kowtowing to her will. Hameeda resented everything about me--my race, nationality, age, that I was divorced with two kids, and mostly that I was keeping her son from moving back to Pakistan where he belonged.

Worse, we had started trying to have children together and were struggling with infertility.

"She's dead on the inside," Hameeda would tell Michael, hoping her pronouncement would break us up so he would be free to marry a nice Pakistani woman who could actually produce a child for him.

When I would ask what Hameeda and Michael were fighting about, he would protect me by saying it was nonsense or that I didn't want to know. Once I got a true inkling of the almost constant arguments, I stopped asking.

I also stopped asking the one question that was on my mind constantly during that first visit and for every visit thereafter: when would they be returning to Pakistan?

The first time I inquired, Michael had angrily replied that in his culture, *when are you leaving,* was the rudest question one could ask. I learned quickly and remained silent wondering when the day would come.

They stayed six long weeks.

Short, compared to the visits they'd make in the future.

Chapter Thirteen

After Frontier Holdings agreed to the deal Michael proposed, his newly minted company, SkyBus, became the owner of seven 727-100s as well as the office space and a staff suitable to maintain and operate seven aircraft. I remember going to a big party for hundreds of employees who had come to meet their new boss right before Christmas of 1984. I clung to Michael's arm as we circulated amongst everyone who was clamoring to say hello. At that time, there were at least thirty pilots, a maintenance staff, tech reps, administrative people, a small engineering department, and an executive/management team that included John Blue and Gene Dessel.

Michael would use the profits from the sale of the planes for operating cash, new equipment, and to pay back Frontier Holdings.

Once he finalized the purchase of Frontier Horizon, he promptly began to arrange meetings with potential buyers including World Airways. They needed 727-100s and Skybus had them available. While these aircraft were all American Airlines airplanes that had been sold to Frontier, they were still in good condition and, if properly maintained, had years of usefulness ahead of them. World Airways sent their executives and technical people to examine the equipment ahead of the meeting. Because of his extensive

PART III

knowledge of every aircraft in the fleet, Gene Dessel was invited to participate in the meeting beside John Blue and Michael.

Gene observed that the technicians were spending far too much time trying to denigrate the aircraft. At Frontier, Gene had been in charge of maintenance and engineering and knew the strengths and weakness of each plane better than anyone. If he didn't speak up, Michael was likely to end up on the bad end of a big deal, so he made it his business that day to disprove their inaccurate assertions. By the time the meeting wrapped up, he was quoting provisions, regulations, reliability programs issues, and all the other factors relating to how they'd been operating the aircraft. As a result, SkyBus ended up in a position of strength and Michael negotiated a price of ten million dollars per plane. The executives at RKO General were angry when they learned the negotiated price was nearly double what he'd paid for the planes, believing they'd been played. They assumed Michael had come to them with a proposal, having prearranged the sale with World and knowing he wasn't paying fair value for the company.

Michael had no patience with their posturing. He'd made both deals in good faith and he'd also taken on all the risk and liability. In addition to having planes to sell, Michael had employees to pay. He assumed the money for the employee salaries would come from the cash earned in the sale of the 727-100s and pay for the transition of operations from Denver to another airport in the future.

World Airways agreed to the deal but wanted the aircraft they'd purchased reconfigured into cargo planes. Under Gene's direction, this work began at World's expense. As a result, SkyBus had to be recertified as a cargo and passenger airline.

After the sale and while Michael was determining how and where to proceed and expand, Michael and Gene leased an additional plane from a broker. That plane was painted SkyBus and actually flew as a passenger aircraft out of Denver for one year.

Michael had been in aviation for a while and had extensive personal flight experience, but he'd never really worked with very large aircraft. John Blue had already proved to be a savvy financial consultant, and Gene Dessel, who'd worked in aviation since 1951, knew the planes inside and out.

During that time, Frontier Services, another subsidiary of Frontier Holdings did all the mechanical work and were, effectively, maintaining the Skybus airplanes. They were to continue to maintain the aircraft until such time as the operation moved—one of the final conditions of the leveraged buyout.

As such, SkyBus was ultimately obligated to leave Denver. And so, with their newfound capital, fledgling airline, and developing plan, Michael, John, and Gene started to look around for an airport where they could permanently establish a hub.

***

In looking around at various parts of the country, Michael decided to start a regional airline in the southeast. His plan developed into entering the Atlanta market using Southwest Airlines format of creating hubs at unused peripheral airports. Charlie Brown airport in Fulton County outside Atlanta fit his parameters—a satellite airport that could support a regional carrier of the size and potential scope of SkyBus.

PART III

With the proceeds from the sale of the 727s to World Airways, Michael purchased two DC9-15s in anticipation of getting the airline up and running. He also began to negotiate potential leasing deals for additional aircraft. The Fulton County community gave SkyBus lip service and seemed enthusiastic about the promise of increased jobs. However, there was an immediate outcry from nearby homeowners and businesses about the increased jet noise at the relatively small airport. Local officials insisted that this and any other issue could be solved by hiring "local" consultants, all of whom turned out to be of dubious reputation and ability, for which they charged Skybus handsomely. Then, local politicians got into the mix and muddied the waters that much more.

Michael and company had done their homework on the technical suitability of Charlie Brown Airport, but hadn't done enough research into the socioeconomic factors at play in the region. The airport was located in a primarily black community which wasn't particularly welcoming to outsiders. In addition, there was already a regional carrier, Air Atlanta, owned by Michael Hollis, a well-known and connected entrepreneur in Atlanta. He and the other executives at Air Atlanta did little to encourage the community to embrace a non-local competitor.

In its scramble to survive, SkyBus bought an advanced 737 which was operated briefly and then leased. SkyBus also operated 727-200s for a period of time. Michael had to buy, sell, and lease aircraft to outside parties to stay afloat, because Skybus wasn't able to operate an actual airline. The "leasing business"—buying, selling, and leasing aircraft—utilized the strengths of Michael's airline connections, bargaining ability, and mastery of knowing the "decision maker" for each airline with Gene's technical evaluation of worth and ability to connect maintenance programs and aircraft engine status to max value. The leasing was separate from SkyBus but critical to generate cash to pay the bills.

Atlanta became a costly misstep. They had no choice but to seek out another airport in the southeast with runways big enough to support a regional airline with larger aircraft.

After looking around at various locations, Michael settled on Clearwater, Florida.

***

When seeking an operating certificate, a company must present a plan to the FAA outlining aircraft type, maintenance programs and facilities, key personnel, pilot qualifications and training, and a variety of issues necessary for safely operating aircraft and carrying passengers.

For SkyBus, which was a small company going from point A to point B, changing FAA jurisdictions and then airplanes, resulted in an enormous amount of red tape.

When SkyBus relocated at the beginning of 1986, they couldn't technically operate as an airline because they had to recertify in their new region. Michael remained in the leasing business for cash flow while working toward starting up the new airline using the DC9 aircraft he'd previously obtained. Because they had no gainful use for employees and dwindling cash reserves, SkyBus was forced to furlough a number of employees and came to Clearwater, Florida with a skeleton crew.

PART III

Michael rented a high-rise apartment on the waterfront, and I shuttled between Clearwater and our house in Genesee to be home with the girls. It was a tumultuous time period, but I was by Michael's side when he needed me. Michael took me on his business trips, brought me to dinners, and introduced me to many of his associates. I met many sharp and experienced business people. Among them was David Brictson who worked as general counsel for Frontier and had known John Blue for years.

David was aware of Michael Chowdry, but didn't meet him face to face until the leveraged buyout of Frontier Horizon. At that time, Frontier was in terrible financial condition and David feared the company was headed for bankruptcy. Anticipating the worst, he left Frontier in 1985, and became general counsel for a smaller carrier called Florida Express. David commuted from Denver to Orlando, working out of his house when he wasn't at company headquarters in Florida. One day, he ran into Michael who was also going back and forth from Florida but maintained the office space near Stapleton airport. In chatting about work and their oddly parallel lives, David asked Michael if he might be interested in trading out office space for legal work.

In short order, David had an office in Denver and part-time legal work. He also found himself in Turkey alongside Michael to negotiate the sale of three 727s that Michael was selling as a side venture to help fund Skybus.

David Brictson, a low-key man who liked to wear his trademark Birkenstocks to work, got a taste of the jet-setting existence that he would come to recognize as trademark Michael Chowdry right away: trips to exotic locales for intense meetings with international executives, stays at places like the luxurious Istanbul Intercontinental hotel, high-end shopping excursions, and, of course, lavish meals.

While David became an invaluable ally and lifelong friend, other business associates were not quite so sterling of character. In fact, Michael was sometimes forced to do deals with less savory individuals. I knew my husband was no angel, and drove a hard bargain, but I warned him against some of the more questionable people I met in the used aircraft business, particularly when they gave me an uneasy feeling. While he needed seed money, I let him know that he couldn't possibly need it that badly, and Michael trusted my instincts.

In truth, he needed funding more than he let on. While working to establish SkyBus, he'd already incurred large startup expenses by leasing planes, making payroll, and dealing with legal bills. Early on, SkyBus held a press conference on the tarmac at the airport in Clearwater. The press gathered on one side of the plane. A cord ran in front of the press corps to keep people away from the aircraft. While it appeared to have been placed there for crowd control, it had actually been set up so no one would see that the plane's engine was missing on the opposite side.

Michael had started pulling income from his aircraft by selling valuable parts from the plane. The whole scene was symbolic of Michael's gambler's spirit as well as faith in his ability to pull rabbits out of his hat. Or, as the case was with SkyBus, pulling valuable parts out of planes, and selling them to pay the bills.

While Michael took whatever risks he deemed necessary to get SkyBus aloft, he relied on the business acumen of John Blue and

PART III

the technical expertise of Gene Dessel to handle the details involved in launching an airline.

***

In making the move to Clearwater, Skybus changed FAA jurisdictions and encountered unfamiliar regulators. Gene had managed to convert and deliver the 727s to World Airways as well as get SkyBus certificated as a cargo carrier. However, Skybus had changed aircraft types from the 737 to the two DC9s and whatever new aircraft Michael leased for passenger use.

The DC-9 aircraft was to become the nucleus of SkyBus operations out of Clearwater. As head of Engineering and Maintenance, it was Gene's job to reconfigure the aircraft interiors. Early in 1986, he upgraded the entire insides from seats to sidewalls, re-certificating them with the new interiors.

Getting an aircraft into flight-worthy condition however, involved a full FAA recertification of the airline including the Flight Department, Engineering, and Maintenance.

Certification also required a complete set of new General Maintenance manuals and an approved maintenance program, the preparation of which continued to be delayed for reasons outside of his control.

As time continued to pass, the financial strain mounted. SkyBus had administrative employees, ten people in the M & E department, and a compliment of pilots for the DC9s, all of whom were being paid. They'd also spent quite a bit to reconfigure the airplanes and upgrade engines. The delays drained the funds SkyBus had in its coffers from prior operations and leasing deals. Michael and company did everything from brokering new leasing deals to managing aircraft to stay afloat in the interim.

"When will we be able to have the GMM (general maintenance manual) approved?" Michael would ask.

"It's ready," he would be told by the department responsible for collecting and creating the necessary materials.

The manuals would be submitted and the FAA would reject the documents. Repeatedly.

There were serious concerns about the materials included in the manuals. For instance, they were operating two engine aircraft but the GMM had an extract from the three engine 727 manual for a "two engine out" operation. Gene was aware of the issues but could say or do little given the office and external politics at that time. Instead, he kept his head down, making sure that all items under his purview: engineering issues relating to how they loaded aircraft, flight department issues, and any number of the other items were taken care of properly.

When asked about the status of the General Maintenance Manual, Gene could only say, "I don't know. My people are doing exactly what you want and they have taken the manuals to the FAA and they've been rejected on several occasions."

There was one aircraft sitting on the ground in beautiful shape and another ready to go, but minus one engine. In addition, the opportunity to fly out of Clearwater was disappearing. The winter weather was warm relative to the rest of the country, but Clearwater wasn't a place people went to winter.

And they still needed to be certified.

PART III

SkyBus ended up going through the full certification—flight attendants, pilots, and all. The FAA sent in a team to ensure they were technically capable. As they left, the FAA gave SkyBus the authority and certifications they needed to operate.

Unfortunately, the company was continuing to maintain employees, expending money for consultants, and paying aircraft rents. The money Michael had made on the buying and selling of aircraft was gone. At this stage, SkyBus was only operating two airplanes and didn't have the capital necessary to launch the airline. SkyBus flew, but not with passengers, for thirty days between Boston, Logan and Washington National, the minimum number of flights required to protect the take-off and landing slots Michael had fortuitously acquired at those airports.

Then, he sold the slots to Continental.

While that income kept Skybus from having to declare bankruptcy, it was evident that Clearwater was not going to work, either. Not one to continue to lose money, Michael realized he was spending all of his capital to establish an operating airline when the market was changing.

It was time to shift directions.

***

All along, and in the midst of the ultimately doomed venture that was SkyBus, Michael was buying airplanes from one airline and selling or leasing them to another. Making money on the leasing side and hemorrhaging money on the operating side.

"We should get rid of all the expenses," he decided. "But keep up the buying and selling."

Skybus was shuttered in Mid-December 1986, having never operated out of Clearwater as a carrier. The two DC9s were sold, the rest of the equipment was either consigned or sold, and everyone moved out of their Florida apartments. Gene joked that he left Clearwater and headed home with four cases of toilet paper and a box filled with airline sized bottles of Mateus wine.

SkyBus was a bust, but Michael Chowdry was glad to get back to his family, the Colorado foothills, and move on to his next venture.

PART IV
AERONAUTICS LEASING
1987-1992

Chapter Fourteen

By the end of 1986, Michael was no longer burdened by the expenses associated with Skybus. The small fleet they had been managing for various entities enabled them to transition into a company he officially named Aeronautics Leasing, a lean operation made up, primarily, of Michael, John Blue, and Gene Dessel.

Initially, Aeronautics Leasing was headquartered in the Denver office space where the SkyBus reservations group had once been located but was soon moved and officially established at 538 Commons Drive near our Genesee home. All they needed was a receptionist, and that was me. I didn't have the qualifications, but my salary demands were zero. To begin with, there were so few calls I would have afternoon naps, propping my head against the phone. Looking back, I can't quite believe things were so quiet.

Michael remedied the situation rapidly.

In order to be successful, leasing companies needed to operate on various levels. Aeronautics Leasing's claim to fame lay not only in Michael's ability to broker transactions and provide consulting services, but a unique expertise in the areas of airplane maintenance and engineering. Much of their business was on behalf of companies with no connection to aviation, but who were interested in leasing aircraft because of the potential return on

PART IV

investment. In negotiating the sale of aircraft from one carrier, and then leasing the planes to other carriers, he developed an income-generating asset. In other words, a financial product whereby the buyer gained an income stream from the lease, and, potentially, appreciation when that aircraft was sold. Additionally, and unlike many assets that can't be moved if the economy drops in a certain area, an airplane can be moved from one airline to another.

Michael was involved in all aspects of the business. He knew about planes. He understood financing. He was, as both Gene and John described him, "the epitome of a Mississippi Riverboat gambler, a risk taker who stuck his neck out financially, and bet the plantation." He figured it was just as easy to sell a big airplane as a small one and it was certainly just as much work. Anything he didn't know, he learned. When he had free time, he'd spend hours poring through stacks of airline periodicals reading all the articles.

He also made a point of familiarizing himself with banks. Financial institutions liked the concept of airplane assets because historically they had gone up in value, but banks did not have the technical competency, nor the ability to form relationships with the airlines. Michael had the knowledge and an industry familiarity that enabled him to start attracting finance from companies like American Express and Pacific Power and Light. More than anything, Michael had boundless energy, enthusiasm, and a desire to meet and talk to everyone. An indefatigable networker, he was constantly on the phone at the office and at home making and maintaining contacts, gossiping about what various airlines were doing, who needed planes, and who had excess planes. He'd hang up with one person and call another.

"What's happening in this world?" he'd ask friends and contacts all over the globe. Michael proceeded to find out what was going on with that company or what they knew about another person or business in the industry. People liked to talk to him because he was always full of information and questions. "Where is the airplane, who has airplanes for sale, who wants to buy airplanes, who is going up in the organization? Who is going down in the organization?"

Michael created a product whereby the bank would finance the purchase of an airplane that he had located. Then, Aeronautics Leasing would find someone who wanted to lease the aircraft. There was an aircraft and a lease, financed 100 percent by the bank, which became a financial product that had more value than just an airplane or a lease. Eventually, Michael was able to sell the aircraft and the bank would get half of the profits and Aeronautics Leasing would get the other half.

As the initiator, facilitator, and master salesman, Michael, along with John, Gene, David, and outside counsel put the negotiations together that were drafted into memorandum of understanding. The MOU covered maintenance divisions, responsibility, who paid for what, redelivery conditions, and other details that would eventually be put into a final, formal contract.

John Blue was the financial expert. After they transitioned from SkyBus into a different kind of venture—one that relied more on Michael's business contacts, John sold his interest in the company to Michael for a minimal amount and took on the position of CFO. John realized that the real value in Aeronautics Leasing was Michael and his ability to generate business and investments.

PART IV

The partnership they had initially established for the purposes of SkyBus wasn't going to be the ideal way to proceed. It was a wise decision that cemented their business relationship for years to come.

Gene Dessel was charged with all technical and maintenance-related concerns and drafted all the contract MOUs. Gene had worked in aeronautics for the Navy and Lockheed Aircraft Service International where he gained a top secret clearance and worked on Air Force One. He'd also spent years at both Frontier and Icelandic Air and was as indispensable to the new business as he'd been to Skybus. He had an encyclopedic knowledge of aircraft and maintenance. He examined every plane and all associated records for each prospective purchase, looking at the hours on the engines, and determining the overall condition of the aircraft and its components. His assessment figured prominently into the overall value and pricing of every deal.

With the triple threat of Michael Chowdry, John Blue, and Gene Dessel, Aeronautics Leasing was missing only one crucial employee: a full-time, in-house attorney to prepare and review MOUs and negotiate deals.

***

For a little over a year, David Bricston had served as general counsel for Florida Express and did part-time work for Michael at a reduced hourly rate. In that time, both companies grew to the point where he had to make a choice: move to Orlando and work full time for Florida Express or take a chance on upstart Aeronautics Leasing.

David had been with Frontier for seventeen years, so he was familiar with large aircraft deals and working at a company of 5,000 employees. While Florida Express would never be that large, it operated on a similar business model.

While working for Florida Express was the sensible choice, negotiating on behalf of Aeronautics Leasing and Michael Chowdry was heady stuff and the only choice for David. He stopped turning in time sheets, negotiated a salary with Michael, and came on as full-time legal counsel, still insisting on wearing his Birkenstocks.

At Aeronautics Leasing, Michael and company, with the help of a new and particularly astute administrative assistant named Janelle Dumerat, were flying all over the world doing deals with carriers like SAS, Korean Air, UTA, and Air France. David had to be aware of foreign law to make sure all procedures were followed correctly.

While there were international treaties about the aircraft mortgages, most of the contracts contained a provision that they were governed by U.S. law. However, every country had its own equivalent of the FAA to deal with, and there were permutations from time to time that would require them to seek outside counsel in the jurisdiction where the aircraft was registered.

Together, Michael, John, Gene, and David made a formidable foursome and provided the foundation for all that was yet to come.

Chapter Fifteen

As Michael began to travel constantly for Aeronautics Leasing, he resented that I was able to stay home. He would return beat and cranky after crossing the globe in economy class, especially if it wasn't a successful trip. I always knew that with a little rest he'd regain his perspective and everything would return to normal. I stood my ground when necessary, knowing that no matter how irritable he was, he'd apologize as soon as he got a good night's sleep.

I traveled with Michael as much as I could, but it was complicated. Not only did I have the two girls at home, but Michael and I had started trying to get pregnant immediately after we were married in 1983.

The girls were thrilled by the prospect of having a baby brother or sister, but the process quickly proved challenging. I had easily conceived the girls in my early twenties, but now that I was in my mid-thirties, I couldn't seem to get pregnant. Six years went by in which I endured various infertility drugs, and countless months where I left the fertility clinic hopeful, only to end up devastated when the procedure failed. The process was stressful, expensive, emotionally draining, and fraught as we tried, month upon month, to conceive.

PART IV

Michael was a man who got what he wanted, so the idea of going forward in life without having his own children, especially a son, was challenging, but he never blamed me. It was just something we faced together. We had a brown Volkswagen Vanagon, we used to call the "loaf of bread." I made and sold homemade whole wheat bread to friends in Genesee which I would deliver in the brown van. When we were really down, we'd get a bottle of cheap champagne, drive to the mountains in the van, drink, cry, and laugh until we felt better.

When I became pregnant and then quickly miscarried twice, we mourned together, growing closer in the process. I then embarked on what would be five costly and painful invitro fertilization procedures.

To complicate matters Hameeda, or Pakistani Grandma, as the family had taken to calling her, and her husband Chaudry Sahib made regular, extended visits. Michael was dutiful out of filial obligation but felt no particular warmth toward his mother or stepfather. I found the relationship with my mother-in-law awkward and sought a balance I could never achieve. I dreaded Hameeda's visits knowing I would never manage to win over my diminutive, demanding mother-in-law who did everything she could to convince Michael that his wife was "dead on the inside."

Luckily, the girls grew to like Pakistani Grandma. They liked that she was tiny and round and had long braided hair, glasses, and funny shoes that would kind of flip and flop as she shuffled around. Pakistani Grandma took to Regan and Jennifer as well, and was as nice to them as she was to anyone. In the early years, she would even smile and half giggle at things they did and said, covering her mouth to hide her missing teeth.

While it was never directly spoken, Regan felt it was the girls' role to entertain her, soften her, and endear her to their mom and America in whatever ways they could. Pakistani Grandma spoke only minimal English and Regan and Jennifer couldn't speak Urdu, so they did a lot of sign language, drew pictures, looked at books with her, and found ways to communicate. Sometimes, Pakistani Grandma would even learn a word or two of English for the girls while they were at school and try them out in the afternoon when they came home.

Pakistani Grandma would look at the girls lovingly and pat their faces with affection. In return, they would make tea and try to cook for the grandparents. One time, Hameeda drew a picture of a black egg. Regan finally figured out that what she wanted was not an egg at all, but eggplant. Having no real idea how to cook, Regan decided to cook the eggplant for her in the microwave.

It exploded.

Pakistani Grandma laughed hysterically and even hugged her step-granddaughter as Regan cleaned up the mess.

The silly moments made up for Hameeda's otherwise perpetual unhappiness and the awful quarrels she had with Michael. He wouldn't explain what had been said, but both girls realized she'd been harsh with him in the same way when he was young. The longer she would visit, the crankier Michael would become. When he did return from a trip or a long day, he'd greet her with a warm hello, and then do his best to avoid her.

No one could really blame him.

***

PART IV

Chaudry is as common a name in Pakistan and India as Smith is in the U.S. Although Chaudry Sahib was no landowner, I was directed by Hameeda to call him Chaudry Sahib. Other relatives insisted he only deserved to be called Chaudry. Although Michael ended up using an Americanized version of the surname, it was out of respect for his biological grandfather, not his stepfather, who, as it turned out, deserved little if any admiration.

Regan and Jennifer both had incidents with Chaudry Sahib which changed the tenor of his already tentative acceptance into the family. Regan and Jennifer took care of the Pakistani grandparents when they were in town, especially Pakistani Grandma. They helped to bathe her, get her dressed, brush her hair, and even cleaned up after her when she snorted tobacco. While Regan found it exceptionally odd, she also dyed Chaudry Sahib's moustache bright orange using Henna.

On more than one of their visits to the states, Pakistani Grandma and Chaudry Sahib accompanied me and the kids to my parent's home in Lubbock. On one of these trips, my mother needed something out of the bedroom where they were sleeping. She sent Regan in to get it while she waited outside the door. While Regan was looking for the item in the bedside table, Chaudry Sahib suddenly sat up, threw his covers open, pulled Regan toward him, and started kissing her.

BJ came running in, grabbed her granddaughter, and immediately pulled her out of the room. She took Regan over to a telephone table in the hallway, sat her down, and asked if she was okay.

Regan was fine, although she wasn't really sure how to process what had happened. Chaudry Sahib had kissed her on the lips in a weird way once before, but Regan had assumed it was just how they greeted each other in Pakistan and didn't give the incident too much thought. Jennifer had also suffered a creepy kiss when he'd happened upon her alone in the basement. The girls had talks about it, concluding that it was totally weird, but that it had to be a cultural thing. They'd both been alone with him many other times and nothing else out of the ordinary had happened.

Grandma BJ told Regan that when she was growing up, a relative had grabbed her and done some inappropriate things and that Regan was never to allow any man to touch her in that way without her permission. Regan felt protected by her grandmother and wasn't terribly worried about Chaudry Sahib trying it again. She was mainly concerned about one thing:

"We can't tell Michael or Mom about what happened," she said.

"Why not?" BJ asked.

"I don't want to cause a problem," Regan said. She knew Michael was under a lot of pressure and had many things on his mind, and she didn't want to cause any more stress in his life. Unconsciously, she also worried that if she told him what had happened, I might somehow be blamed for the incident. She took on the burden of family harmony as her responsibility.

BJ told Regan to let her know if anything at all ever happened again. She also let me know what Chaudry Sahib had done. I was angry and horrified, but I confirmed Regan's intuition by not telling Michael either. I simply made sure my daughters were never alone with Chaudry Sahib again for any reason.

***

PART IV

Despite some of the unexpected trials and tribulations, Jennifer has fond memories of walking with Michael, driving through Poudre Canyon outside Fort Collins while listening to Chuck Mangione, cooking bouillabaisse out of the Vanagon, and just driving up to Vail for a stroll through the picturesque ski town.

She especially remembers Michael opening their world to new types of cuisine. There were always good smells in the house when he cooked, even if the food was sometimes questionable. Chicken brains, for example, were not very tasty, particularly for a girl who liked eating mac and cheese and apple juice every day.

Michael was a lesson person. He would point out that they lived in a bubble and had no concept or clue how the rest of the world lived. For example, Jennifer didn't like rice but kept telling him she was planning to join the Peace Corps.

"Rice is a staple in every country where you'll be sent," he said with a chuckle. "You'll starve to death."

As she made her way through high school, Jennifer recognized that there were qualities she liked about Michael and times when she really enjoyed his company, but that he could be a difficult and sometimes unfair person.

Regan's high school experience would ultimately prove even more challenging than Jennifer's.

Golden High School, where she started ninth grade, wasn't a good fit. Her best friend, a boy named Seth Richardson, lived on nearby Lookout Mountain and went to Mullen, an all-boys Catholic school in Denver. Our families were close through their ties with the church and youth group. When I came to her with the news that they were going to let girls into Mullen the following year, and that I'd let her go if she got accepted and could get a ride with Seth, Regan jumped at the chance. At the time, the $3500 tuition was a stretch, but we made it work.

Regan thrived at Mullen both academically and athletically. She played on a different team every season and was a natural athlete.

As the girls got older and learned to drive, their peers regularly got cars for their sixteenth birthdays. They knew this wouldn't be the case for them. Michael dealt with them on financial matters through me and I kept them on a tight leash. Jennifer and Regan had to work for the car they would eventually share. By saving up babysitting, chores, birthday, and pooling their Christmas money, the girls accumulated $2000. Michael and I matched their earnings and gave them an additional $2000. An extensive search turned up a used Suzuki Samurai convertible of questionable road worthiness and safety. The girls were thrilled with the freedom that came from having their first car even if sharing the car proved challenging and led to fights and resentments.

Michael did, however, foot the bill for various other expenses and events like Jennifer's graduation dress and the party itself (which he declined to attend because her father, Stephen, would be there). When she was getting ready to go to college, Michael said to Jennifer, "Pick any school and I'll pay for it."

His grand gestures, although sometimes unpredictable, went a long way with the girls.

***

PART IV

After six years, Jennifer and Regan thought of themselves as experts on infertility when at thirty-nine, I announced I was not only pregnant but that we'd heard the heartbeat and a baby was on its way. The whole family celebrated the announcement and enjoyed one of the happiest periods of our lives together.

I felt great, and nine smooth, complication free months followed.

This baby chose to make his entrance into the Chowdry family during a blizzard on New Year's Eve of 1988.

Certain the baby wouldn't dare come without him at home, Michael was away on what he insisted was an unavoidable business trip to Kuala Lumpur. Jennifer was babysitting for a family in Genesee when she got the phone call that I was in labor. Regan had gone to a New Year's Eve party and become stuck in the snowstorm. I wasn't upset at Michael for being away, or unhappy with the girls for their absence. Still, I had no choice but to drive myself to the hospital.

As I labored, Michael got on a plane. My mother rushed into town and over to the hospital. In the excitement, my mother forgot her suitcase and had to wear the maternity outfit I'd packed for the hospital until my dad brought her clothes when he arrived a day later.

James Michael Akbar Chowdry, who Michael insisted be named after my father Jim, was born January 2, 1989 at 2:20 a.m. Michael wasn't there, but called at exactly the right time and heard Jimmy's first cries via phone.

The baby and I were happy, healthy, and back home when Michael arrived with gifts of pearl necklaces for everyone to commemorate his joy.

His infant son was the greatest gift of all.

All the memories of years of struggling to get pregnant faded on January 2. I reveled in new motherhood. Michael was beyond delighted to be a father. Jimmy became a sacred thread of sorts that ran through the family. He was a unifying force with the Pakistani grandparents because I had produced an heir that looked like them. Regan and Jennifer adored their baby brother and devoted themselves to his care.

As a young girl, Regan's neighbor and friend had had a porcelain baby doll that was Indian. It had white clothes and she'd been fascinated with it. When Jimmy was born, she put him in a white onesie and thought, "I finally got my baby doll."

Chapter Sixteen

Aeronautics Leasing didn't house or store aircraft, but facilitated what were known as Dry Leases, in effect, operating leases where an aircraft was purchased from one carrier via financing from a bank or other financial institution, leased by another, and integrated into its fleet where it was manned and serviced by the lessee. In a typical transaction, a bank fully financed the airplane and received all rents plus 50 percent of the profits on the lease. Atlas took the other 50 percent of the profits. At the end of the lease term, either the lessee owned the plane or Aeronautics Leasing regained possession of the aircraft. Due to demand, the planes were quickly sold or re-leased to yet another carrier.

Michael had put together the nucleus of a very effective and efficient group of people whom he trusted implicitly. Together, the principals of Aeronautics Leasing did deals with everyone from Federal Express to Lufthansa, but it was Michael's contacts, credibility, people skills, and abilities on multiple fronts that led to the companies' immediate and exponential growth and set the groundwork for all the success yet to come.

He was the rainmaker—expert not only at developing relationships with airline executives and decision makers all over the globe but providing the technical expertise that financial institutions like Amex, ING, Pacific Power, and Hong Kong Bank depended upon to invest in aircraft.

The value of an airplane lay in its condition. The difference between an aircraft that required a heavy maintenance visit and one that did not could be five to six million dollars. An older 747 could be closer to ten million depending on the airframe and the engine condition. A 747-400 could exceed six million dollars per engine in life-limited parts alone. Airplanes were bought and sold as-is and Aeronautics Leasing bore the full responsibility for knowing what they were getting. If they paid $20 million dollars for an airplane, they had to be certain of the status of the maintenance, engine, airframe, and major components. Aeronautics Leasing made money for themselves and others because of their ability to assess these important values. Any missed details came straight out of their pocket.

A majority of the aircraft that were bought, leased, and sold had been in service, often in foreign countries. While these planes met the requirements in their jurisdictions, a lot of work done on them may or may not have met the Unites States FAA requirements. For example, when Aeronautics Leasing was doing work for American Express with Philippine Airways, the aircraft were operated under U.S. rules, but being maintained and serviced overseas. There were also obligations under federal air regulations to export an aircraft in accordance with the rules of the importing country.

Most aircraft were built in the United States so an Export Certificate of Air Worthiness is issued to all aircraft delivered outside of the country. This verifies that the plane meets U.S. rules on export. When Aeronautics Leasing was to take redelivery of an aircraft, it was to be brought back to the U.S. ready to go into service. In order to do that, Gene was tasked with making certain all repairs accomplished by the foreign operator were in accordance with Boeing and the FAA. This meant dealing with export issues, jurisdictional regulations, and certification of air work. Not only did each airline have its own regulations, but the country in which they were based had unique import requirements as well.

Michael sent Gene to meet with Royal Jordanian Airlines to inspect a 747 Combi (an airplane that can carry freight as well as passengers and features reinforced floors to accommodate cargo pallets) and negotiate redelivery conditions. Aeronautics Leasing planned to buy the plane, then lease or sell it to another company. They soon found themselves in the midst of a bidding war with the sales price topping $70 million. The cost rose out of their range, but Aeronautics Leasing held the mandate and negotiated a deal in which Gene would do all the required due diligence on the aircraft. As a result, they were able to take a multi-million dollar brokerage commission.

To celebrate, Michael flew in from the States for a big dinner at the Jules Verne in the Eiffel Tower. Throughout the evening, and with Sacre-Coeur lit up in the background, Michael kept saying his one and only sentence in French, "Dom Perignon s'il vous plait."

By the end of the meal, there were many, many bottles of champagne on the table.

Another multi-plane deal involved an Angolan airline and Equator Bank in Denmark. Aeronautics Leasing had collected deposits of four million dollars per DC-10. Equator Bank wanted to back out by saying that the planes would not be allowed to be exported by the U.S. because of a technology transfer with a country that was on a watch list. Aeronautics Leasing had already viewed any barriers to the export of these aircraft to Angola and found that the U.S. approved. The bank still wanted out of the deal, so Aeronautics Leasing kept eight million dollars in deposits.

Aeronautics Leasing soon managed a fleet of over thirty planes in which they held an equity interest. Some, they owned outright. During this period, half of Virgin Atlantic's fleet of airplanes were leased through Aeronautics Leasing. In addition, the company placed six 757s with Air Europe, two with Air Espana, four with MarkAir, three 747-200s with Philippine Airlines, and a number of 727s were leased to Pan American Airlines. They also bought and modified DC8 aircraft from Air Canada and sold them to UPS. Atlas did deals with the Venezuelans on three 757s and bought two 727 advanced aircraft that could fly over water, which were subsequently leased to Donald Trump's airline.

Michael maintained good relationships and contact with everyone in the industry, even leasing airplanes to Michael Hollis, the president of Air Atlanta who'd played a role in keeping SkyBus from operating in the Atlanta area.

Hollis's business model was to create an airline that provided a superior level of service in a semi-first-class configuration including leather seats, high-end cuisine, and a boarding area that was set up as a lounge. Because Hollis was the dashing, successful local boy whose father had been a train porter, he was admired, connected, and funded by the community. Most of the money for his venture came from investments made by Georgia-Pacific and other large companies in Atlanta and wasn't as profitable as projected.

The overhead of maintaining a quasi-first class airline was high and Air Atlanta primarily only flew back and forth from Florida.

The Wall Street Journal interviewed Michael for an article on the aviation business and Air Atlanta, to whom he'd leased planes. As part of the conversation, he told the reporter that airlines need to have a hub to bring in as many flights as possible and connect to other cities from there to create critical mass and thus profitability. When asked whether or not Air Atlanta was capable of reaching the critical mass he said, "No, they're a critical mess."

A comment which did little to endear him to his client but was unfortunately correct.

Air Atlanta which had been on shaky ground, went bankrupt in 1987. Michael needed to get the three aircraft leased to the company back ASAP. Gene was sent to retrieve the planes. Taking an aircraft back from a bankrupt company was difficult to begin with, but when Gene got to Atlanta, he discovered that expensive components like cascade thrust reversers were missing. Air Atlanta had a fairly large fleet with a lot of old equipment. They'd taken some components off Aeronautics Leasing's planes and put them onto other aircraft. Other parts were simply in storage. All told, millions of dollars worth of equipment was scattered in different directions.

Gene had to pay former Air Atlanta employees to identify where specific parts were and remove them from various storehouses. In one case, he had to remove components off one plane only to re-install them on the Aeronautics Leasing plane so the aircraft could be flown back.

It was a messy and drawn out ordeal.

PART IV

One of Michael's bigger deals was the purchase of two DC-10 30s from SAS for nearly $20 million dollars each. In September of 1989, Gene and David went to Kuala Lumpur to sell the aircraft to Malaysian Air System. Just as they were wrapping up negotiations, Michael called and said to tank the deal—a UTA DC-10 carrying 170 passengers had gone down due to a bombing. A replacement was needed immediately.

After a great deal of back and forth, they ended up selling one plane to UTA and the other to Malaysian Air System for over forty million dollars apiece due to immediate demand. Additionally, MAS didn't want to take delivery of the aircraft for a year, so they actually leased the aircraft to World Airways in the interim. At the end of the lease terms, World returned the plane and Aeronautics Leasing ferried the plane to Kuala Lumpur.

On another occasion, Michael and David flew over to Ireland to negotiate a contract for multiple airplanes with a big organization that had huge resources. They could borrow money cheaper than Michael and were known to be tough negotiators. Sitting across the table from each other, they kept asking for better terms, all of which led to a long drawn out meeting that lasted through the night.

By 4:00 AM, David was making what was supposed to be the last change to the contract. As he read over what was to be the final draft, he saw they'd purposely neglected to put in an agreed upon term.

David lost his cool.

Instead of getting angry at David for calling out a customer, Michael told him that the leasing company knew what time their plane would be leaving and were using it as a negotiating tool. The closer it got to flight time, the harder they were squeezing. Michael told David that the 4:00 AM push was simply a tactic.

Michael smoothed things and the deal was inked, but not at that meeting.

David felt badly for losing his temper.

"You were just tired," Michael said to David afterward.

At that moment, David realized just how savvy Michael truly was and admired his grace under pressure that much more.

The team continued to travel together in various combinations, depending on who they were going to see and where the company was located. When they traveled, Michael made sure everything—flight, hotel, and food, were always first class.

Michael once said to Gene, "If you fly coach, you can buy a new suit."

Gene turned him down because he didn't want to give him the chance to say, "Well, if you can fly coach today – you can fly coach tomorrow."

He needn't have worried. Michael traveled more than anyone, and understood the importance of comfort, particularly on long haul trips. Still, Gene traveled so much that at one point, he came home at the end of December, stayed through January 3, left for what was supposed to be two weeks, and returned three months later. Upon walking into the office, he discovered they had changed receptionists.

Just for fun, he asked her for an employment application.

Chapter Seventeen

Aeronautics Leasing was officially located in Colorado, but Michael's customer base was almost entirely overseas. He traveled back and forth to England to meet with customers so frequently that he decided to rent a short-term apartment in Kensington where he ran the office and stayed for two to three weeks at a stretch. I greatly enjoyed London and often traveled with him. Jimmy was a baby, and the apartment, Thorney Court, was walking distance to Harrods on Hyde Street, and Hyde Park.

Regan and Jennifer were less enthusiastic about my frequent absences. I would always have a family friend stay with them while I was traveling, but it was not ideal. Getting rides to and from school and extracurricular activities proved challenging and the girls complained that I never left enough cash or grocery store coupons for them. Worst of all, they hated that I took their beloved baby brother Jimmy away from them when I left.

Both girls were in high school during this time. Michael and I were busy with the business, travel, and the baby and we weren't able to come to many school events. This lifestyle was hard on Regan. Even when Michael and I were in town, she couldn't play afterschool sports the way she wanted to because the driving from practice interfered with the business. I always worked for Michael

PART IV

at Aeronautics Leasing in some capacity and frequently needed Regan home to babysit for Jimmy. When Regan's new boyfriend Ryan invited her to his lacrosse game, I said she could go, but had to take her brother along with her.

I loved working with Michael at whatever he was doing. I was happiest and most fulfilled in his presence. While I felt a constant sense of internal conflict, Michael's gravitational pull did, at times, outweigh the needs of the girls.

Regan, in particular, grew increasingly resentful.

In 1989, when Jimmy turned six months old, Michael and I decided to spend the summer in London, taking a large flat, big enough not only for the girls, but Pakistani Grandma and Chaudry Sahib who planned to come to the U.K. as well. At the end of the school year, Jennifer and Regan picked up tickets at the Aeronautics Leasing office and made their way overseas to meet up with all of us.

As always, Michael traveled during his parents' visit. I was again saddled with my mother-in-law for an extended period of time. Even with Hameeda's grunting acknowledgement of the adorable, smart, male heir I'd managed to produce, there was still the issue of caretaking my in-laws. I did not know how to drive on the left side of the road, so excursions required taxis, making things that much more difficult and complicated. Luckily, we were living within walking distance of Harrod's and the famed food halls which served cuisine from all over the world. I lost ten pounds that summer making trips back and forth in the heat for Pakistani food but was thankful for the simple mealtime solution.

***

Aeronautics Leasing was so busy, the girls generally spent their days helping out with the business, tending to the Pakistani grandparents, and caring for Jimmy. They often loaded Jimmy into a baby backpack and headed out on excursions through the city of London.

At one point, I took Regan clothes shopping in England. Michael got upset over how much we spent, but it wasn't just about the money. I agreed to items Michael didn't find appropriate, including short skirts. He frowned upon the girls wearing lipstick, and he barely tolerated any mention of boyfriends. It was hard for Michael because he didn't like the freedom afforded girls by Western culture. He was both worried and displeased about the amount of time they freely ran around London having fun. He remembered what life had been like when he was a youth in London and struggled as he watched how independent Jennifer and Regan had become.

This adherence to his Pakistani cultural roots would prove to be an increasing source of tension, even in a business setting. Everyone working with Michael was considered an "uncle" and addressed as such. They all seemed to be nice people, but one of the "uncles," a man from France, had his eye on Jennifer. He began to hang out at the penthouse after hours, coming up with excuses for why he had to stay late, and then lingered until dinner time.

One night, over pizza, Regan shut him down. "I don't know what you think is going on here, but you need to cut it out."

He backed down and they all pretended the incident didn't happen.

Another of Michael's business associates tried, unsuccessfully, to get Regan to come up to his hotel room after she was instructed to drive him home after a dinner party.

PART IV

The girls didn't say a word about any of this. They knew not to cause a ripple or a problem with anything that might interfere with the business of Aeronautics Leasing.

When the doorman of the apartment building acted inappropriately toward Jennifer, she did mention that she didn't like coming or going for fear of having interchanges with him. Jennifer hoped he would get fired, but he remained employed as a doorman. As a result, she felt trapped in the apartment.

After that first summer, we returned to the States. With the prospect of constant back and forth travel, Michael decided he needed to be in London full time. In 1991, we rented a house in Surrey County, in the town of Worplesdon just outside of Guildford. The house, which was big, beautiful, and featured an indoor pool, sat on three immaculately groomed acres. At ten thousand pounds per month rent, it was a world away from Michael's meager days back in London driving a cab and working at a Pakistani market. While he enjoyed nice things and living the high life, it wasn't money he cared about. Success and achievement were everything to him. Given how far he'd come, the trappings he was now able to afford were that much sweeter.

I liked England and was excited to live there permanently. Plus, after another failed attempt at in-vitro, I had become pregnant again and didn't want to travel back and forth. Jennifer had started college at Seattle Pacific University. Only Regan, who was to start her senior year in high school, was left with a difficult choice to make. One solution was to move with us to England and finish at a nearby American school. Moving to England was a tempting but challenging option because she was happy in Denver, had friends in Genesee, and loved Mullen High School. While she didn't want to be away from the family, Regan had been invited to live with the pastor from their church. It was another less than ideal arrangement but would allow her to graduate with her friends and her class.

On the fence about what to do, Regan consulted with her father.

Stephen pointed out that everyone at Mullen was taking their SATs and ACTs, going on college visits, and doing all the necessary groundwork to apply for college admission. Because she had no parents at home, she hadn't done anything in the way of college preparation, nor had she gotten the support she needed to pursue athletics or a scholarship to play on a collegiate team. In fact, she didn't know if she was going to college or not. Her father suggested it was time for her to focus on her education and what she wanted to do with her life. He also suggested that the only reason Michael and I wanted her to live with us in England was to babysit Jimmy.

One day, shortly before we were due to leave, Regan came into the kitchen where Michael and I were sitting.

"I just can't go to London and be Jimmy's babysitter," she said. "I have to think about my future."

"Where did you get these ideas?" Michael asked.

"I was talking to my dad," Regan said. "He's concerned I'm not prepared for what my path in life will be."

Michael was silent for a moment.

At that point, Michael was more stressed than usual. He was successful, but still on the cusp of a boom or bust. Money was going out. Lenders were starting to call in loans. He was looking at having to pay to park unleased jets in the desert. Whether he truly was irritated over the loss of our most trusted help with Jimmy

PART IV

or jumping on the prospect of removing himself from an increasingly difficult relationship was uncertain, but his stepdaughter had somehow pushed a crucial button.

"Okay, you don't have to go with us," he finally said.

"Okay," she said, somewhat relieved at the prospect of a decision everyone agreed was for the best.

"But you're not going to live in Genesee, either."

"What?" she asked, certain she'd heard wrong.

"You're going to move to Wichita Falls, Texas to live with your dad."

"Wichita Falls?" Regan asked, mortified by the thought.

"Start packing your bags," Michael said.

His word was final.

Regan was blindsided.

Although I was furious with Regan's father for planting the idea in her head, I didn't object the way I should have. There were times when I knew there was no confronting Michael, but, as a result, Regan felt permanently cut off from the family. Brokenhearted, she stuffed whatever clothes and things she had and drove herself down to Texas. She was so numb and upset she made the drive barefoot in a straight twelve hours.

Her world had literally fallen apart in a matter of minutes and her journey through many tumultuous years had just begun.

***

For Regan, Wichita Falls was as bad as Cheyenne had been for me. She was a girl who'd come from a background of good education and world travel, and the town felt like a cultural wasteland that was lost in time.

Regan enrolled in a school called Old High. When she brought in her transcripts from Mullen, she was told that she'd already taken all the senior classes and had no choice but to retake courses she'd already completed at her old school. By forcing her to move to Texas, Regan felt her parents, now far away in England, had even further thwarted her chances of academic success.

In Wichita Falls, she didn't know anyone but her father and she was lonely for her siblings. She was deeply hurt and very angry with Michael and me, spoke with us infrequently, and was left trying to deal with the huge blow of feeling that by speaking up and caring about her future, she'd been kicked out of the family. When she did make friends, they were from the wrong crowd.

Stephen had never really experienced the challenges of full-time parenting and was strictly hands off. He was so uninformed about his daughter's budding vegetarianism, he threw a pig roast in a friend's back yard for Regan's graduation.

She fell into the numbing effects of drugs and alcohol.

***

By September 1991, the family was spread out across the world. Jennifer was at school in Seattle. Regan was in Wichita Falls. Michael, Jimmy, and I were in England.

It was a dark, gray, November day in Guildford, Surrey. I went into my local ob/gyn for a routine ultrasound. The doctor was somewhat alarmed by the small size of the baby. He referred me to

PART IV

Harley Street in London where all the top specialists practiced. He wanted a second opinion.

I traveled alone to London later that week unconcerned and anticipating a clean bill of health for my unborn baby. I remember being so carefree, I had a haircut before my appointment.

The doctor performed an ultrasound that lasted for forty-five minutes.

"We've found abnormalities," he finally said. "They are consistent with Edwards Syndrome, a fatal mutation of Down's Syndrome."

I was completely stunned, and my heart pounded as he continued.

"This child will likely not be born alive. If she is, then she'll only live for a few months at most."

A nurse escorted me into a small office where I called Michael.

"I need you to come to the doctor's office in London. He wants to speak to us together."

Michael, who was coming from his office at Gatwick, arrived as quickly as he could.

"I recommend that you terminate the pregnancy," the doctor told both of us.

"No," we both said immediately, despite his advice.

"I'm going to let nature take its course," I said.

Michael, already grieving, simply nodded in agreement.

I was forty-three at the time and unlikely to ever conceive again. I immediately went into a state of mourning that lasted the remaining month of my pregnancy.

Both Jennifer and Regan were an ocean away and felt utterly helpless. When Regan got the news that the baby wasn't going to survive, she had an image of me sitting in dreary England, in a dark house by myself and wished more than anything that she could be there to comfort me. Regan's vision was accurate. I felt completely alone. Michael and I were simply unable to console each other.

To add to our impending personal disaster, the airline industry began to nosedive. Michael's biggest clients were suddenly afraid about their investments. I spent night after sleepless night worrying about my pregnancy and overhearing Michael's heated late night phone conversations with executives at American Express and other investors.

Despite stress that was all but impossible to bear, Michael had little choice but to continue to try and salvage as much of Aeronautics Leasing Incorporated as he could. I had literally one acquaintance in London—a woman from Michael's business—and otherwise knew only the nanny I'd hired to care for Jimmy. With no one for support, particularly after counseling sessions on issues like how to ship the infant's body back to the United States, I began to pray.

I continued to pray morning and night for the next month.

I was scheduled to be induced on December 14, 1991. If the baby was born alive, the staff was not to take any special measures.

Mother and Daddy came over from Lubbock for the birth and to help me deal with the emotional aftermath. Michael and BJ drove me to the brand new Royal Surrey County Hospital that icy, gray morning. I spent the day in light labor while Michael paced and talked on the phone, and my mother sat anxiously at my bedside. I was given Pitocin to speed along the process, as well as an epidural. I'd suffered enough pain with the pregnancy and didn't want to endure any more, emotionally or physically. At eight p.m., the midwife turned me on my side to encourage contractions. The doctor was to be paged, as soon as I was fully dilated.

At ten p.m., the effects of the epidural were wearing off. I was still laying on my side with my knees pulled in towards me. The midwife was sitting in front of me, next to the bed. I felt something and there was a small noise. The midwife stood and looked at me with no small amount of panic.

The baby had been born and the cord was wrapped around her neck.

The midwife paged the doctor. She'd been assigned to me because of her prior experience with Edwards Syndrome and had been present at hundreds of normal births.

She began to examine the baby. "There is nothing visibly wrong with her."

Even though there was a Do Not Resuscitate order, the midwife cut the cord and began to massage her limbs, which quickly turned from blue to pink.

Olivia Chowdry, born on December 14, 1991 took a big, miracle breath and emitted a healthy cry.

"This is a beautiful Pakistani baby," pronounced the midwife, who also happened to be of Indian descent, and had seen Michael coming and going from my room.

Had any other doctor or midwife been in attendance, beautiful, healthy Olivia would not have been resuscitated. Because no one expected the baby to be born alive, there was not even a small blanket to wrap the tiny infant. My mother took the pink cashmere sweater from around her shoulders and helped wrap her new granddaughter.

Michael and I cried tears of delirious shock and joy.

While it had been confirmed by top medical professionals that there was no chance, no possibility, that this was going to be the outcome, I'd spent a month praying day and night for my baby to be born healthy.

And God listened.

The first night, I didn't want to go to sleep because I feared I would wake up and discover the whole day had been nothing but a dream.

The doctors kept Olivia in the hospital for a week, testing her in every way possible while I recovered physically and mentally (with help, in part, from a Jerry Lewis and Dean Martin film festival that happened to be playing on the hospital TV). To protect us mentally and emotionally, Michael wouldn't allow anyone but family to see the baby until the doctors determined she not only didn't have Edwards Syndrome but was as healthy as the midwife had pronounced.

When Regan got a call from Michael, they had not spoken since he'd sent her to Texas. "Your sister has been born. She's okay, and your mother is okay. It's a true miracle."

Regan cried tears of joy for me and her healthy infant sister.

Plans were already in motion for her to come to England that summer, so as soon as she graduated, she would not only get to see Jimmy, and also meet her new miracle sibling, Olivia.

***

Jennifer flew to England that Christmas during winter break from college. She was taken by how beautiful her new sister was but

PART IV

couldn't miss how stressed and emotionally spent everyone seemed to be. The mood of the household was very fragile.

My mother and the nanny got into an irrational fight over who would go to the grocery store to get the ingredients for Christmas dinner. Because BJ wasn't familiar with shopping in England and had no idea how to drive on the left side of the road, I suggested the nanny go. BJ was deeply offended and made my daddy change their return flight to the States. They left before Christmas Day. Looking back, I believe the extreme stress we all had endured set the stage for that irrational decision.

Soon after, Hameeda and Chaudry Sahib arrived and she began to spin her own tall tales. Despite now having two beautiful grandchildren, Hameeda was still consumed with trying to get rid of me so Michael would return to Pakistan. Although it appeared to be a losing battle, she had no intention of giving up the fight and began to tell her son that I wanted them to leave immediately as well, even though I never said a word to that effect.

Michael, who was as stressed as he'd ever been over business, started to believe his mother's nonstop crowing about me and how I was mistreating my in-laws. In addition, he continued to get planes back from various airlines. It was becoming more and more difficult to work with the banks to refinance anything. There were endless late night phone calls with lenders across the globe.

The multiple stressors put an enormous strain on our marriage and Michael and I were arguing constantly.

One evening, in the heat of the moment, Michael said, "How much money do I have to give you to just go away and leave the children with me?"

"You don't have that kind of money," I said. "I'm leaving and taking the children."

In late January of Jennifer's freshman year, I called her at college. "I'm taking the kids and I'm going home to Lubbock. Don't count on Michael for any financial support. He says he won't pay for any more college. I'm afraid you're on your own."

That was all I said and we hung up.

Michael was dark, angry and brooding, but it was a turning point because he knew I wouldn't back down like I had in the past.

He soon apologized and asked me to stay.

We had weathered a lot together and began to work through our issues.

In the end, we resolved everything but Jennifer's college bill. Unfortunately, she was left dealing with the financial fallout of our conflict.

Jennifer had little choice but to figure out how to stay in school on her own. Had she known Michael expected her to pay, she would not have picked an expensive private school like Seattle Pacific University. At the time, Jennifer was dating Chad, the young man who she would eventually marry. Before he met Michael, Chad recalls that Jennifer was distraught because she'd gotten the call from me in London saying that Michael wasn't willing to pay for her schooling anymore. Thankfully, Stephen had been claiming her as a dependent and she was able to use his tax information to get financial aid. Every quarter, she went to the financial aid office to work through what loans she needed to take out. In addition, she got a part-time job, and was granted twenty hours a week of work study over the course of her college years.

PART IV

Although it was traumatic and troubling, Jennifer transformed into a better student and a more mature person as a result. During her first semester with Michael footing the bill, she'd behaved like a typical freshman--partying, not necessarily going to classes, and not being entirely responsible or clear as to why she was there. Losing her funding served as a turning point. Because she was paying, she never missed a class or the opportunity to maximize her education again. She had to work while going to college which really taught her how to manage her time and money which she considered a great life skill. Jennifer channeled her pain and the financial uncertainty into getting good grades.

Chad was less forgiving than Jennifer. He met Michael and I for the first time at a Chinese restaurant in Seattle. Chad's impression was that Michael liked to take charge, ordering an abundant amount of food for everyone. He also felt that Michael was testing him by offering him whatever he wanted to drink. Not yet twenty-one, Chad was surprised to be offered alcohol and was careful not to drink more than a single beer. He and Michael enjoyed a cordial meal, but he gained a clearer understanding of Jennifer's challenges.

A chance meeting with Michael at the Metropolitan Grill in Seattle, further confirmed his reservations about her stepfather. Chad was working as a valet parking cars when Michael came out of the restaurant accompanied by Boeing executives.

They looked at each other in surprise.

"Don't tell Jennifer I'm here," he said. "I would have stopped by, but I'm in and out of town."

Chad agreed and thought it best not to tell Jennifer, knowing she would be hurt.

***

Regan returned to London for the summer of 1992. She helped me with the babies and worked for the company. We also traveled as a family. Regan enjoyed being the nanny. She loved her baby brother and infant sister and she was paid, which would help to defray some expenses at Colorado State University where she'd been admitted as a freshman that coming fall.

Regan relished her time with Jimmy and baby Olivia. She enjoyed taking walks out in the countryside around Worplesdon where Jimmy fed apples to the horse that lived across the street. It was a happy time for her as she cherished the miracle that was beautiful Olivia, but her communication remained awkward with Michael. He had sent her away, so their conversations were limited and primarily consisted of pleasantries. There was no addressing what had happened. For the most part, Regan remained wary, and kept quiet. She wanted to stay in Michael's good graces because she was very attached to her small siblings. For her, they were the anchor for staying involved in the family.

Jennifer also returned to England that summer. She helped the family by babysitting Jimmy and Olivia. Jimmy was three at the time and was attending a local preschool. He had a sweet little British accent for a time which he would eventually lose after the family moved back to Colorado.

While living in London, the family went to visit Michael's old friend Naseem. He still lived in the humble neighborhood where Michael had rented a room so many years ago. Naseem and his family were a very warm, happy group of assorted relatives living traditional style under one roof. One of Naseem's nieces had recently married and showed them the bright colorful bedroom she shared with her new husband. She was in full Pakistani clothing and had her nose pierced. Regan thought she was indescribably lovely and wanted her nose pierced from that day forward.

They were all gracious, kind people and their house was filled with different, delicious smells. Sometimes, when I accompanied Michael to their house for dinner, Naseem's wife and daughters stayed in the kitchen and waited until we had finished eating. I struggled with the awkwardness of being left to eat with the men, even forgetting about business for a while.

On this evening, however, we enjoyed a simple, delicious family meal. Michael was clearly comfortable, relaxed, and connected to these good old friends. It was a nice, revealing side of Michael we all felt fortunate to experience.

As soon as dinner was over, the plates were cleared and a large box of Pakistani mangoes was set on the bright yellow plastic cloth, covering the table.

"You're going to want to get in on this," I said to Regan.

"What are we doing?" she asked.

"We're going to eat mangoes Pakistan," I said, like it was a big activity. "It's the best thing you'll ever have."

We pushed our sleeves up and began to enjoy the delicious flavorful fruits while juice dripped down everyone's fingers and cheeks. We laughed and ate until we were full. After dinner, we all sat down on the low-lying couches around the dining table and let our bellies relax.

Regan felt joyful and Michael was happy too. It was clear he enjoyed the mangoes and having family and friends around for meals and gatherings. He craved the harmony of large Pakistani families.

We left that night in two cars. I had the little ones in car seats in my vehicle, but Regan went home with Michael in the Mercedes with Pakistani music blasting, and the sunroof open as he talked on his big brick cellphone.

It was a good moment she wished would last.

***

Regan applied to and was accepted at Colorado State University in Fort Collins, Colorado. At the time, I was overwhelmed living in England, dealing with Michael and two kids. Regan filled out all the paperwork, got everything sent in, and was accepted not knowing exactly how it would be financed, but not thinking too far ahead either.

After a second summer with the family abroad, she left England. Regan's father, Stephen, met her back in Denver and drove her up to college. She signed in and moved into the dorms with her belongings and the $1000 she'd made over the summer. When her dad left, Regan made a discovery that had become all too familiar in the Chowdry family: her tuition for the semester had not been paid. Jennifer's first semester had been taken care of, but like Michael years before, Regan was told she couldn't live on campus and couldn't start school.

"We already gave you $1,000," I said, when Regan called in a panic. "Michael says it's more than he had. You'll have to figure it out."

PART IV

I was overwhelmed with family and moving and the business and the babies, but it's no excuse. To this day, I can't believe how cold and uncaring I was toward my own daughters. I'll never understand what I was, or more likely, wasn't thinking.

Regan had no choice but go to the financial aid department, tell them what had happened, and throw herself at their mercy. Unlike Michael back in his Minnesota days, Regan, ironically, couldn't get financial aid because we made too much money. In order to get a student loan, she had to sign paperwork saying Stephen was her sole parent. She held back tears in the financial aid office of CSU as she signed an affidavit saying she no longer saw Michael or me as her parents.

Chapter Eighteen

Aeronautics Leasing's business model had been effective and profitable. It was also a time in the industry when airlines were doing well, used aircraft were relatively inexpensive, production of new equipment was slow, and in many cases, carriers were not aware of the value of their used equipment.

Suddenly, everything began to change quickly and precipitously. First, there was the bombing of Pan Am flight 103 which exploded over Lockerbie, Scotland, on December 21, 1988, killing all 259 people on board and nearly a dozen on the ground. In the aftermath, people were afraid to travel. There was also a general downturn in the whole industry. Planes were being parked in Arizona.

Desert Storm followed.

At that time, Pan American had 747s which were considered Civilian Reserve Air Fleet aircraft (CRAF) meaning they had a side cargo door, interiors that were easily removable, and a reinforced main deck so that in case of a national emergency, they could be turned into freighters for military use. Michael had sold and financed the CRAF 747s to Pan Am which were conscripted during Desert Storm. Pan Am, which had been in difficult financial straits before the war, quickly verged on bankruptcy. And although the conflict only lasted ten days, the planes that were sent off to the military were returned in a deteriorated condition.

Strapped for cash to refurbish their fleet, Pan Am faced giving the planes back to Aeronautics Leasing. The airline needed to stay afloat and Michael needed Pam Am to remain solvent enough to keep their planes. He was able to convince ING Bank of the Netherlands to buy Pan Am's cargo-configured airplanes for just over $50 million per plane. He then did a sale leaseback to PanAm for $54 million in which they paid Aeronautics Leasing $870,000 a month. A full payout plus arrangement, Pan Am was to lease the aircraft owned by ING through the agreed upon period. Aeronautics Leasing made a monthly profit, while the bulk of the lease payment paid off the full amount of the ownership cost plus residual and carrying charges. At the end of the lease, Pan Am would own and could sell the aircraft.

While the issue had been artfully negotiated (and seemingly solved) the industry-wide problems were becoming more persistent. Boeing, who'd not been building many new aircraft, began to ramp up production. The AirBus A300 grew in popularity. Airlines who'd been eager to buy used equipment began to use their money to buy new planes as well as parts which had not been readily available.

And then, despite the cash infusion, Pan Am went bankrupt and the planes came back anyway. Other carriers started reneging on their airplane leases as well. Aeronautics Leasing had limited options because fewer carriers wanted the used planes for passenger service. Michael had to park a Fed-Ex 747 in the desert and feared there would be more. He also began to get middle of the

Chapter Eighteen

Aeronautics Leasing's business model had been effective and profitable. It was also a time in the industry when airlines were doing well, used aircraft were relatively inexpensive, production of new equipment was slow, and in many cases, carriers were not aware of the value of their used equipment.

Suddenly, everything began to change quickly and precipitously. First, there was the bombing of Pan Am flight 103 which exploded over Lockerbie, Scotland, on December 21, 1988, killing all 259 people on board and nearly a dozen on the ground. In the aftermath, people were afraid to travel. There was also a general downturn in the whole industry. Planes were being parked in Arizona.

Desert Storm followed.

At that time, Pan American had 747s which were considered Civilian Reserve Air Fleet aircraft (CRAF) meaning they had a side cargo door, interiors that were easily removable, and a reinforced main deck so that in case of a national emergency, they could be turned into freighters for military use. Michael had sold and financed the CRAF 747s to Pan Am which were conscripted during Desert Storm. Pan Am, which had been in difficult financial straits before the war, quickly verged on bankruptcy. And although the conflict only lasted ten days, the planes that were sent off to the military were returned in a deteriorated condition.

Strapped for cash to refurbish their fleet, Pan Am faced giving the planes back to Aeronautics Leasing. The airline needed to stay afloat and Michael needed Pam Am to remain solvent enough to keep their planes. He was able to convince ING Bank of the Netherlands to buy Pan Am's cargo-configured airplanes for just over $50 million per plane. He then did a sale leaseback to PanAm for $54 million in which they paid Aeronautics Leasing $870,000 a month. A full payout plus arrangement, Pan Am was to lease the aircraft owned by ING through the agreed upon period. Aeronautics Leasing made a monthly profit, while the bulk of the lease payment paid off the full amount of the ownership cost plus residual and carrying charges. At the end of the lease, Pan Am would own and could sell the aircraft.

While the issue had been artfully negotiated (and seemingly solved) the industry-wide problems were becoming more persistent. Boeing, who'd not been building many new aircraft, began to ramp up production. The AirBus A300 grew in popularity. Airlines who'd been eager to buy used equipment began to use their money to buy new planes as well as parts which had not been readily available.

And then, despite the cash infusion, Pan Am went bankrupt and the planes came back anyway. Other carriers started reneging on their airplane leases as well. Aeronautics Leasing had limited options because fewer carriers wanted the used planes for passenger service. Michael had to park a Fed-Ex 747 in the desert and feared there would be more. He also began to get middle of the night calls from concerned investors who had financed the planes, including American Express and Hong Kong Shanghai Bank.

Michael had fallen into yet another of the down cycles in his already established pattern of making big money on a good idea, building on it, riding on the concept, watching the concept crash, and losing the money. Only this time his pro forma net worth had risen to almost $100 million dollars and was threatening to fall into the negative multi-millions.

At one point, Michael and John Blue determined they could sell one of the returned planes owned by Hong Kong Shanghai Bank to Virgin Atlantic. Virgin Atlantic was interested but only willing to pay seven million dollars.

Hong Kong Shanghai Bank said, "Your loan with us is for $15 million. Feel free to sell it for seven million, but how are you going to pay off the remainder?"

Aeronautics Leasing incorporated each aircraft, so if they got in trouble on one, or it crashed, that was the limit of their liability. The bank however, required Aeronautics Leasing to sign on the debt. Michael and John knew they had no choice but play hardball.

John Blue said, "We can sell this aircraft for $7 million dollars, but you aren't capable of selling it at any price. You do not have the technical capability, nor the relationship with Virgin Atlantic to get one cent for it. If you want your $7 million dollars, this is the deal and you'll eliminate our debt. Otherwise, you can sue us for the $15 million dollars. We have nothing to lose."

Hong Kong Shanghai Bank had little choice but to accept the deal.

As part of the arrangement, the airplane was overhauled and painted in Virgin Atlantic colors. Either because of rivalries that exist in the airline industry or possibly sheer negligence, the maintenance was completed but the plane was never cleaned. The waste in the tanks fermented, causing the smoke detectors to go off and the odor of sewer to permeate the entire aircraft. After a thorough cleaning the plane was cleared for flight and delivered to Virgin Atlantic.

Aeronautics Leasing continued working to eliminate their debt. By the summer of 1992, they had only the two 747-200 freighters that had been returned by Pan Am. ING had a huge loan on these airplanes and were none too happy that they were sitting unleased. ING was out on a limb and so was Michael.

Aeronautics Leasing, which had enjoyed stratospheric success, was headed for a fall.

However, Michael had an idea that would set the groundwork for his next business accomplishment.

Chapter Nineteen

Through his extensive networking, Michael had forged a relationship with Peter Yap, the Vice President of Cargo for China Airlines. As a result of their discussions, Michael knew they needed freighters. He believed he could lease the 747 freighters to China Airlines. Because they had been CRAF aircraft, they already had a substantial portion of the cargo system capability. The floors were modified and they had cargo doors. The planes could go to Boeing in Wichita where they maintained a conversion factory and have the sidewalls removed, barrier nets added, an automated loading system installed, as well as any other necessary modifications.

Michael then met with the executives of ING Bank who was carrying the financing. He proposed that they put up ten million additional dollars so Aeronautics Leasing could convert the airplanes from partial to full freighters. He argued they needed to invest the money in order to make the aircraft viable.

"You don't have a lot of options here," Michael told ING. "We're broke, and this is the only hope for getting the money back on your investment."

Michael was well-regarded and capable, as were Gene, John, and David. Despite the downturn in the industry, they had a good reputation. It was still something of a miracle however when ING agreed not only to put up the money for the planes but didn't ask for some percentage ownership given they were injecting money into a defunct, negative worth company.

Michael went to China Airlines and negotiated a deal with them whereby they would lease the heavily indebted-aircraft, once they were configured, for pure freight.

The one stipulation China Airlines had however, was that they didn't want to have their pilots operate the aircraft. They wanted what is known in the industry as a Wet Lease. Wet leasing (also known as ACMI--Aircraft, Crew, Maintenance, and Insurance) meant the airline not only got the aircraft, but crew, maintenance, and insurance through Aeronautics Leasing. In these agreements, Aeronautics Leasing was not responsible for fuel costs, thus protecting them from the volatile jet fuel market.

In order to do a wet lease, a company has to have an operating certificate from the FAA, which was something Aeronautics Leasing didn't have. Michael went to his friend Morris Nachtomi at Tower Air, a passenger/cargo airline out of New York that was certificated for both. Michael explained that he had the aircraft and the client. They negotiated a deal to conduct the wet lease under the operating certificate for Tower Air. The Tower Group would make risk-free money on the deal as Aeronautics Leasing would be responsible for the costs associated with the operation of the aircraft.

Almost as soon as the ink was dry on the overall deal however, Tower Air began approaching China Airlines and asking why they were working with Michael Chowdry when he didn't have an operating certificate? They then offered the same services for less money.

Peter Yap from China Airlines, who respected the relationship he'd built with Michael, both personally and professionally, honored his contract with Aeronautics Leasing, but Michael knew it was time to take the next step.

A day later, I found myself standing around the kitchen table at the house in Worplesdon with Michael and Gene.

"I have an idea," Michael said. He had recognized that airlines were reluctantly buying cargo planes, a capital expenditure which affected their profit and loss statements. Providing cargo planes to China Air had given him the idea of creating a company that would fill a needed niche. He would invest in aircraft, bring them up to a standard that was at least as good as or better than anything else in the industry, and then lease cargo aircraft, complete with the crew, the maintenance, and the insurance.

"What's it going to be this time?" Gene asked.

"Air cargo. All I need is a name."

Gene and I both knew that despite any of the obstacles we were certain to encounter, it was on to the next chapter.

"Atlas," I said, the idea simply occurring to me. "Atlas Air Cargo."

Michael thought for a second. "Atlas Air Cargo it is."

PART V
Atlas Air Cargo
1992-1996

Chapter Twenty

In order to begin operations on his new venture, Atlas Air Cargo, Michael needed a Federal Air Regulation 121 certificate. The FAR 121, which is the highest level of certification, allows airlines to operate without further restrictions. Atlas Air would have had to have an approved aircraft maintenance program, a pilot training program, a flight dispatch center, maintenance and ground handling services, all manuals approved, and much more. At the end, there would be a proving flight. In addition, they would have to be granted a Certificate of Necessity and Convenience proving there was a market for what they were going to do.

Finalizing the documentation for SkyBus had been challenging, but creating a major cargo carrier meant submitting to the full scrutiny of the FAA. In other words, it was a huge undertaking.

Undaunted, Michael moved forward.

Atlas owned two freight airplanes. He and Gene started the process with a Boeing 747-200 with tail number N505MC. The N signified United States registration and the MC for Michael Chowdry. All Atlas-owned aircraft would have the MC designation. Rated for the highest load capacity of any 747 at the time, it was one of the passenger planes that had been converted to a freighter. One of the reasons Michael had been able to get the contract with China Air, which enabled him to start Atlas Air, was because of the planes' higher load capacity.

In order to certify and operate N505MC, they needed to complete a major overhaul known as a D check. Atlas had a maintenance agreement with KLM which was utilized to get the D check done. Gene was sent to Amsterdam to handle the technical details, while Michael, John Blue, David Brictson, and the small contingent of people who made up Atlas proceeded to set up the company per the dictates of the FAA operating certificate.

Michael thought about basing his new airline in San Francisco because of the proximity to China. Gene encouraged him to look toward New York because there were nearly a thousand trained, out of work, Pan Am employees in the region, one of them being Ron Morasco, a former Pan Am executive, who would oversee the technical details needed for the operating certificate.

While he liked the idea of establishing his company on the west coast, Michael decided Gene was right. They settled on John F. Kennedy Airport where they had a readymade workforce with all the right qualifications.

Headquartered in Denver with operations out of JFK, Atlas Air's primary business model was wet leasing or ACMI: aircraft, crew, maintenance, insurance. Atlas could also fly on a charter basis when an airline had cargo they needed to ship but didn't need a cargo plane full time. Because Atlas would be small and nimble, airlines could use their services in a variety of ways—even to test whether a certain market was viable for them. One of the geniuses of this idea was that, previously, when an airline bought an airplane, they needed to operate it full time. Most airlines did not want to purchase an aircraft devoted entirely to freight until they knew it would be financially workable. Leasing was much more attractive and financially sensible.

It would take a year and a half to get the Operating Certificate, a time period in which Michael had no choice but continue to subcontract with Tower Air. Morris Nachtomi tried to convince Michael that he didn't need to start his own airline. When Michael didn't listen, he tried to convince Gene and the other principals of the company.

"He's making a mistake," Nachtomi said.

"Michael knows what he's doing," Gene would say.

And he did.

Atlas was, and would remain, Michael's undisputed brainchild. As a result of his business acumen, uncanny ability to develop and nurture relationships, and a sixth sense for surrounding himself with capable people, the company would quickly grow to the point where they were operating for airlines all over the world.

***

One of the most notable, longest serving hires from Atlas's first year in business, was Jim Matheny. A career naval aviator, who had finished his military stint, Jim was amongst the people hired to work on getting certification for Atlas Air.

When Jim joined the company in December 1992, Atlas was made up of a total of eight people. They initially worked from temporary offices in Uniondale, Long Island. They soon relocated to a cold, cavernous space leased from American Airlines at JFK. At first, the Atlas offices were devoid of cubicles or furniture beyond a table and a single phone. Jim worked at the company for a few months before ever meeting Michael.

The two men finally met in Manhattan along with John Blue. Over dinner, Jim told Michael he'd been the commanding officer on an aircraft carrier. Michael was fascinated by every detail and continued to ask questions. At the end of the evening, Michael said that if Jim could tell him that much about the engineering of an aircraft carrier, then he ought to be able to run operations for Atlas Air.

It was a decision neither would regret.

The corporate headquarters of Atlas Air remained in Colorado and Michael had already hired Dave McElroy, an experienced airline executive, to head up the JFK operation. At that time, Michael typically spoke directly to McElroy. Jim Matheny, on the other hand, was involved in organizing the various operational functions--the air crew being the most challenging aspect.

The core of Atlas Air technical people—pilots, flight engineers, dispatchers, maintenance, and engineering personnel—were former Pan Am or TWA employees with extensive experience operating 747 aircraft. At that time, both Pan Am and TWA had ceased operations so there were a number of qualified people available. Atlas hired as many of them as they could.

The initial operation was to consist of three trade rotations from Taiwan to New York each week. Each rotation would take thirty plus hours to complete. The flight would originate in Taipei, go through Anchorage, terminate in New York, and then backtrack to Taipei. This plan required very efficient crew utilization because they were time limited as to how long they could operate the aircraft before there had to be a personnel change or the crew would have to take a rest period.

Just as the details were being finalized, China Air decided that instead of those three rotations, they wanted the middle rotation to go to Luxembourg through Dubai. This change would result in a tremendous strain on resources because it meant that Atlas would have to leave a crew sitting in Dubai for a week waiting for the aircraft to come back.

The reason China Air wanted this change had to do with marketing. The primary market for air cargo went from Asia to the US. It was also time sensitive because it was far more expensive to ship by air than by ground—two to three dollars per kilogram versus approximately five cents. And surface shipping took many days longer. On the other hand, the market between Europe and the U.S. was basically saturated because of what is known as belly freight, or freight that a passenger plane carries in its belly. Because there were so many flights going from Europe to the U.S. most shipping needs were satisfied by utilizing spare space on passenger jets.

This became a factor when Atlas operated its second aircraft, N808MC, part time for China Air and part time for KLM. Generating enough revenue to cover positioning costs across the Atlantic to operate a weekly rotation for KLM from Amsterdam, and then back to New York for the China Air flights was a challenge. However, Michael was willing to sacrifice some of the profit to grow Atlas's customer base.

The proving flight was from New York to Anchorage to Taipei, Taipei being the home of China Airlines. Upon the successful

PART V

completion of the proving flight, Atlas was awarded the FAR-121 certificate and could start operations.

They began operating immediately by hauling revenue cargo back to the states.

Jim Matheny recalls standing in their new facility at JFK Airport and seeing the N505MC with the new Atlas Air logo land on the runway right in front of the window. Jim was awed by the sight and the incredible risk Michael had taken to get Atlas Air up and running.

Michael's mother, Hameeda Begum

Jazzy Akbar, crop dusting days

Jazzy Akbar, a student in Crookston Minnesota

Uncle Salim and Auntie Khurshid Rama

Jazzy Akbar and Becky Stolheimer

JANUARY 2001   A REED BUSINESS PUBLICATION

AIRLINE BUSINESS

STRATEGY FOR AIRLINE BOARDR

STRATEGY
Low cost survival in Europe

SPECIAL REPORT
Service seeks the personal touch

INTERVIEW
Michael Chowdry
The man who made Atlas Air

Michael Chowdry, 747 cockpit

The delivery ceremony of 747-400

Jimmy cutting ribbon with Sheila Gaillard of Boeing upon delivery

Jim Metheny, COO, and Michael

Gene Dessel, David Brictson and Michael during Aeronautics Leasing days

Gene and Judy Dessel in Genesee home in the kitchen with Michael and Linda

Olivia, Linda, Michael, and Jimmy at the New York Stock Exchange. Atlas goes public!

Company clam bake party, 2000 at Genesee home

Host Michael

John and Sandy Blue

Prague, 1999

Nap after fishing, Colorado, 1997

Bird hunting in Colorado, 1999

Jimmy, Regan, Jennifer and baby Olivia

Olivia, Michael, and Jimmy fun in the Genesee home pool

Masood and Michael, New York City, 1997

Shazad and Michael cooking in Genesee home, 1998

Virginia Kiely, 1999

Michael and Linda at the opening of Museum of Flight, Seattle, 1997

Michael Pictured with L39, 2000

Chapter Twenty-One

We returned from England in October 1992. For the first time we bought, as opposed to rented, a house in Genesee and settled into a busy, happy existence. I had sold all of our furniture to avoid the cost of shipping it home. As a result, the first few months we lived in the house with outdoor furniture and mattresses, again on the floor. At that time, we were just happy to be back in Colorado, especially Genesee, where we had friends and a church home. We had weathered the stormy parts of our marriage and Jimmy and Olivia were energetic toddlers. This time around, instead of the haphazard childcare I'd cobbled together for the girls, I hired the help I needed—starting with young au pairs from Europe. I was forty when Jimmy was born. By the time Olivia came along, I was forty-three and any and all extra hands were welcome and appreciated.

Michael adored the kids and did his best to spend as much time with them as possible but continued to travel extensively. He was on the road as many as 220 days per year. At Christmas, he was more excited watching Jimmy and Olivia open all the presents than they were about their bountiful visit from Santa Claus. To Michael, his time with his kids was far more valuable than any hours logged flying above the horizon, any load of freight, or any deal done.

PART V

I never resented his absences. I'd always appreciated his ambition, was proud of his success, and loved him for it. I got involved at both Lookout Mountain preschool in Genesee and then Colorado Academy, the school the kids attended. While I participated in all the mom activities I'd missed with the girls, I still preferred being with Michael and staying involved in the business. I truly enjoyed parenting, but I was happiest when I was with Michael doing whatever he was doing.

Michael appreciated how I handled my role as a mother. He also depended on me at Atlas Air. I not only lent Michael direct support but was as detail-oriented as he was. I saw flaws and sought perfection. As the business continued to grow and pressures mounted, he depended on me to help him work through whatever issues he faced and help him to reestablish balance in his life. We really did work together as a team. Michael trusted me and valued my input. Jennifer remembers a ritual I had; I would go through and update his entire address book with all of his business contacts. I have nice handwriting, good attention to detail, and an ability to recall phone numbers by memory. I was content to help out in any small or large way I could.

Unfortunately, the skill and finesse required to maintain family harmony, particularly where the older girls were concerned, would prove to be one of our most difficult joint challenges.

***

Regan stayed at Colorado State University for one year and decided she wanted to transfer to the University of Montana. She got a ride to Missoula from someone she worked with whom she barely knew. She became interested in environmental and social issues which clashed, in her mind, with our endless pursuit of money and the materialistic life she felt we had come to live.

Regan was working two jobs to support herself and going to school full time while we traveled the world. She lasted one semester. Then, she worked just enough to get by and party. She was hurt and disillusioned with life and her answer was to numb herself. Michael treated her with disdain for her choices but did allow me to try and help her by sending small amounts of money. The money only went to finance her habits, so, sadly, I stopped sending it and, for a time, lost track of my daughter.

I spent countless nights over the next five years worrying that Regan was not only becoming lost to me, but irreparably gone.

***

Jennifer and Chad got engaged in June 1996 immediately after Jennifer gained her diploma and a teaching certificate in elementary education. Chad had graduated in 1995 and landed his first job at Microsoft.

Once she graduated, Michael stepped up and paid off all her student loans.

Jennifer never completely understood his thinking. She accepted that it was all part of the Michael Chowdry rollercoaster ride. It had been a difficult emotional process, but she gave herself credit for clearing the financial and academic hurdles she faced as a self-funded student.

PART V

They decided to get married the following Thanksgiving. Michael offered to pay for the entire wedding—including a lavish ceremony and reception at the posh Woodmark Hotel in Kirkland, Washington.

Despite ongoing friction, Regan came to the engagement party in Seattle to support her sister. She did not hide her feelings about Michael or conceal the pain she felt that I never stood up for her.

She did, however, conceal the fact that she'd become pregnant while living in Montana. Regan. While she wasn't yet showing at the engagement party, she certainly would be by the time the wedding took place.

Michael was furious when he learned that his stepdaughter was going to be an unwed mother.

The family, minus Regan, were in Lubbock for Grandpa Jim's 70th birthday when Michael announced that Regan was not welcome at the wedding.

"You can't demand those things," Jennifer said, uncharacteristically furious.

"She can't be seen in public in her condition," Michael said. "Not in front of our family and friends."

"She is our family," Jennifer said. "She's my sister and she's going to be there."

"If she's invited, I'm not coming," Michael said.

Jennifer was heartbroken at the prospect of having to make a decision of this nature, but she was also an adult now. She and Chad talked it through and came to the same conclusion.

"This is our wedding and we invite who we want to invite," Chad told Michael. "Regan included."

"I won't pay if she's there," Michael said.

"Then, we'll figure out how to do everything ourselves," Jennifer and Chad said.

"I won't come and I won't allow Jimmy or Olivia to come," Michael said. "I don't want them to see their sister in that condition. She will humiliate our family and it sets a terrible example."

Jennifer and Chad were young, and Jennifer did not like confrontation, but Chad gave her the confidence to hold firm.

"Regan is invited to our wedding," Jennifer said.

"I will be taking Olivia and Jimmy to Disneyworld during that time," Michael said.

"We will truly miss having everyone there," Jennifer responded.

The whole situation had become infinitely more difficult, but Jennifer and Chad made the best of it. They had put a nonrefundable deposit at the Woodmark but were allowed to apply it toward food which they served at a cost-effective but charming old schoolhouse that had been transformed into a venue for parties and weddings.

I was upset and angry with Michael, but knew he wasn't going to change his mind. Michael knew I wasn't about to let my anger get in the way of helping my daughter with whatever she needed to have a memorable wedding day. Over the course of our relationship, we'd learned to function effectively despite any issues that existed between us. Often times, when there was an undercurrent of tension between us, we managed to maintain an outward calm and an ability to work alongside each other, if not together.

Michael relented in that he did nothing to stand in the way of my role in the preparations. I flew back and forth to do all the

PART V

regular mother/daughter wedding appointments and organizing. Experiencing a sense of déjà vu, I went back to the craft store and got the supplies to create two four foot tall topiary trees, matching table centerpieces, and a variety of other wedding decorations which I paid for, and then assembled at home. Michael was well-aware that the items were being charged on our joint credit card but said nothing. I spent many happy hours with the glue gun in the loft of the house looking forward to Jennifer's upcoming wedding day.

Because Jennifer and Chad got married in late November, they decided to have a Thanksgiving feast as their rehearsal dinner. I brought cornbread stuffing and frozen gravy in my suitcase and Michael sent me first class. He also paid the airfare for my parents. He simply wouldn't pay for the wedding itself, nor attend the ceremony. I had spent many days designing and assembling the trees. I felt they came out beautifully. Apparently the guests agreed, because at the end of the evening, all the small centerpieces had disappeared. Jennifer was able to hang onto the taller trees and used them for Christmas decorations for years until they began to disintegrate beyond the repairs she could make with her glue gun.

The wedding was simple, touching, and devoid of any tension that Michael's presence would have brought. Jennifer was sad that Jimmy and Olivia and weren't there, but she and Chad had everyone else they really wanted in attendance, particularly Regan, who was teary, joyful, and deeply touched to be part of the celebration. The wedding was warm, loving, and much more reflective of who they were than it would have been at the Woodmark.

In the end, Jennifer felt relieved that her dad didn't have to share the day with Michael. Most important, their wedding day wasn't on somebody else's terms.

***

Tired of chopping wood and being cold in Montana, Regan managed to save enough for a ticket from Montana to Hawaii where she'd decided to live and raise her baby. She stayed with a midwife in the rainforest outside of Hana on Maui in a little shack with no running water, no electricity, and no screens on the windows. While she was there, she kicked her drug and alcohol habit cold turkey for the good of her unborn child and herself.

She has remained sober ever since.

As her due date approached, I flew over to Hawaii with my longtime friend, Lindi Kirkbride, who was Regan's godmother. We arrived to a scene straight out of a B movie: Regan laboring in a green plastic swimming pool full of hibiscus blossoms on a deck overlooking the Pacific Ocean. There were young nude girls running around in an almost worshipful manner as part of a makeshift ritual birth.

Lindi and I were shocked, but as devout Christians we prayed over the whole scene. "Lord this is evil. What's going on here is weird. Please protect this little baby."

When we weren't praying, we were holding parasols and putting sunscreen on everyone. In a situation like this, we had no idea what else we could do.

PART V

As we said our prayers, my first grandchild, a healthy boy, was born.

At the end of the day, we went back to the hotel room and killed a bottle of wine. By the time we finished, we'd had a good laugh. We spent the next day at the hardware store buying screening material to staple to the ramshackle little cabin and determined to make the best of it all.

A local lady from Hana village gave him the name Nalu - which meant big wave because he was 10.5 pounds at birth. In keeping with Hawaiian culture, Regan renamed him Suka (which means sweet) on his first birthday.

We stayed for two days before I had to get back to Michael, Jimmy, and Olivia. I hated leaving Regan with an infant and no visible means of support, but Regan wanted me to go too. While she wanted me there for the birth, we were still at odds with each other.

During this more than difficult period, Regan did what she had to do, working odd jobs and sleeping on people's couches to scrape enough together to support herself and the baby. At one point, she worked harvesting bananas with Suka on her back. Finally, however, she began to get in touch with the family again. She spent some time with Chad and Jennifer in Seattle, and I visited her and Suka in Hawaii when Michael traveled to the islands on business.

Michael and Regan were completely estranged, so he didn't join me. While Regan was pregnant, Michael had written her out of the will. Regan had no idea, but felt he was cruel and wicked and totally materialistic and felt no desire to see or acknowledge him in any way.

A few years later, she wrote him a letter trying to work through some of their issues and resume communications.

He never responded.

Sadly, they would never have the chance to repair their badly damaged relationship.

Chapter Twenty-Two

Michael's interaction with Peter Yap had provided the basis for Atlas's initial success and China Air would continue to be their biggest customer. What truly allowed Atlas to grow, however, was that they filled a niche in the cargo market, offering wet leases on what was known as big ugly cargo. In other words, cargo planes with lift capability that other aircraft didn't have and freight that traveled on metal pallets or in shipping containers as opposed to small UPS style express packages. FedEx and UPS carried, and continue to carry palletized freight, but only on a limited basis. Atlas offered affordable air shipment of time sensitive cargo, such as clothing, electronics, and perishables as an alternative to shipping by sea.

Their second customer airline was KLM and many more followed. The business deals were, by and large, a result of Michael's ability to make friends with the decision makers and navigate the differences in culture at companies like Emirates, Alitalia, Thai Airways, British Airways, Korean Airlines, and the South American carriers. He was perceived as knowing everyone in the industry, and likely did. He knew what others were doing and he always knew how to turn that to his advantage.

PART V

Michael operated with confidence that he could solve whatever problem surfaced. Plus, he was always willing and able to expend funds where he deemed valuable.

David recalls with humor a business trip to Paris where they stayed at Le Meurice Hotel. In the middle of the night, Dave heard Michael on the phone yelling at someone in China. Soon, the guests in the adjacent rooms began pounding on the walls and telling him to, "Shut up and go to bed!"

He worked the phones twenty-four hours a day because there was always someone awake somewhere in the world with whom he needed to speak.

***

The Atlas business model was an all-around win-win. There were plenty of airlines in the world that had 747 freighters, but it was an enormous expense to purchase a new aircraft, train pilots to fly it, and then have the cargo department commit to generating revenue. In many cases, it was cheaper to have a company like Atlas come in and fly routes instead.

While the air worthiness certificate was kept at JFK airport, the planes were based and often maintained by the customer airline. If the aircraft had to be sent to another location for specialized maintenance, Atlas and the customer would attempt to arrange a revenue flight to accommodate such movements.

Atlas Air was selling lift in some cases on a wet lease basis, and in other arrangements flying under its own certificate, utilizing Atlas Air international traffic rights. No matter what, Atlas went out of its way to accommodate customers. For example, if they had a delay, they tried their best not only to make it up, but to reduce costs or somehow operate an extra flight.

Most of the cargo on the 747s was carried on ten-foot aluminum pallets and loaded via an automated system. Load preparation was an involved process. Pallets were covered with a cargo net that had to meet FAA specifications. If a cargo net was damaged in any way, it had to be replaced or repaired before the flight could proceed. Along with loading and securing the cargo, Atlas had to make certain that everything was done per specifications.

There was an FAA approved loading manual and many restrictions of what could and couldn't be carried. For example, hazardous cargo had to be treated per regulations and in some cases, couldn't be dealt with at all. Other items had to be packaged in a certain way and had to be identified and clearly marked as a hazardous chemical. Of course, all cargo had to be loaded efficiently and properly ensuring a stable fit, and in compliance with aircraft weight and balance requirements.

Now and then, Atlas would get a request to ship construction equipment or some other outsized items that couldn't be put on an airplane. As long as a load was able to be shipped via standard ten-foot pallet (or, in some cases, twenty foot pallets) that met the height and weight restrictions in accordance with their FAA approved loading manual, the Atlas crew would figure out how to make it happen.

One of the early challenges was not so much the freight itself, but their limited fleet with which to recover from any flight

PART V

disruptions. Atlas started with the one freighter, then went to two for a considerable period of time before they got a third.

While there were fifty airplanes when Jim Matheny left the airline, the first few years were a different story. If an aircraft had a mechanical problem and the flight got delayed, the customer doing the shipping and the airline were both very unhappy. Atlas had to make every effort to catch up if a disruption or problem occurred.

A famous example of one of the challenges they faced was an airplane full of fish that experienced a mechanical problem in India. The fish rotted and the aircraft reeked. For years after, they were known to be the airline with the rotten fish odor.

If they were having a delay or an issue, Peter Yap would call Jim, sometimes at 3:00 a.m. and say, "Jim, you're giving me a head itch."

Jim would laugh, knowing he meant headache, and did whatever it took to ease Peter's mind and solve the problem.

The company-wide policy of attention to customer service led to the quick, exponential growth of Atlas Air.

Chapter Twenty-Three

It was 1993 and Michael was going through executive assistants regularly, so when he told me he had found someone who had proven to be a fit, I was, of course, anxious to meet her. He suggested I take Vicki Foster to lunch and get to know her and hear her story. We met in a nice restaurant on the west side of Denver where Vicki shared her experiences from her first few months at Atlas.

When Vicki stepped into our Indiana Street corporate offices in Lakewood, Colorado, Atlas Air consisted of a small team and four airplanes. She told me she knew they were in the air cargo business and that they were looking for an executive assistant. That was all she really knew.

The first thing she noticed was that the lobby had a calm, pleasant atmosphere and was somehow unlike any of the other places where she'd interviewed.

And then she met Michael.

From the moment he offered his firm, welcoming handshake she knew there was something different about him and his company. Michael's confidence, body language, and instantaneous ability to connect made her feel as though she was a good friend he'd known for years. Although he barely topped 5'6" and Vicki was

5'10" Michael's big personality and self-assurance stood out even amongst the top executives she'd met in the past. From the start, it was clear that he came from a place of unbridled enthusiasm about his company and its offerings.

The interview proceeded with Michael mentioning in his matter-of-fact way that he'd just returned from Dubai and was leaving for London for the christening of Virgin Atlantic's first Airbus A-340 airplane. As though that tidbit of information wasn't compelling enough, he added that Princess Diana had named the plane, "Lady in Red" and would be breaking champagne over the hull of the plane.

Vicki had certainly heard of Virgin Atlantic and Princess Diana but she had no idea what or where Dubai even was.

Michael continued the interview by saying he was looking for someone who spoke German, French, or perhaps Chinese.

Vicki had minored in French in college, but to say she actually spoke French was something of a stretch. She was so intrigued however, she decided then and there she would do whatever stretching needed to be done, by learning everything about Dubai or conversing in a foreign language.

On her second interview, just before Michael offered her the position, Vicki asked about the amount and duration she would be required to travel.

"There'll definitely be some travel," Michael told her. "But the longest you'll ever be gone is two weeks."

Vicki Foster became Michael's executive assistant in January 1994. Her job description, which included everything from handling calls and correspondence to eventually managing all public relations and marketing was complex and ever-changing. In other words, Vicki spent her time doing whatever was needed to assist Michael achieve his goals for Atlas Air. Some days she made his favorite Assam tea and tracked down McVities English biscuits, and some days she handled all the logistics of a trade show in a foreign destination.

***

Vicki was scheduled to go on her first trip, to Singapore for a trade show, a little over a month into the job.

Prophetically, she was gone for sixteen days.

Despite the length of the trip--the first of many, many lessons Vicki would learn about the actual demands of being Michael Chowdry's executive assistant--her visit to the Far East would prove equal parts exhilarating, educational, and eye-opening.

Aviation tradeshows are held in convention centers around the globe. They are gigantic, impressive, international affairs, which feature everything from simulated military compounds and exploding exhibits to breathtaking airshows. The Singapore show was no exception. Alongside the aircraft and engine manufacturers, major airlines, and other staples of the aeronautics industry were the biggest players in the air cargo business like UPS and FedEx. Not to mention Polar Air Cargo—Atlas Air's toughest direct competitor at the time.

One of the primary secrets to Michael's superior salesmanship was his ability to connect with people. He talked to many, many people each day, not only about business, but the other important milestones in the lives of family, friends, and clients alike.

PART V

Vicki, who had one of the Palm Pilots that were all the rage in the early 1990s and some extra time during her first weeks at Atlas, took it upon herself to input all of his contacts into the device. She figured it would come in handy eventually.

Eventually came as quickly as the first days of the trip to Singapore.

Vicki arrived early and got everything set up. Michael arrived soon after, inspected the booth, and started looking for a potential client whose number he'd forgotten to bring along.

"I'd really like to invite him to come by the booth for a meeting. It's probably too late now."

"No problem," Vicki said. "I have his phone number."

"How do you have his phone number?" Michael asked.

She pulled out her Palm Pilot.

"You're going to make it," he said. "You have what it takes."

Vicki was glad to hear it. Keeping up with Michael at the trade show, and in general, would prove to be something of a larger-than-life task.

Atlas Air, with its four planes, was not only a new venture and a bit player, but brand new to the world of trade shows. Intrinsically aware of the importance of first impressions, Michael set about creating a booth that would not only impress but establish his company as the undeniable rising star in the air cargo market. He saw to every last detail of the booth's design from the huge backlit picture of a 747 to the decision to have two of Atlas's pilots, dressed in uniform, present at the booth.

The pilots outlined the basics and answered questions, then introduced potential clients to Michael who'd invite them to have a seat at the conference table inside the booth itself. While this set-up evolved at later trade shows into a more elaborate arrangement including a separate meeting room, Michael was in his element meeting, mingling, and convincing industry stalwarts that Atlas Air had a winning business model whose time was now. The indelible impressions Michael made as a persuasive, personable, generous CEO at social events outside of the venue itself also paved the way for Atlas's skyrocketing success.

Vicki, who had come to Singapore as the advance person to set up and tear down as well as manage everything during the show itself, was surprised when Michael asked her to accompany him on a shopping trip. He was to host a dinner for executives of China Airlines and wanted to bring gifts to each of the attendees. As part of her job, Vicki found herself giving him advice on fine wool suiting fabric for the men and pearl necklaces for the wives who'd be attending. She also helped him pick out a stunning bracelet to bring home to me.

To her shock and surprise, he also had Vicki pick out a necklace for herself.

Vicki learned that Michael's generosity, which extended to clients, employees, family and friends alike, was part and parcel of his business style and personality. So was his sharp sense of humor. Before she left on her trip, Vicki's mother in South Dakota was a nervous wreck. Her daughter had traveled internationally before, but never to the Far East.

Before Vicki left, she gave her daughter a stern warning: "Don't eat any fish."

That evening, Vicki found herself as the only woman sitting at a long table of men. The server put a platter of raw fish directly in front of her.

PART V

She'd never had sushi in her life.

"My mother told me not to eat any fish," she said quietly while seated amidst the men. "Now, I'm about to eat raw fish."

One of the gentleman seated beside her, waved his chopsticks and said, "Oh, it's fine!"

Not wanting to look simple and unsophisticated, despite feeling exactly that way, she picked up a bright orange piece of sashimi, put it in her mouth, and began to chew. She prayed the cool, slimy texture might become an acquired taste.

"Well, I wouldn't eat it," Michael said.

"Now you tell me," she said, having just swallowed.

Michael smiled.

Vicki knew that if nothing else, she had a fun story to tell.

***

Upon their return to Denver, Vicki took anything and everything that was thrown at her as a personal challenge. Learning the details of the job proved easier than mastering the demands of working with the explosion of energy, tasks to be done, and mayhem that often came with assisting Michael Chowdry.

He had a weight room installed in the basement of the building so the employees could exercise on site. In other words, he could find them at a moment's notice. Hence, the phone on the workout room wall. More than once, there would be a knock on the door while Vicki was showering after exercise.

"Michael wants to talk to you."

"He's going to have to wait just a few minutes," she would say.

Michael laughingly joked about needing to have a phone installed in the bathroom itself.

She knew that waiting was excruciating for her boss, particularly when there was a question that needed answering. While his executive assistants couldn't hack his tendency to micromanage, Vicki inherently understood how much he cared about fine details. She got that her boss was only pressing to do what needed to be done and that he was simply impressing the high standards to which he held himself on those around him.

Despite her total commitment, there were moments when Vicki would say to herself, "This time I'm going to say no. I'm not going do it."

On one of these occasions, Vicki walked into Michael's office and said, "All right, I can either do project A or I can do project B, but not both."

"I need them both done," he said, in his usual matter-of-fact way.

"There's not enough time to do both," she said, holding her ground. "Which one will it be?"

"I really need both of them done," Michael said, not giving an inch, either.

"I can't do both," she repeated.

"I have every confidence in you," Michael said, heading for the door to her office. "Go make it happen."

Despite what seemed like too tall an order, Vicki also realized that by accomplishing the tasks he needed undertaken, she was ultimately saving herself later headaches. She knew that if she didn't get the jobs done, he would simply spend extra time finding someone who would—hence creating more for her to do.

PART V

So, she got down to it.

Michael was, of course correct. Despite having to stay late, Vicki got both projects done.

***

Vicki's commitment to *making it happen* resulted in numerous novel challenges. One such incident pitted her against Jim Matheny, who ran Atlas operations from New York where the pilots were based and dispatching was managed. Atlas had started working for KLM. On one particular day, a number of flights were scheduled but one especially important flight—the inaugural flight for KLM—was delayed.

Michael burst into Vicki's office perturbed. "The flight is delayed, it cannot be delayed. I want you to call and get that flight off the ground."

"I have no control over the schedule," she said. "That's Jim Matheny's job."

"Call dispatch," he said. "Tell them I said to get that flight off the ground."

Vicki had worked for Atlas long enough to know that if she didn't handle the issue, he'd find someone else. No matter what, there would be problems. She'd made a point of getting to know everyone in the New York office personally or by phone and reasoned that it made the most sense for her to take whatever heat resulted from Michael's request. Vicki took a deep breath, phoned the dispatcher and, in as friendly a tone as she could possibly muster said, "Hey, just want to let you know, Michael needs that plane off the ground right now."

"I'll get on it," he said.

The delay continued.

Numerous calls back and forth followed.

Eventually, Jim and his team got the flight in the air.

Later that morning, she got a call from a furious Matheny.

"Vicki," he said. "Who do you think runs this airline?"

"Michael Chowdry," she answered.

"But I run the operations," Jim responded. "Never call my dispatch and tell them what to do, ever again."

Vicki took a deep breath. "Jim, I, personally, would never call your dispatch and tell them what to do, but if Michael tells me to call your dispatch and tell them what to do, I'm going to do that."

He repeated. "Never tell dispatch what to do."

"I think you need to talk to Michael about this."

"I'm talking to you, right now," he said.

"I'm going do what Michael tells me to do. It's my job," she said. "Let me connect you to him."

Half an hour went by and Vicki had a knock on her office door.

Before she could say *come in*, Michael was in the room in front of her desk.

"So," he said…

Her heart was racing at what she felt would be her inevitable demise, but she met her boss's stern gaze.

"If I ever tell you to do that again, tell me *no* until I take no for an answer."

***

PART V

From the very beginning of her time at Atlas, Vicki found herself working on and learning how to resolve issues she'd never imagined she'd undertake. As a result, she learned a great deal. She typically felt fully engaged and her phone never stopped ringing--often with demands from Michael. She continually learned to do more, better. Over time she learned to anticipate what he was going to do or how he would decide to handle certain situations.

One evening, they were in New York, having dinner with a group of bankers. Given that Michael and Vicki had been invited, the bankers would theoretically be picking up the tab. As dinner unfolded, Michael began to command the attention and admiration of their dining companions.

Vicki assessed the situation, considered his generous nature, and decided Michael would want to pay for the dinner of excellent food and wine. While it was something of a gamble on her part, she knew his affinity for bold moves. She excused herself and took care of the hefty bill, confident that she was thinking ahead for him.

The dinner went on in grand fashion. Just before the arrival of dessert and coffee, Michael got up and excused himself. When he returned, he looked a little perplexed.

She leaned over and told him, "I took care of the tab."

"You did?" he whispered back.

"That's what you wanted, right?" she said, a tad nervous, but mostly confident.

He smiled broadly and nodded. "Nice work."

***

Vicki transitioned from viewing her job as a challenge to overcome to realizing her boss was truly a great man who worked harder than anyone she'd ever come across.

She had accompanied Michael on a trip to Anchorage, Alaska. At that time, the pilots were discussing the possibility of unionizing, so Michael embarked on something of a world tour to persuade them otherwise. On this particular leg of the journey, Michael scheduled lunches or dinners with a different group of pilots every day, but there was also an unexpected amount of free time.

It was on this trip that Vicki saw a different side to Michael. She learned how truly passionate he was about airplanes and talked in between naps on the flight to Alaska (another Michael Chowdry trademark) about all things aviation. While he didn't like excess down time on a business trip and preferred to be home with family, she learned he also liked adventure. One evening, over dinner, a flight engineer mentioned that he was going to rent a light plane and go flying the next day.

He invited Michael and Vicki to join him.

"Sure," Michael said.

The flight engineer was clearly excited about the prospect of taking the CEO of his company up in a small plane.

The next morning, Michael picked up the rental fee and the three set off, enjoying the stunning scenery, and looking for and spotting animals in a nearby national park. At one point, the young man, who was as nervous as he was enthusiastic, accidentally hit a wrong button, and every alarm in the cockpit signaled danger.

PART V

Vicki panicked, but Michael maintained his usual composure. He assessed the situation, looked over the control panel, found the problem, reset the controls, and calmed his shaken co-passengers.

When they were safely back on the ground and out of the plane, Michael simply shook his head. Vicki feared the young man's days at the company were sharply numbered, but Michael only said, "I'm glad he's just a flight engineer."

Vicki was glad to be alive and ecstatic as ever to work for Michael Chowdry.

Chapter Twenty-Four

When they first came to visit us in Genesee, Hameeda and Chaudry Sahib would come for a minimum of six weeks at a time and Chaudry Sahib would stay for the entire trip. In the early years, Hameeda needed her husband to advocate for her in court. After the case was settled and she gained control of the land, Hameeda dangled the money to entice him to stick around.

Their marital arrangement, although far less than ideal, and certainly lacking in love or affection, remained somehow workable. That was, until one night, when Michael got a call from one of Chaudry Sahib's sons in Pakistan and learned that they'd had Pakistani Grandma declared mentally and physically incompetent. Michael explained to me that because his mother was a woman, and thus had few rights, they'd managed to persuade her pharmacist to say she was unfit to take care of herself or her affairs. As a result, they were going to be able to take away the deeds to her land. Chaudry Sahib felt that he was well within his rights to do so. He'd been instrumental in settling that court case, and Hameeda hadn't rewarded him properly, in fact, at all. Having outlived her usefulness, Chaudry Sahib's family would have kept her in an outbuilding with minimal care.

PART V

The entire time Michael and I were married, he had no desire to return to his home country and had spent at total of six days in Pakistan. After that one phone call, Michael was furious and fumed for the rest of the night. He was on a plane, bound for Pakistan the next morning.

Michael returned to the United States three days later with his ailing mother in tow. To this day, I have a vivid mental picture of Pakistani Grandma scooting down the stairs of the plane on her bottom. She could figure out no other way to navigate them. Incredibly, she was accompanied by her ne'er do well husband Chaudry Sahib. While Chaudry Sahib had been a party to having her declared incompetent and had seized her jewelry and the deeds for the land, he still made the trip. I was shocked by the sight of him but knew better than to ask what he was doing there. Instead, I said nothing to him at all.

Thankfully, soon after they arrived, he turned around and left, never to return.

Family rumor was he'd married one of the servant women and lived happily ever after, courtesy of Hameeda.

Pakistani Grandma, who had nowhere else to go and nothing to her name, had come from her home to America to stay in Genesee, of all places. No one could fathom her isolation and loneliness.

While sympathetic to my mother-in-law's deeply unfair plight, I wasn't exactly delighted about the prospect of having Hameeda with us indefinitely. While she wasn't mentally incompetent as purported, she had diabetes, high blood pressure, and Parkinson's. She was in increasingly frail health and needed someone to attend to her around the clock.

Luckily, Michael and I were blessed with the means to hire help to take her of daily needs.

Hameeda didn't feel quite so blessed. She'd lived in Pakistan her whole life and had lost the land that had served as her driving force for staying in her home country. Now she was elderly, broke, in poor health, and trapped in the home of her erstwhile daughter-in-law. Happiness had never been her plight in life, but she was now truly unhappy and bitter.

I tried to make the best of hosting Hameeda and hired an ever-revolving cast of caregivers. One day, I was out in the garden while one of the home health providers was inside the house giving Pakistani Grandma a shower. The woman came outside soaking wet because Pakistani Grandma had turned the shower head on her. It was one of many such incidents that occurred during that time, as miserable, broken Hameeda made it a point to get rid of the vile American helpers on a regular basis.

***

Life was challenging and stressful, but then we hired Virginia Kiely. Virginia was working at both Mt. Evans Hospice, and as a special education assistant at her ten-year-old daughter's school when a friend named Lupe asked if she could come spend the weekend with the elderly Pakistani lady who was in her care. The scheduled nursing assistant who was supposed to take the weekend shift had suddenly quit--a regular occurrence. Lupe explained to Virginia that the elderly woman's family was in Europe and that she herself would be out of town and couldn't take the extra shift. After the tragic death of her husband, Virginia was struggling and needed the money, so she agreed to step in for the weekend and a couple other nights until the family returned. Lupe called me to vouch for her friend Virginia, and then brought her to our home where she was introduced to Hameeda.

Lupe left, and Virginia remained in the large house with the tiny little Pakistani woman who didn't speak English but gave the evil eye better than anyone she'd ever met.

Virginia, both a worrier and a warrior by nature, was extremely stressed by the responsibility of the angry foreigner in her care. She, quite nervous, wondered why the family would hire someone they didn't even know. What if something happened while she cared for Pakistani Grandma? Most importantly, would she make it through to Sunday night?

Hameeda's Parkinson's caused her to move slowly and unsteadily, so Virginia carefully kept her from falling. She was afraid to be on her feet and spent a lot of her time in a wheelchair, but Virginia helped her shuffle around the large family room for exercise. Virginia bathed and tried to ease her anxiety about getting around, so the poor little woman didn't feel like she had to hang on for dear life.

Somehow, they not only survived the weekend together, but at the end of the shift, Hameeda scowled, grabbed Virginia's hand, and pulled her. This was her way of showing affection and that she didn't want her to leave.

Virginia learned from her friend Lupe that Hameeda had broken an arm that had not been set properly which contributed to her fear of falling. She also learned that another of the caretakers had forgotten to set the brake on her wheelchair and she'd gone careening down the driveway and crashed into the bushes—a comical sight but terrifying for the old woman.

That first weekend and in the remaining days she filled in, Virginia not only took every precaution, but had a demeanor that made Hameeda feel safe. She was protective by nature, and Hameeda not only seemed to respond, but wanted her around more often.

When we returned, we saw how competent Virginia was and instantly hired her to come in two days a week, for twenty-four hour shifts. Virginia was delighted and relieved. We paid her well enough so she could give up her current hospice job and stop driving throughout the foothills to care for other elderly people at a much lower wage. She could work with one person, in one place, two full days a week. The job also allowed her to be home more so she could spend time with her daughter.

At first, Virginia didn't interact a lot with us because she primarily spent her shifts with Hameeda down in her room, separate from the rest of the house. When she'd come upstairs to prepare Hameeda's meals, we all got to know her and she soon became part of the family.

I told Virginia she brought sunshine when she came to the house and that her shifts were the best two days of the week. Plus, she had the patience of a saint.

Virginia also grew increasingly connected to Hameeda. She liked to take care of people and Pakistani Grandma needed the attention. There were two other caretakers who came a couple of days a week, so they traded off and would stay twenty-four hours, sleeping in a twin bed in the same room as Hameeda. These women only did what was absolutely necessary and displayed little care. Hameeda sensed they were there for the money and resented their attitude. These caretakers came and left on a regular basis, a constant worry for me. Virginia, on the other hand, would take Pakistani Grandma for car rides, Indian food, and, of course, to Burger King. When her shift was over, Hameeda would scowl. When she returned for her next shift, Hameeda blessed her with her nearly toothless smile.

Michael and I had his mother fit for dentures, a big ordeal with many trips to the dentist. She never wore them, but always carried her dentures in her pocketbook. She was never without her purse, trusting only Virginia to take possession of it for her.

Virginia noted that the kids were somewhat scared by Hameeda and her toothless smile, so she began to encourage them to sit near her and hold her hand. She also did the same thing with the dogs. Michael was an avid hunter, and we always had labrador retrievers. Dogs in Pakistan had been wild, roaming the streets scrounging for food. As a result, Hameeda was terrified by the big, gentle household pets. Virginia would sit and pet the dog. Hameeda would look at her like she was crazy, but Virginia would just say, "Nice dog," pet it, and have the kids do the same thing. It didn't take long before the kids would come in, sit down next to their grandmother in uncomfortable silence smiling and holding her hand.

Virginia not only managed to make her feel comfortable, but made sure Pakistani Grandma knew she had someone at her beck and call. If she made a peep, Virginia was right there, especially at night when the old woman had a habit of shouting out several times.

The first time it happened, Virginia was startled and concerned something terrible was wrong. She popped out of bed and turned on the light. Hameeda was sitting up looking at her. Virginia patted her arm, talked to her, and asked her what was wrong. Hameeda just lay down and went right back to sleep.

Until it happened again.

And again.

Virginia tried leaving a night light on, but it didn't make any difference, so she just got used to the nightly drill. She didn't ignore Hameeda but got up and attended to whatever she needed.

Virginia learned a few words of Urdu from Ali, Michael's college-aged second cousin who came to live with us for a year.

She learned how to tell Hameeda she looked pretty, and ask her how she felt. Hameeda would just laugh at how badly Virginia was butchering the language but seemed to appreciate the effort. When they'd drive in the car, Hameeda would pinch her arm and hold out her hand. Even though she was driving, Virginia would allow Hameeda to grasp her because it made her feel safe. Virginia was pleased to be able to crack through and build some rapport, especially when so few things made the little old lady happy.

Once a month, Hameeda would shuffle into her room, pull her suitcase out of the closet, and try to pack her bags. The first time it happened, Virginia asked Ali what she was doing. Ali asked Pakistani Grandma and learned she was preparing to go back to Pakistan to kill Chaudry Sahib.

No one paid too much mind to the understandable ritual and even found it to be comical, but when Hameeda started packing once a week, Virginia decided enough was enough. She took

PART V

the suitcases and put them in the garage. Once the suitcases were gone, Hameeda seemed to forget about her desire to murder her husband, which was a relief to everyone, particularly Virginia who preferred to direct her charge to more positive activities.

She washed and braided her long gray hair and often did the same for Olivia.

A favorite was a weekly pedicure.

Because she had a young daughter who liked brilliant colors, Virginia always wore bright nail polish. Hameeda would look at her fingers and toes. One day, Virginia motioned to her feet and Hameeda nodded, so Virginia gave the old woman a pedicure and polished her toes with hot pink nail polish. From then on, every week or so, she would soak Hameeda's size three feet, and give her a pedicure in another bright color.

While the other caregivers complained that Hameeda was mean, Virginia found her to be a kind soul. She understood that Hameeda was unhappy by nature and a fearful woman in a foreign country trying to make the best of her difficult situation.

Virginia was only three or four years older than me, but quickly became a mother figure to all of us. Although she started out as Pakistani Grandma's caretaker, she became a beloved second mother to the kids, and she soon became indispensable. She helped cook, grocery shop, tidy up, and even fill in at school events. Virginia didn't meet Regan until much later but met Jennifer and Chad a few times when they'd come to visit.

Other than her penchant for Burger King, Hameeda ate Pakistani food almost exclusively. Virginia appreciated the exposure to the new cuisine and liked that her workplace was filled with the rich aroma of saffron, curry, garlic, and exotic spice.

One morning, Virginia was downstairs with Hameeda. I was at church with the kids. Michael and Ali, who was visiting, came in from the garage with a big black garbage bag.

"Don't come upstairs," Michael said.

She soon heard crashing, hammering, assorted noise, and endless roaring laughter. She wondered what in God's name was going on.

Until she started smelling a delicious aroma…

A couple hours later, Ali came down with the big black garbage bag again and said. "Don't look in the trash."

When he came back in, Virginia asked, "What's going on?"

"Oh, we just cut up a sheep's head. We're cooking the brains."

They cooked it and ate it. It smelled delicious, but Virginia, who was a fairly adventurous eater, decided to take a pass.

Michael enjoyed having Ali around for (mis)adventures of this nature and Virginia found his presence helpful when it came to caring for Hameeda, but it escaped no one's attention that Michael took the boy out and bought him a brand new Subaru hatchback.

We all understood that he bought a car for Ali to show off to his Pakistani family. We knew the purchase was meant to illustrate that he was doing well and living the American dream. Still, the girls made mention of the difference between how a male cousin was treated compared to them, his stepdaughters. They both wondered if things might have been different were they boys or he'd been able to adopt them, but assumed it was more a bloodline and a boast to the family back home.

PART V

Ali drove it into a ditch and wrecked the car within days.

I remember sitting on the front porch with him as he sobbed in remorse.

Jennifer eventually ended up with the vehicle after it had been repaired and Ali left town, but Michael didn't gift the car to Chad and Jen. Rather, he had them take over the payments. Perhaps if Michael had insisted on Ali taking more responsibility, it wouldn't have ended up wrecked.

***

Michael traveled much of the time, but the first thing he did upon returning home was to come into his mother's room, kneel in front of her chair and speak to her in Urdu in the way of an obedient son. Her room was downstairs, close to the door to the garage, so he'd stop in and talk to her whether he was coming or going. Before he would leave, he would tell Virginia to take his mother to her favorite Indian restaurant and out for drives.

Virginia was aware that he had many difficult memories from his upbringing and that Hameeda was often mean, so she was impressed by how kind and respectful he was to her, no matter what.

When he was leaving, she gave him her infamous scowl, but when came back home from a trip he'd stop in to talk to her before he greeted anyone else in the family. I think this made her feel she held a superior position to the rest of us, particularly me. Although unhappy, she was always pleased to have him back at home so she could complain to her heart's content.

Chapter Twenty-Five

As Atlas grew, they continued to buy airplanes and convert them: six aircraft from Thai Airways, five 747s from Fed Ex, and the list went on. Not only did Michael take in used planes, but he would eventually start buying new 747-400 freighters directly from Boeing, right off the line--ten in 1997 and two additional 747-400 aircraft orders by 1998.

A 747-200 could carry about 100 kilotons. A 747-400 could carry 125 kilotons. Of course, that depended on the cargo density and on the range, so the fuel load had to be balanced with the payload to achieve maximum range. While a plane could usually take-off with a predetermined payload, downward adjustments had to be made to account for situations where it was very hot, like in Dubai in the middle of the day. In that case, they'd be limited by a lower weight for take-off.

At that time, wide-body aircraft carried significant cargo in their belly along with baggage. As a result, the yield on cargo across the Atlantic between Europe and the US was very limited. It was not practical for an airline to operate a 747 cargo airplane across the Atlantic. Shipping across the Pacific was a different story, though. All the clothing sold in the Limited stores, for example, came through Hong Kong and was manufactured in China.

PART V

Designers in New York would come up with a logo for a pair of jeans, send the logo to China, China would manufacture the clothing, and send it on to Hong Kong, where Atlas waited.

The highest yield cargo at that time was leaving Hong Kong on Sunday morning and arriving in either Chicago, New York, or Los Angeles on Sunday night where they gained between thirteen and sixteen hours. The clothing, already on hangers and in plastic bags, that left Hong Kong on Sunday morning would be for sale in places like The Limited stores on Monday morning. If it arrived two or three weeks later, it was too late. This was the case in clothing, electronics, perishables, and anything else that had rapidly changing demand.

The ultimate challenge in operating from Asia to the U.S. was getting a payload to go back. Most of the revenue was generated on the eastbound trip and very limited revenue available going back westbound. To remedy this, Atlas arranged some creative payloads that, at times, even included animals. Atlas carried a polo team, a load of pregnant cows destined for New Zealand where they were having trouble breeding cattle, and even alligators made their way from one zoo to another aboard Atlas planes. Transporting live animals wasn't predictable and could sometimes result in momentary havoc if a creature got loose, but it was a lucrative market.

More typical were flights to and from Chile where Atlas planes flew in seabass and salmon from the big fish farms. Atlas transported asparagus from Peru. In Kenya, salads were premixed and packaged in plastic destined for supermarkets in London. Atlas could transport almost anything that was time sensitive or perishable for the market.

At Christmas time, Fed-Ex and UPS became overburdened with packages, so they would wet lease Atlas 747s to account for the increases. FedEx and UPS needed these aircraft and paid a high price for the short-term leases.

In South America, one of the key cargos was flowers. At one point, fifty percent of all cut flowers sold in the U.S. came through what became Atlas's third office in Miami. The inherent challenge coming from South America was drugs. Not only was there an extensive screening process, but the rule at that time was that if drugs were found aboard, the authorities confiscated the airplane itself. The possibility of losing an airplane was an ongoing issue because drug dealers hired airport employees to stow contraband on aircraft. Atlas never had an airplane confiscated, but drugs were discovered onboard from time to time. Because they didn't have multiple flights going to the same destination every day, Atlas had to position or carry spare wheel assemblies. More than once they found wheel assemblies that had been loaded full of cocaine.

At one point, the Venezuelans sequestered an Atlas aircraft. Gene and Dave had to travel to Caracas to negotiate the release of the plane. A whole phalanx of people including generals and high level bureaucrats came into the meeting. All were adamant that Atlas didn't have a proper license, which was an entirely trumped up charge. In the end, the Venezuelans released the plane without demanding a payout of any kind, but no one was too happy about having to face Chavez's henchmen or the tense hours they'd spent in a country that was, for all practical purposes, a dictatorship.

Chapter Twenty-Six

Pakistani Grandma was well cared for and received proper medication. She had been integrated into daily family life. While she and I never grew close, and the arguments between her and Michael never fully ceased, we made it work.

Despite three calm, safe years and no outward signs of new or acute illness, Hameeda seemed to decide her time was nearing the end. She began to grow less alert. At that point, Virginia was at the house three days per week.

Michael, the children, and I were out of the country when Hameeda began to decline food and drink. Virginia called the hospice and they sent nurses. She called Michael's assistant and let her know she thought Hameeda's time was coming and that we needed to cut our trip short.

Michael had once asked Virginia to get something out of his desk when he was traveling and she remembered he had old, familiar Pakistani musica tapes. She went upstairs, retrieved them from an old cassette player, and put them on in Hameeda's room so she would have something comforting and familiar to hear.

The tunes made Hameeda smile.

Virginia played the music while Hameeda was drifting in and out of consciousness. As the nurses tended to her medical needs,

PART V

Virginia brushed her hair, wiped her face with a cloth, and comforted her.

Hameeda passed away at noon in Virginia's arms as she rocked her in a recliner and played the soothing Pakistani music.

We hurried back from Europe, diverting to Boston's Logan Airport to refuel so we could make it back to Denver more quickly. Michael got word his mother passed while en route and began to sob over her death. Jimmy tried to comfort his grief-stricken father. I was both sorry and surprised to see Michael so distraught, but I had never had much of a relationship with Pakistani Grandma beyond knowing Hameeda didn't like me and that it had been three long, difficult years.

Virginia knew the owner of the only local funeral home authorized to prepare bodies for a Muslim service. She arranged for Hameeda to be picked up and provided the proper rituals for burial which included being bathed by Muslim women, all of whom were quite shocked to see Hameeda's hot pink toenails. While she waited for the hearse to come, Virginia dressed Hameeda, put lotion on her, and braided her hair.

As soon we arrived, Virginia took us directly to the funeral home. Along the way, she let Michael know that his mother had died peacefully and had been transported within an hour of her passing.

Michael hesitated in the doorway of the funeral home, but eventually entered the beautiful candlelit room to say his goodbyes to his mother. I stood by him and was filled with deep sadness for his grief.

The next day, we had a Muslim funeral at a local mosque in Aurora, Colorado. Because Muslim funerals are conducted as part of the regular worship ceremony, I was permitted to watch from the upstairs balcony amongst the women, but because Michael was a Christian man he wasn't allowed into the mosque at all. He had no choice but to wait in the foyer during his own mother's funeral ceremony.

Both Jimmy and Olivia were in attendance, but neither of the older girls came back to Denver. Michael and Regan were completely estranged. I called Jennifer at Michael's request to let her know Pakistani Grandma had died and that she needed to come to Colorado right away.

Stephen had just arrived for a visit with her in the beautiful Northwest. Jennifer remembers weighing what to do. She recognized that her dad felt like she'd been forced to choose Michael over him throughout her childhood years. She knew Michael would assume that her non-attendance would be a payback for his actions regarding Jennifer's wedding. While it was sure to cause another significant ripple in their relationship, Jennifer decided to stay in Washington with her father.

On a cold, snowy day, Michael, Olivia, Jimmy, Virginia, and I accompanied Hameeda's body to a Muslim area of a cemetery in Denver where she was lowered into the ground.

Nobody ever knew exactly how old she was.

While his mother was demanding, critical, and anything but easy to please, Michael realized that she'd given him his firm resolve. He had survived a childhood with Hameeda and his current success was due, in part, to lessons he'd learned from her, no matter how harsh.

Her legacy would live on through him and his children.

PART V

***

After Hameeda passed away, seven-year-old Olivia came to us about Virginia on behalf of herself and Jimmy. "We know Virginia was hired to take care of Pakistani Grandma, but we've had so many nannies and we don't want anybody else but her. We want her to live with us forever."

Luckily for all of us Virginia stayed on. Her presence took a huge load off me. I was able to travel with Michael while the kids could stay in school and do their activities.

Michael and I were always appreciative, and Virginia enjoyed her dual role as a second mother and my assistant. On a typical day, she'd take the kids to school, tidy up, buy groceries, prepare a nice dinner, set the table, and go home. She was doing what she'd done for her husband and family.

During the early years, Virginia got to know Michael well through her time making his breakfast in the morning. Once her own daughter left for college, she had time to spare and would come over to our house at 7:00 a.m. and then stay until 7:00 p.m., sometimes later when necessary. When Virginia was cooking, she'd ask Michael what he wanted for dinner. He'd either tell her, "little chickens" (Cornish game hens), lamb chops, or steak. She would get whatever it was he wanted, knowing he'd be happy with anything that involved rice, veggies, and meat.

He even liked what he called her "boiled meat." On St. Patrick's Day one year she said, "Should I make corned beef and cabbage?"

"What is corned beef and cabbage?"

"It's like a brisket cut that you simmer with carrots and potatoes and cabbage."

He gave her a funny look and said, "Oh, okay, but have something else in reserve."

It came out so well he had her make it repeatedly over the years.

When we traveled as a family, Virginia accompanied us on ski trips, to Santa Fe, and to Sea Island, Georgia where we stayed in a big house on the beach. The kids would usually invite friends, so Virginia kept all of them busy building sandcastles, baking cookies, and swimming while Michael and I entertained guests.

Virginia grew to become a member of the family.

On her birthday, she arrived to a giant bouquet in the entryway. Michael and I toasted her with champagne on the patio. As she was leaving for the evening, I insisted Virginia take her flowers with her. The bouquet was so huge, Virginia didn't think it would fit into her tiny Toyota Tercel. It did, but only after she belted the vase into the front seat and opened the sunroof. She drove away with flowers coming out the top of the car. When she got home, she put the bouquet on a table behind her sofa, and her daughter, Bridget, looked at it and said. "It's so big it's like a room divider."

As the kids got older, they each got their own bedrooms and we fixed up Pakistani Grandma's old bedroom for Virginia. When we were out of town, or out late, she had her own space in the house. We also let her drive one of our safer extra cars so she didn't have to worry about getting stuck somewhere with the kids in what she called her old jalopy.

Virginia or V as the family called her, watched the kids grow into teenagers, helping them with their homework, going to school functions, and driving them where they needed to go. She took Jimmy to tennis and went back and forth for novice horseback riding lessons in Evergreen with Olivia.

Once, Michael came to watch one of the lessons. He sat there for about fifteen minutes, looked at Virginia and said, "She just rides around in circles."

Another fifteen minutes passed and he said, "I'm going outside."

They came out an hour later and he was asleep in his car in the sun.

"Riding in circles," he said when he opened his eyes. "And I'm paying for this?"

Chapter Twenty-Seven

Atlas started out in 1992 with two 747-200s. Michael liked the 200s because they could be acquired for less and provided lower cost lift than the 747-400. The price tag on a used 747-200 was around twenty million dollars, depending on the age and condition of the aircraft. Then, it had to be converted, which typically ran up to another twenty million. At the time, however, it was still much less expensive than a 747-400.

As the 200s aged and the cost differential made less sense, the 400 became a more viable option. The 200s had much less lift capability than the 400s. Michael felt that his company had moved forward as an outsource provider and had to have the best equipment. It was a gradual transition, but one that Michael decided upon and proceeded to work toward.

Due to the high cost, getting the first 747-400 was a major step for Atlas. These were pure factory freighters designed as such, and they had tremendous benefit over the 200s. Atlas Air bought five new 747s from Boeing. Given the price tag, the deal was enormous. Negotiations were intense and time consuming. They had to settle on the price for the aircraft, the technical aspects of the deal itself, maintenance and maintenance training, as well as pilot

PART V

training. For a big airplane, the technical part of the contract alone took at least twenty days to finalize.

Upon delivery of the first 747-400, Michael and I, along with a small entourage including David Bricston and Gene Dessel, went to a fabulous party at the Museum of Flight in Seattle.

Atlas ended up as one of, if not, the lead purchaser of Boeing 747-400s and invigorated the greater market for this aircraft.

***

In early 1996, Atlas decided to create a procurement department. Jim Matheny, who was heading Operations, put out feelers amongst his contacts in the Navy for someone who was ready to retire, interested in working in the airline business, and was willing to relocate to New York.

A month into the search, Larry Gibbons, a retired captain in the Navy, got a phone call asking him to sit down with a recruiter to see if he might be the right fit to head up Atlas's new procurement group. Larry had a background in aviation logistics with the Navy. He was one of the senior people when it came to providing everything necessary for maintenance on airplanes, and did a lot of procurement, buying parts, and services, which was exactly what Atlas needed.

A few weeks later, Larry went to New York and interviewed with Jim Matheny. They were looking for what was known as aviation material management--someone to come in and head up that group to help Atlas get to the next level in growth. It was clear Larry Gibbons had the ideal skill set.

In the spring of 1996, Larry was newly employed by Atlas and working in the offices at building 151 at JFK Airport in New York, which was now fully built with offices and cubicles. Michael and I stopped by the office to say hello. In those days, the office area was set up like a bullpen and everybody came around to greet us. It was the first time Larry had met Michael and says he was struck by how relaxed his boss was. Not one to put on airs, Michael seemed like another one of the guys. Wanting to make a good impression and please Michael, I always tried to be warm and friendly as well. We were both as interested in talking to people about what was happening in their lives as we were about business. Michael would always ask his employees about their lives and the family. He had a genuine interest in people, which came out again and again. Larry was as impressed by the comfortable, casual atmosphere at Atlas as he was with Michael as a businessman.

At the time Larry was hired, Atlas owned six planes. A few weeks later, when he arrived for his first day of work, there were eight due to an Alitalia deal Gene had made. They were taking in 747-200 passenger airplanes at a brisk rate and having them converted at multiple locations.

Procurement and arranging for the purchasing of goods and services is important for any sizeable company, but especially one that was growing as rapidly as Atlas. Larry learned quickly that Michael took an interest in making sure Atlas was acquiring on sound terms. He started dealing with Michael directly as they continued to expand and had to negotiate contracts for heavy maintenance, airframe maintenance, and engine services.

PART V

Once the 747-400s joined the growing fleet, Atlas needed to enlist a company to provide component and off-wing engine support. Larry put out a solicitation and Atlas got bids from Lufthansa, KLM, and Air France. Michael was concerned that KLM was too small, and he had concerns Atlas's operations might be impeded with Air France due to frequent strikes. They settled on Lufthansa.

During the following negotiations, Michael said, "I think we can do better."

With Michael, the deal was never done. When everyone else thought they were at a place where the terms were satisfactory, Michael always wanted to go back and see what else they could get as icing on the cake.

Larry and Michael met with the CEO of Lufthansa Technik. Michael proceeded to push for better terms.

"Michael, we can't go any lower," he said, pointing to Larry. "He has gotten every cent out of us that can be had. Hopefully, we can have a relationship with you guys, but understand, we just can't go any lower."

After an hour of back and forth, but no change in the terms, Michael was finally satisfied that they were getting as good a deal as they could possibly get.

When they were doing any kind of a major deal, Michael was either involved or insisted on being briefed on the details. Michael encouraged his top people to be engaged and very proactive in negotiations. In conversations, Michael was not one to sit on his position, or lead the discussion, because he always wanted to learn. He was very collegial and wanted input. He would provide commentary on what he wanted, where he thought the deal should end, and what he thought needed to be included. He was a great sounding board when contracts were being negotiated.

Initially, all of the airplane engines were serviced under a deal with GE and later, KLM. When the arrangement with KLM stopped working effectively, they put out a solicitation to all of the major providers for proposals on servicing the engines which were used on the 747-200. They settled on a company called MTU out of Hanover, Germany.

***

In addition to running the business, Michael stayed in very close contact with the operation even as Atlas grew to be much larger than any one executive could manage.

At one point, Gene had been to Tel Aviv and was working all over Europe. Michael called him and said he needed to head over to Jordan.

"I have to get a visa," Gene said, "How the heck are they going to let me into Jordan? I have an Israeli stamp on my passport."

"The deal is for $75 million dollars," Michael said. "For that kind of money, you don't have to worry about whether you have an Israeli stamp in your passport, but I'll make a call."

The Jordanians were more than happy to let Gene into the country.

It was not uncommon for Michael to call anywhere--even into Atlas's global control center to talk with the people on shift and ask, "Hey, how's it going? What's that aircraft doing? How are we doing over in Asia?" It would catch the people off guard and at the

PART V

same time, they welcomed his interest and that he was passionate about the all the details of business, customer service and aviation, as well as the employees.

Chapter Twenty-Eight

Michael always provided expertise where client issues were concerned, creating solutions for any situation that needed to be resolved. He could be confrontational and direct when necessary with one notable exception—his employees—particularly the people he worked with most closely.

Michael valued loyalty in others, but his own loyalty could be somewhat transactional. He was very task-oriented and was 100 percent behind an employee as long as he thought of the person as relevant to accomplishing the task on which he was currently focused. If, however, he considered someone to be superfluous or, worse, they made a costly mistake, did subpar work, or there was some sort of disappointment or miscommunication, his attitude changed quickly and precipitously.

Because of the fast-paced, high-stress nature of the business, disappointing Michael, at least at some point, came with the territory. Disagreeing with Michael, even on a simple issue, could be tricky. Everyone found themselves on Michael's Do Not Call list at some point or another. While Vicki Foster learned to wait it out until he got over whatever had angered him, others weren't so lucky. Firings, some permanent, most temporary, were something of a common occurrence. Michael, who avoided hands-on management whenever possible, typically didn't fire anyone personally, but assigned that particular task to someone else. This translated to family life as well. Whenever there was difficulty with Jennifer and Regan, or if there was a household employee who needed to go, Michael had me deliver the news.

Employees with a middle manager to cushion the blow, or entry level staff were somewhat protected from his mercurial nature, but those who worked directly with Michael all knew the telltale signs that they were the subject of his displeasure: coldness, distance, and, sometimes, a messenger with bad news.

John, David, and Gene were Michael's most trusted advisors and his closest friends. They understood he was creating value and wealth, and all three enjoyed being part of the process. Whether in boom times or during the frustrating, difficult periods, they were always helping Michael make the business work. Because Michael respected and appreciated their expertise, they felt like equals and spoke their minds. They also understood that at some point they would possibly be fired or would be instructed to fire someone—often each other, and on multiple occasions.

John was let go by David two of the three times he was fired, but never did leave the job.

Michael was almost entirely hands-off where David was concerned. He was confident that David knew what he was doing and let him do it. He'd never lost his temper at David and he'd never come down on him for anything. His job would only become threatened in lean times when Michael would say, "David is surplus, get rid of him."

During one of these periods, Michael dispatched John to do his dirty work. John slinked into David's office and, sheepishly said, "Things aren't going well and we're going to have to let you go."

"I don't know, John," David said in response. "I have a fairly specific contract with Michael."

They talked about the particulars but came to no conclusion. After John finally left his office, David looked over his employment contract. Michael sent a copy to an outside lawyer. The issue of whether he could actually be fired sat out there indefinitely. In the meantime, David kept coming into the office and Michael kept paying him.

No conclusion was ever reached and David remained employed.

As for Gene, Michael was particularly dependent upon his technical expertise. He was very good at operations, knowing FAA rules and maintenance programs, and was truly crucial to every venture Michael ever undertook. Because they worked together so closely, however, Michael would periodically feel it necessary to fire him.

On one occasion, Michael did take matters into his own hands, saying, "Look, I think you ought to leave."

"I have a contract," Gene responded.

"Okay," Michael said. "Then you'll be here at nine a.m. in the morning and you won't leave work until five p.m."

Although Gene had always worked far more than forty hours per week, coming in early and leaving late, but on his own schedule, he found himself contractually obligated to be at work every day by nine and not leave before five. He did so without fail for two or three months until the issue, whatever it was, had been forgotten.

PART V

Another firing resulted in Gene being "replaced" by a smart, capable former Air Force pilot and engineering/maintenance supervisor.

As capable as the new supervisor was and continued to be, Gene's intricate knowledge, honed by years on the job, was quickly deemed invaluable once again. Soon after his "firing" he saved the company several million dollars on a maintenance deal and was back at his desk. The new hire stayed with the company and proved to be a valuable asset as well.

The fact was, getting fired was a somewhat normal occurrence without any real implications. Mostly, when John, David, or Gene would get fired, whoever had been let go would walk out of the office saying something to the effect of, "Yeah, I got fired, I'll see you soon."

The situation would blow over and they'd be back.

In Gene's case, the outcome was often a net positive because of his value to the company. John would typically be given the responsibility of firing him and David was always in charge of negotiating Gene's severance agreement. He would negotiate a package deal, where Gene would get a certain amount of money over a period of time.

A week or a month later, Michael would need him and ask John to hire him back.

Over time, Gene and David had a running joke that all David was doing was giving him bonuses because they both knew he was going to be hired again.

"I am the best thing that ever happened to you," David often told Gene.

All three were hired and fired periodically over the course of the years for various reasons, all of which were minor and funny in hindsight. While their job security was sometimes iffy, it was balanced by the upbeat, positive work energy in the office.

Despite his quirky interpersonal skills, Michael was admired by all three men—personally and professionally. I'm told every employee at the company felt much the same way about his character and the business.

PART VI
GOING PUBLIC
1996-2001

Chapter Twenty-Nine

By 1995, Michael had built a business worth hundreds of millions, yet his wealth was largely on paper. He had the finesse, ability, and assets to get the money he needed to grow, but he was dependent on banks and investors for loans to increase his fleet of 747s. His business model made solid financial sense, but Michael needed access to more and more cash to fund the rapid expansion of the company. Although control was of paramount importance to him, the obvious and most sensible solution was to take the company public.

After numerous trips back and forth to New York to meet with investment bankers for tumultuous meetings, which were inevitably followed by interminable heated phone calls, the various hurdles involved in going public were negotiated and the IPO was prepared. Michael would retain control of 51 percent of the stock. Because of his capability, and in fact necessity, as the undisputed leader of Atlas, he would also have a nucleus of other stockholders who supported him.

Atlas first went public on NASDAQ via Merrill Lynch. At the time, there was a requirement related to IPO value that precluded Atlas from going directly to the NYSE. Once the issue was rectified however, Michael, Jimmy, Olivia, and I, plus a contingent

PART VI

of Atlas executives, flew to New York City. We were welcomed at the New York Stock Exchange by a large banner that said CONGRATULATIONS ATLAS AIR CARGO! We proceeded to a catered breakfast with the CEO of the exchange. Afterward, he escorted us out to the famed balcony above the trading floor. Michael, reveling in the moment with all of us beside him, didn't want to sound the opening bell himself, but gave the honors to five-year-old Jimmy.

Jimmy, who sensed something important was happening, and was a bit puzzled, but thrilled beyond belief, rang the bell.

Atlas Air Cargo became a publicly traded company.

After the initial offering, Michael went from a business owner worth several million dollars to a CEO worth $800 million.

David had become Goliath.

***

Atlas Air Cargo had stockholders, plus a board, and an audit committee. Michael held the controlling interest and remained heavily involved in all aspects of the business. Atlas continued to deal with foreign entities that had a different mode of operation, and different expectations than U.S. companies, all of which Michael understood.

Still, it was a challenge to transition from private to public company. For the original gang of four, the new, improved, publicly-held Atlas had some notable downsides.

John Blue was CFO up until Atlas went public, at which time Michael brought in another person to do the IPO. Shortly after,

John left Atlas but remained with Michael as his personal financial consultant, helping him navigate his wealth through the turbulent ups and downs inherent in aviation and the market in general. John was a trusted advisor then, and remains involved in our family finances to this day.

Because Atlas also needed to hire New York counsel to do the IPO, David Brictson had little to do with the process. Michael wanted him to take on the role of general counsel, but that would have meant a move to New York, which David had no intention of making. He stayed on, but worked for Atlas on a salaried, part-time basis while two acting general counsels took care of the bulk of the company's legal needs from New York.

Gene had suffered his most recent "firing" just before Atlas went public but was brought back on soon after, where he would remain. He was well-compensated and stayed with the company for the duration.

Michael pushed forward harder than ever. Despite something of a persistent war cry from the board to relocate the corporate offices to New York, Michael was reluctant to leave Colorado. He would fly out for long stretches, but somehow managed to run Atlas from the offices in Golden.

The company would continue to grow exponentially, purchasing aircraft, adding hubs, and important employees along the way.

Chapter Thirty

Tina Ferry met Michael for the first time in Seattle. She was there with her godmother, Vicki Foster, to help care for Vicki's newborn baby boy. Leaving the baby with a hotel sitter, Tina was invited to attend a dinner where she met not only Michael, but was introduced to Jimmy, Olivia, and me. Only seventeen at the time, Tina was impressed by everything about the trip--from the downtown Four Seasons hotel where we all stayed, to the opulent dinner at the Museum of Flight.

Two years later, in 1998, Tina started working as a summer assistant in the Atlas offices. She had heard all about the whirlwind that was Michael Chowdry from her godmother, but seeing was believing. From the moment she started working, it was clear that everyone in the office was doing everything they could to try and keep up with the boss. While her job description as Vicki's assistant was to file, get coffee, and do whatever general gopher work she was assigned, she saw that her main goal, above all else, was to make sure Michael had what he needed, exactly when he needed it, ready to go.

At that time, Vicki was in charge of marketing and Michael's current assistant was expecting her first child. Tina was surprised and incredibly intimidated when she was asked to cover for the assistant who had to leave one afternoon for a doctor's appointment. Tina was so nervous when the phone rang, she jumped in her seat, but knew her only choice was to feign confidence. She'd noticed that the people who succeeded at Atlas could read Michael. He appreciated those who could think for themselves and saw that asking him too many questions was bothersome to him. When he asked her for something, no matter how outrageous, it meant *just figure it out*. As a result, Tina and Michael hit it off and she ended up working at Atlas full time.

Michael preferred to have two assistants because he always wanted someone available to answer his, and all other, calls. The office phone would ring at 7:01 in the morning and Michael would be on the line, from wherever he was. "What's going on in this world?" he would say.

At first, it was standard procedure for Tina to try and cover up the fact that she didn't actually know what was going on in the world. Soon though, she discerned what Michael needed to know for that day. She also knew that he liked a good joke. She would drive into work thinking up a good answer to the inevitable question. If he needed an uplift, she was ready. If she needed to be serious and tell him what the market was doing as quickly as possible, she was ready for that, too.

While Tina's overall job description was to be available, answer calls, balance schedules, and accomplish typical executive assistant tasks, she never really knew what was coming her way. Like an emergency room, she never knew what was going to walk through the door. Anything could or did happen and ranged from working with airline heavyweights in a foreign country to figuring out how to gut a walleye fish in the middle of nowhere.

One of the many qualities Tina admired about Michael was his determination. If he wanted something to happen, he was going to accomplish it. He expected everyone around him to have the same mentality.

Michael's office was down the hall from Tina's. Because of the layout, when someone went in to talk with him, they'd stop at her office first. On more occasions than she could count, whoever it was would vent that Michael was going to want something impossible and that there was no way it would or could happen.

Tina would wait for them to come out and inevitably say, "I don't know what happened in there, but I guess now I'm doing this and I really feel like I want to, so here I am."

"No," was simply not an acceptable answer because Michael would constantly ask for whatever was necessary to make the business and his life function smoothly. Most of his requests, no matter how far-fetched, directly contributed to the success of Atlas.

On one memorable occasion, Michael called her at five in the morning, elated because he couldn't wait any longer to tell her he'd had a great night's sleep with no back pain on a mattress at the Peninsula Hotel in Hong Kong.

"I want this mattress," he said.

"Great," Tina said, knowing how big a deal this was for Michael, who had chronic back pain and sleep problems. "I'll find out what brand it is and we'll order you one."

"No. I want this mattress. The one I slept on. I don't care how many people have slept on it. It's perfect."

PART VI

Tina spent the next few days working out the details to buy the broken-in mattress, tipping the bellman from continents away to have it removed from the hotel room in Hong Kong and delivered to his new business jet so it could come back home with him to Genesee.

Michael and I slept on the mattress from that day on.

In those days, Tina drove a Honda Civic. One day, Michael borrowed her car while his was in the shop so he could get a haircut.

He wasn't halfway to the salon before he was calling Tina.

"The CD player. It's stuck."

"It worked when I was in the car," she said.

"No, no, it's broken," he insisted.

As it turned out, he'd jammed one of his Pakistani CDs into the changer not realizing there was already a disc in the player. When Tina got her car back she had to listen to music that sounded like a screeching cat in a bathtub until she could get the vehicle repaired.

Tina often shook her head, or quietly laughed, but she saw it as her job to make sure to do whatever it was Michael needed done. Just as she knew this was part of working at Atlas, she also understood the puzzles inherent in solving management and personnel issues. It was common knowledge that Michael was uncomfortable with interpersonal confrontation. In fact, one of the things someone told her when she started working was that when she did something wrong, inevitable in the fast-paced, high-stress world of Atlas, "You won't know what you did necessarily, you'll just know Michael is unhappy with you."

The day Tina made her first mistake, she knew she needed to be proactive.

Because she was young, driven, and planned to be the assistant that lasted, she walked into his office, sat down in one of the chairs opposite his desk and said, "I understand that sometimes it's uncomfortable to talk about mistakes, but I know I made one and I want to talk about it because I want to be the best assistant you've ever had."

"Okay," he said with a nod.

"We both know this job is demanding. I know changing assistants is challenging for you. So, I'd really like to know what I do wrong, when I do it wrong, so I can fix it. That way I can do my best."

"Great talk," he said. "May I have a cup of tea?"

Tina knew it was his way of saying she was in the clear.

Soon after, Michael forgot his billfold in Miami, so he flew Tina and her boyfriend on the corporate jet to retrieve the wallet, treating them to filet mignon along the way. It was an errand she would never forget and more than made up for the stress of being Michael Chowdry's assistant.

Tina kept her head down at the office because her position was coveted and exercised the weight and power that came with her title. She never told anyone she was only nineteen when she started. When she turned twenty-one, however, a co-worker in human resources looked into her file and discovered her secret.

They put Happy 21st Birthday on a big cake and invited the whole office.

"You're just twenty-one?" Michael said, shocked and more than a little impressed.

Tina was embarrassed she'd been found out but was also proud of her ability to excel at her job, despite her youth.

PART VI

A year and a half into working eighty-plus hour weeks, Tina decided she really needed to take a vacation. She went to Michael and said, "You know, we go to Lake Powell usually, but I skipped last year."

"Okay," he said.

Because of the nature of working with Michael, she literally took a phone with her when she went into the bathroom, so she knew she needed to add a qualifier. "Here's the thing. There's no cell service in most of Lake Powell."

"What?" he said, but with a smile. He knew she'd more than earned the vacation, and he wanted her to get away.

The day before she left she said, just for fun, "What's going on in this world?"

"Well," he answered. "I've been reading the news and I hear that there have been multiple shark attacks at Lake Powell."

Tina laughed, but knew that if he could have sharks added to the lake, he probably would.

***

In 1997, Sheila Remes-Gallard was one of Boeing's top salespeople. Along with her female sales team, she was one of few women who had risen to that level in the male-dominated airline business. She currently serves as vice-president of strategy for commercial airplanes. At the time, her husband Van Rex was vice-president of sales for Boeing in Central America.

She met Michael along with Gene at an Italian restaurant in Denver.

When they met, she handed Michael a duffel bag full of Boeing goodies for the Challenger jet he owned at the time. It would be the first of many gifts they'd exchange and the beginning of a close friendship between Van Rex, Sheila, Michael and me.

The topic of discussion that evening was, of course, airplanes. Cargo carriers in particular. From that point on, they developed a rapport and trust. Sheila interacted extensively with Michael, negotiating on behalf of Boeing for the 747-400s sold to him.

Sheila grew to know Michael well from both a personal and professional perspective. No stranger to gender discrimination, Sheila was impressed by how Michael never treated her with anything but the utmost regard.

In a business setting, he was always well-dressed. If he was going to be a few minutes late, he always called to say so and apologized in advance. He was very good about working within the system and was respectful of everyone, but was a tough negotiator. He always knew exactly what he wanted, was laser-focused on making it happen, and never vacillated.

***

In 1999, John Dietrich was living in Chicago working as a young lawyer at United Airlines headquarters when he was contacted by Tom Scott, the general counsel at Atlas Air, about interviewing for a position. At the time, Atlas wasn't necessarily a household name, but John was intrigued by the success and the growth of the company, as well as the business model and the entrepreneurial energy of Michael Chowdry.

PART VI

A born and raised Midwesterner, there were only a few places in the country John and his wife were willing to move, much less raise their young children. Denver was one of those cities, especially given the opportunity to serve as assistant general counsel for Atlas Air at the Golden offices, which somehow felt more family-oriented than corporate.

John met Michael shortly after he was hired and began working with him on a variety of projects. At the time, Atlas was growing, bringing on new customers, and adding aircraft units with existing customers. Michael had recently purchased a Boeing Business Jet and was in the plane headed somewhere, constantly cultivating and building relationships.

John, like everyone else, was amazed by Michael's consummate salesmanship and his huge presence. As a newly employed young lawyer, John was guarded and intimidated, but wanted nothing more than to be in the middle of the action. One morning, he was called into a business meeting about an aircraft deal. He saw that Michael placed a lot of emphasis on trust, discretion, confidentiality, and the viewpoints of his various advisors. John saw that he commanded respect, and that people worked very hard to please him. He returned their hard work, not only as career developing opportunities, but also with the chance to engage in interesting and exciting international business.

On one particular Friday, Michael called him into his office. Atlas had bought a number of new 747-400s and Michael had a question. It was very vague and he was in a bit of a hurry as he was due to leave on a business trip.

"John, I'd like you to take a look at some of the sections of the contract," he said. "I have some questions I want to run by you. Let's catch up on Monday."

John spent the entire weekend studying the contract inside and out so he'd be ready for any questions Michael might have.

When Michael came into the office after the weekend he said, "I hope you got to know the contract; my question has been answered but let's chat anyway."

They proceeded to have a discussion about the importance of a new asset coming on board. John quickly knew that Michael realized he'd worked very hard to learn the contract and didn't just want to say, "Oh, I got my answer, don't worry about it." Instead, he engaged him with questions about his thoughts regarding deliveries.

John appreciated the acknowledgment. Michael appreciated the commitment and he soon consulted John on a number of matters with China Airlines, Korean Airlines, Cargolux, and LAN in Chile.

John's importance to Atlas would continue to grow.

Chapter Thirty-One

Michael knew how to sleep on the floor, but he preferred his bed from the Peninsula Hotel. He would always be the same character as when he had no money, but he enjoyed the finer things: custom made clothing, Cohiba cigars, great food and wine, and collector's items like vintage watches, and his prized $75,000 handmade Italian shotgun.

One night he and I were invited over to Sheila and Van Rex's home for dinner.

"Why do you have so many paintings?" Michael asked.

"We love art," Van Rex said.

"How much for that one?" he asked pointing to a painting he admired. "I really like it."

"It's in your budget," Van Rex said, and then named a very generous price.

Michael bought it, we took the piece off their wall, and brought it home that evening.

A few months later we invited the Gallards to an art auction, black tie, limo and all, where we bid on and acquired a number of paintings. Michael and I were exhilarated by the experience and started what was to be the foundation of our art collection. I continued to collect art over the next twenty years. Later, I came to a place in life when it was time to lighten my load, and as part of it, I began to sell my art collection piece by piece. Not surprisingly, the paintings Michael had purchased appreciated the most by far. He had such an eye for quality.

Michael was always looking for items of value to purchase. He enjoyed both vintage and fast cars. While in France, he made a fun purchase, buying a Deux Cheveux--a small, antique convertible. I swear, the car had a lawn mower engine. He brought the vehicle back to the United States and Gene managed to somehow get it into the country.

While the Deux Cheveaux could only be driven on special occasions, and never fast, Tina remembers flying up I-70 in Golden, Colorado with Michael in the new canary yellow Porsche he'd just purchased.

"Watch this," he said, turning to her with a telltale twinkle in his eye.

He started weaving in and out of traffic at top speed. As he rushed to pass a car and between two others, Tina assumed he was going to slow down, and not try to thread the needle. Instead he smiled and zoomed right through.

As Tina's life flashed before her eyes, Michael couldn't stop laughing. "Porsches are made for this kind of driving."

"I don't make enough money for this," she uttered.

He just laughed that much harder.

The only thing that increased Michael's enjoyment of fine things was sharing them with close friends and family. He had Kobe beef in Japan and enjoyed it so much he bought and flew home enough to feed a large dinner party. The grand gestures came naturally to him.

NO MAN'S SON

***

And then there were the aircraft...

From the moment he could make the payments, Michael owned a plane for personal use. Starting with the Cessna he'd financed for $2800 per month and used when he worked as an air ambulance pilot, he was forever trading up to better, faster aircraft.

Michael chose to fly commercial until 1992 when Atlas was incorporated. At that point, a used, eight-passenger Cessna Citation caught his eye. Gene examined every detail about the plane and approved the purchase.

Michael loved the freedom of having a corporate jet, albeit a small one.

For one of our first trips on the Citation, we flew to Scandinavia. As we cruised along in the middle of the night, wrapped in our winter coats due to the frigid temperature inside the aircraft, we had the beautiful, otherworldly experience of flying past the Northern Lights—a dazzling, shimmering, moving curtain of magic that I will never forget.

On another occasion, we flew to Puerto Vallarta, Mexico in the Citation. Michael was pilot, and Chad, Jennifer's fiancé at the time, was up front as well. Jennifer, the kids, and I were in the back. The wing flaps got stuck. When landing a plane, the pilot has to pull the flaps, but they wouldn't go past 30 percent. It was dicey and tense, but Michael remained calm. They had no choice but to come in really hot and fast, and it was a bumpy landing.

When we were finally safe on the tarmac, Chad's heart was pounding. He needed a moment to regroup before he could even stand.

PART VI

Michael, who hadn't broken a sweat, handed him a bag. "What's this for?" he asked.

"Just carry it through security," he said.

As soon as Chad got through the screening process without incident, Michael took the bag back. He was much more concerned about whatever he'd brought into Mexico than he'd been about the scary landing, so Chad began to sweat that much more. Surely there were cigars inside, but Chad wondered what else he was afraid to have confiscated by customs.

He knew better than to ask.

***

Michael liked the Citation, but its range was limited and it did not have a stand-up cabin. By 1995, he'd sold the plane and purchased a Challenger which was faster, had a longer range, required two pilots, and featured a stand-up cabin. The Challenger quickly became a luxurious corporate perk.

David and Michael were headed to different places in the Far East. Michael suggested that David go with him to Hong Kong and then the plane would take him on to Malaysia.

David boarded the Challenger at the private jet hangar at Denver. He was impressed by how luxe the plane and amenities truly were.

"Would you like something to drink?" the flight attendant, typically an Atlas employee, asked him.

"I'd like a beer," he said.

"What kind?"

"Anchor Steam is my favorite," he said.

"Oh, I'm sorry, we don't have any of that," she said, giving him a Heineken instead.

Their first refueling stop was in Anchorage. When they got back on the plane to take off again, the flight attendant handed him a fresh beer. "Here Mr. Brictson--an Anchor Steam for you."

Michael had arranged for her to buy David's favorite beer in Anchorage.

Their second stop was the Kamchatka peninsula in Russia, the site of big earthen domes used for storing MIG jets. As they took off from Kamchatka headed to Hong Kong, Michael flew stretches of the journey.

David, who had grown accustomed to Michael's hospitality and generosity, was still overwhelmed by the experience of flying on the Challenger with him across the Pacific and on into Asia.

The first big trip Jimmy remembers taking with his father was on the Challenger, bound for Seoul, South Korea. The trip was at Christmas. I remember Jimmy being with us at the Atlas holiday party in Denver. He was asleep at the table in my lap when Michael picked him up and carried him out to a car waiting to transport them to the airport.

During the flight, they were preparing to make a scheduled fuel stop in Russia where they would have to deplane. Michael handed Jimmy a temporary landing visa with the warning not to lose it, because he would need this important paperwork in order to leave the country. Jimmy decided to tuck the visa safely underneath his pillow. When it came time to deplane, nine-year-old Jimmy spotted two soldiers on the tarmac holding AK-47 rifles. He panicked and couldn't remember where he'd put that visa.

PART VI

In Jimmy's mind, his father had logged more miles than anyone, so when he calmly told him not to think about the soldiers, Jimmy remembered where he'd hidden the visa and they were able to proceed with the refueling stop and re-board the plane.

When they got to Seoul, Jimmy was worried because he'd heard Koreans eat dog. The mere idea was unthinkable. First, his father teased that they were definitely going to be served dog, then got him a regular American hamburger. He did, however, insist that Jimmy try the Korean "Fuji apple drink." The early exposure Jimmy got to different foods made him an adventurous eater. The cultural experiences he had with his father were informative to his childhood and his adult identity as a citizen of the world.

***

In addition to the Challenger, which was used exclusively for business and family trips, Michael located and purchased a vintage DC-3 with a passenger interior.

We thought of the DC-3 much the same way another family might look at their Suburban—a means of transportation for the kids, the pets, and the whole family. When Olivia would go somewhere on the DC-3 she would check five or six books out of the school library and fill a backpack with her reading material and stuffed animals. There was no way she could take that much luggage on a commercial airline, but Michael didn't say a word. He loved her enthusiasm about the flight ahead.

Once, we went to Mexico in the DC-3, and, on the way, stopped in Lubbock to pick up my brother, his kids, and lots of toys. The airplane was soon filled with kids and tricycles for the trip south of the border.

We also took the DC-3 to the Grand Canyon and flew below the rim.

On the 4th of July, we would get take-out Chinese food from the Imperial restaurant in Denver and Michael would take the plane up and circle the city for everyone to watch the fireworks below.

The kids would run up and down the aisle in the plane and thought it was the greatest fun. Because Atlas Air was headquartered in Golden, near I-70, at the base of the foothills, Michael would circle the office where everyone would come out to watch. He proudly tipped the wing for the employees.

Gene avoided a catastrophe in the DC-3 on the way home from a trip from an airshow. Michael was not onboard, but Jimmy, Olivia, Gene's wife Judy, and I were. A former United captain who was working for Atlas in Wichita piloted the plane. Along the way, we dropped off another passenger, an ex-Boeing employee and current Atlas vice-president named Don Hickey.

We were on the ground after dropping off Don. Gene and the captain went to the fuel desk and personally presented a fuel slip for 100 octane. To be sure, Gene told the young man working the desk, "Remember it's 100 Octane, which is not jet A or jet fuel."

They received the fuel and the captain went out onto the wing to fill the first of two reserve tanks. As Gene was doing a preflight walk around the plane, the fueler came running out. "I think something's wrong. It looks like they're putting Jet A into the engine."

Gene ran over. Sure enough, the captain was on the wing fueling the auxiliary tanks with kerosene, jet A, into an airplane that

PART VI

required gasoline. Had this mistake not been noticed, the reserve tanks would have been filled, which would have gone to the mains, mixing the fuel with what was in the tank already.

We'd likely have gotten off the ground with what was in the lines and then the plane would have exploded. I thank God for Gene's astute awareness, knowledge, and the care he took of our family.

***

In 1999, Michael had completed a deal with Boeing for ten 747-400s plus an option to purchase five more. As a perk, they sold him one of the very first Boeing 737s in what was known as the executive configuration. Known as the BBJ or Boeing Business Jet, it was a $30 million dollar "green" aircraft whose price tag neared $50 million once all interior installation was complete. The BBJ had a 737-700 airframe and the wings of a 737-800, giving it a relatively long distance capability. The aircraft had the range to fly from Asia back to Denver without having to make the standard stop. To make certain the BBJ could make the longer legs, they did a modification at a site down in Georgetown, Delaware where fuel tanks were added to provide even more range for the airplane.

The BBJ was important for a number of reasons. As CEO, Michael was the face of Atlas and needed to be able to be all over the world meeting with customers and vendors. Ornate and impressive, it was also a major sales tool. Michael was not only easily able to fly overseas to meetings but could conduct negotiations and entertain potential customers within its luxe interior.

Michael, Larry Gibbons, and I worked with Lufthansa and a host of suppliers to come up with the design for the airplane exterior and interior. Michael and I took a tremendous interest in the layout of the interior space. It was great fun. The empty shell was designed with a master suite in the back, a smaller bedroom, a conference/multi-purpose room where some of the seats converted into beds, sleeping accommodations for up to three pilots, and a galley for the preparation of elegant meals. Magnificently furnished, the cabin had the feel of a walled-off, five-star hotel suite. The BBJ interior featured fabrics from Europe and all the wood had been specially handcrafted by a company in Como, Italy.

Michael was one of the first customers to own and fly a Boeing Business Jet. The finished aircraft was so well engineered and beautiful, both inside and out, he was asked to work with Boeing to promote the plane. The design served as a model for the select few future owners of Boeing Business Jets.

I went with Michael to Europe on one of his first trips in the BBJ. Along the way, we made stops in London and Brussels. When we got to Rome, it was sunset. The pilot talked to air traffic control and got permission to fly low over Rome during a stunningly beautiful pink sunset, another Michael memory which I will never forget.

The BBJ proved to be the most luxurious perk imaginable for us, our friends, and countless employees. Michael called Larry one day and said, "I understand you're going to Germany. We'll pick you up in New York."

Larry felt hesitant about traveling on the Boeing Business Jet with the head of his company, but as soon as he was aboard,

PART VI

Michael made him feel so comfortable that he found himself relaxing and getting to know Michael, not as his boss, but as a fellow traveler while they crossed the Atlantic together. The most social time he would spend with Michael was on business trips when they were headed to and from international destinations.

***

While there was no denying the appeal of the BBJ, or any of the planes Michael had owned over the years, my husband's passion for aviation intersected with his penchant for collecting rare and interesting items when he learned of an Aero Vodochody L-39 Czech military jet trainer for sale.

Anyone with a passing interest in aviation would jump at the chance to merely fly in such a jet. Michael purchased the plane in Prague. Painted red, white and blue, the L-39 was his pride and joy.

On Saturdays and Sundays when he wasn't traveling, Michael and Jimmy would climb into the Porsche Carrera 4. Michael would blast Pakistani music and head down the curving back roads to Front Range airport, breaking the speed limit the whole way. They would pull into the airport, prep the plane, and take it for a joyride.

"I'm going to take us up to altitude and then you're going to push the joystick left," Michael would tell Jimmy. He not only wanted his son to feel what it was to experience the power of flight but taught him to do a barrel roll in the Czechoslovakian fighter trainer by the time he was ten years old.

I was just glad I didn't know until after the fact.

From the beginning, the plane made me terribly nervous.

Chapter Thirty-Two

Having come from a modest, middle class background, I enjoyed the jet setting and the parties and thought our lifestyle was great fun. Michael experienced the full gamut of success, including gracing the cover of Airline Business Magazine and being named one of the Forbes 400.

Through it all, Michael's generosity was arguably more important to him than making money and he relished spreading his financial blessings and hospitality. Because the Atlas Air offices were ten minutes from home, it often seemed as if the business was in the house and the executives from the company were part of the family. He loved cooking, entertaining, taking people on trips, and gift giving. Intermingling Atlas with his home life was the only way he wanted to do business.

When at home, Michael always made time to be in the kitchen. He cooked restaurant quality Karachi chicken, lamb with garlic, Basmati rice with peas and raisins, and a variety of other delicious Pakistani dishes. He'd prepare the Kobe beef he flew in by slicing it thin, cooking it on a hot marble slab in the middle of the dining table, and then serve it with peppers and onions. Introducing Jimmy and Olivia to foods from around the world was of great importance to him.

PART VI

The kids loved coming home to the aroma of oil, onions, and garlic permeating the whole house. They knew dad was done with work for the day, in his house slippers, and cooking Pakistani food in the kitchen.

Olivia had a huge sweet tooth which he indulged by preparing a Pakistani dessert called Gulab Jamun which is basically balls of sweet dough in a syrup of rosewater and cardamom. Even when she was too full to finish her dinner, she would surreptitiously make room. Michael would say she had an extra compartment in her stomach just for dessert.

Michael invited Gene, John, Dave, and their wives over for dinner on a regular basis. The men would often prepare the meal together, making a contest out of everything from the grilling to who could handle the spicy food best. He would hold a napkin to his forehead to blot the sweat with one hand, while often adding more spice with the other.

Ever the consummate host, Michael enjoyed throwing dinner parties. He'd always have more food than his guests could ever possibly consume. One evening, he had Virginia prepare four pork tenderloins for a dinner party with twelve guests. For another party, he gave her a food and wine magazine that had a recipe for cherry-sauced quail on mashed potatoes. She'd never cooked it before and didn't know she was supposed to debone the body of the quail. She otherwise prepared the meal according to the recipe and plated what appeared to be a perfect creation. When the guests cut in around the bone, the meat was still pink and bloody. She felt awful when Michael had her put the quail in the microwave. Luckily, he wasn't mad—he couldn't be given the culinary successes they had produced together for guests over the years.

Michael was his loosest and most talkative at home in Genesee after a meal with family and friends, especially when they'd go outside around the fireplace to enjoy a glass of brandy and the then illegal Cohiba cigars he'd bring in from Cuba.

Everyone appreciated getting an invitation for dinner.

***

Michael and I threw fun, elaborate parties for our friends and employees. Every year, Atlas hosted no-expense-spared Christmas events as a thank you to employees for their hard work and commitment. Because he was constantly traveling or away from the office, Michael spent the whole evening chatting, shaking hands, and saying hello to spouses and significant others, all of whose names he knew. Because he wanted the evening to be a reflection of how much he valued the people who worked for him, the party was always held at top venues. Incredible food was, of course, a focal point of the evening. Because Atlas's main hub was in New York, the executive offices were in Denver, and a smaller hub had been opened in Miami, we spent three weekends in December attending Christmas parties, one in each city—New York on the first weekend of December, Miami the second weekend, and a grand finale in Denver.

Another highly anticipated annual event was the summer clambake. A rarity in landlocked Colorado, the clambake attracted a crowd of over a hundred to the backyard of our mountain home. The party was a notoriously fun event. It had a comfortable, relaxed, open house vibe with free-flowing food and alcohol. Michael was a casual, warm, and welcoming host, even though there were still business deals going on. I greeted all the guests although I wasn't adept as Michael at remembering names.

John Dietrich remembers his first clambake at our home with fondness. He was new to the company and had very young children at the time. He recalls how Michael and I embraced him as a new employee and welcomed his wife and family. He saw that we treated all employees with warmth and appreciation, not just the executives. John believes the value we placed on relationships with everyone at all levels helped form a family-oriented culture that remained at the center of Atlas as a corporation.

***

Instead of always doing business over the phone, Michael would get on a plane and personally meet people. He was tireless in his efforts to connect and he knew the power of face time.

Michael liked to travel, but he loved it when he could take others along with him.

In general, his approach to being a tourist was to drive by and take a look at the big attraction of whatever country he was visiting. Gene was working in Egypt and Michael wanted to see the Great Pyramids. Gene knew what to do—he hired a car and had the driver take them past Giza for a look. Michael napped along the way. They saw the Coliseum in Rome the same way. Michael was always talking on the phone or taking a nap between sites. Much more important to him was the hotel where they were staying and finding the best restaurants in the city.

Whether his jet setting was for business or pleasure, he preferred to create fun for everyone that accompanied him. Michael stayed in the nicest hotels and he treated his employees to the same accommodations--especially David, John, and Gene.

In 1989, Michael brought the Blues, the Brictsons, and the Dessels along with us to the Paris Airshow, a huge event held every other year in June. Originally, he'd planned to take the whole group on the Orient Express out of Paris afterward. He wanted to, but couldn't quite talk us into wearing tuxedos and gowns to sit on a train, especially given how much we were already enjoying our stay at the gorgeous, historic Le Meurice Hotel. Michael wanted to bring Jimmy to Paris but he was only five months old and he didn't have a passport. I remember spending a harried day in Miami literally walking his application through the passport offices while an Atlas employee's wife babysat Jimmy. So often, Michael would make a request that seemed impossible. I learned to handle such a variety of difficult situations just to please him. I grew in confidence as I took on what seemed to be insurmountable tasks and I am thankful for that to this day.

On another occasion, he invited South American clients to the Aspen Food and Wine Festival. They enjoyed tent after tent of wine tasting, the finest food and entertainment including lectures, cooking demonstrations, and art gallery tours.

As a seasoned international traveler, he understood the challenges faced by his employees whose jobs had them on the road. From its inception, Atlas put its pilots up in nicer hotels in acknowledgment of their service. He truly cared about their quality of life both at home and in the field.

PART VI

One summer, they had difficulty booking accommodations for flight crews in Alaska. When Operations was unable to solve the issue, Michael suggested renting luxury RVs which could be parked in the lot of the hotel. The pilots who were given the overflow accommodations were delighted to discover they were staying in swanky motorhomes.

"Can we take them fishing?" more than one asked, delighted about the possibility of utilizing the RV for wilderness activities.

"That's certainly what I would do," Michael said.

Years later, the pilots were still talking about the time they'd gone camping and fishing in the motorhomes Michael had rented for them.

As a true aviation aficionado, Michael attended the OshKosh Air Show for a number of years, once bringing in both the DC-3 and the L-39.

Made famous by the clothing company of the same name, Oshkosh, Wisconsin is also world renowned for hosting the largest annual aviation event in the world and was, naturally, one of Michael's favorite events of the year.

On the last week of July, 600,000 people from 90 plus countries and 7 percent of all the aircraft in the country fly into the region to celebrate all things aviation. As a result of the popularity of experimental aircraft, and aviation in general, the Oshkosh Airshow attracts everything from astronauts to Piper Cub owners. The show honors all of the hallmarks of aviation from airplanes built at home to antiques, and Apollo 13 astronauts to Doolittle's remaining Raiders. People see planes they've only heard about or watched on the news, and can speak with and talk to the pilots, crew, mechanics, builders, veterans, and survivors.

Some of these planes are flown during the show, so everybody on the ground can see them in the air as airplanes are meant to be seen and enjoyed.

During the show week, up to 12,000 airplanes arrive. All the hotels fill to capacity and 36,000 campers drive in and stay in the campgrounds. Sometimes enthusiasts even camp under the wings of their plane. The residents of Oshkosh often move out of their own homes and rent them out for the week. In fact, Airbnb may have gotten its idea there, because, since 1953, people by the thousands organize their homes to host attendees.

Michael rented the same beautiful house on the north shore of Lake Butte des Morts every year for us, assorted family members, and friends. He also rented one or two nearby homes for the employees and crew he always brought along. The entire week was spent enjoying the best food, great wine, and appreciating everything the aviation world had to offer.

It was at Osh Kosh that Michael and I met Greg Anderson, an avid aviator with over 3200 hours of flight time. A graduate of the Air Force Academy he was an Air Force pilot who had grown up in the region of Wisconsin where Paul Poberezny founded the Experimental Aircraft Association in his basement in Milwaukee in 1953. The EAA grew to become one of the largest aviation membership organizations in the world.

The EAA hired Greg in 1983 as a director of development at their newly built facility in Oshkosh, Wisconsin. Greg stayed with the organization for twenty-one years helping them develop their new world headquarters which included the world's largest aviation event every summer in Oshkosh, Wisconsin. Greg became vice president and then executive vice president of the organization.

Michael and I were first introduced to Greg by Dick Taylor, a vice president of Boeing, but we got to know him through our attendance at the airshow and he became a good friend.

Greg appreciated that Michael was just as happy looking at a little RagWing ultralight as talking to a vice president of Boeing about their latest airliner. He spent much of the airshow down on the flight line, fascinated by the airplanes, talking to the people who'd flown them. He was a pilot's pilot who wanted to know how this particular design or that particular plane performed in the air.

At the Oshkosh Air Show, Michael was truly at home amongst the assemblage of people who shared his sense of wonder and imagination about flying and aviation.

***

Wherever he went, Michael always came home with whatever Jimmy and Olivia were into at the time. He brought Olivia the rare Princess Diana Beanie Baby when the plush little animals were her prime focus. She also liked coloring, drawing, and painting, so he brought back the largest art supply kit she'd ever seen. He got her a rocking sheep in Scandinavia and a dark purple velvet dress with kimono-like closures from Southeast Asia that was so beautiful she wore it to her spring piano recital and for many days afterward.

As Michael was headed out the door for a trip, Jimmy would say, "I want Legos!"

When he'd return a few days later, dazed from extreme jet lag and whatever was on his mind after the trip, Michael always had the Legos with him.

***

Any time anyone got married, had a birthday, a baby, and even when there was a funeral, Michael was the first one with the phone call, flowers, and an apropos gift. To know Michael Chowdry was to be treated to his friendship, flights of fancy, thoughtful nature, and unerring attention to detail. It also meant knowing there were no limits to either his kindness or, sometimes, his expectations.

When Vicki Foster became pregnant with her first child, Michael was ecstatic for her.

"From now on until your baby is born," he said, "I insist you start keeping banker's hours."

A week later, Vicki's phone rang at 3:00 a.m. It was Michael calling from Europe.

"I thought I was supposed to be keeping banker's hours," she said, trying to wake herself up enough to deal with the issue he needed to have managed.

Michael laughed. "Here, it is banker's hours."

We had such fun working together on a baby gift for Vicki. She was a special part of our lives and we wanted whatever we gave her to reflect that. We decided to let Vicki create her dream nursery. It was fun for her and a true pleasure for us.

When she brought the infant into the office to show him off, Michael spotted a tag on the baby's collar he was certain was uncomfortable for the newborn. He stopped all the festivities until he could snip off the tag with a pair of scissors.

His care, generosity, and concern was exponential when it came to Karen, a flight engineer who was diagnosed with cancer while working at Atlas Air. Although she couldn't work due to her illness, Michael insisted on paying her salary until she could return to the flight line.

This sort of generosity and interest in the well-being of his employees was expressed in a variety of other ways as well. From top-of-the line events to plush pilot accommodations, he sought to create a work environment that was both engaging and fulfilling.

***

Some of his gifts were extravagant, like the grand piano he gave to Peter Yap at China Airlines, and the 50th birthday trip to Paris on the Concord for a stay at The Ritz he gave to John Blue and his wife. There were many notable others. When he hosted a dinner, he regularly gave gifts to the attendees which included items like pearl necklaces and custom-made suits.

His grand gestures were often appreciated, but sometimes proved to be unsuitable for whatever reason. On one occasion, he bought a diamond Rolex for a Chinese general's wife. Upon discovering the gift would be considered inappropriate, he didn't return the pricey watch, but gave it to me. I knew it was meant for someone else but couldn't have cared less as Michael fastened it onto my wrist. It just wasn't in my makeup to turn down a diamond Rolex.

Michael understood that gift giving, particularly of his magnitude, was somewhat more common and accepted in the culture he came from than other places, particularly in the United States. Undaunted by the knowledge that his level of generosity could be looked on with suspicion, he continued to do things in a big way because he understood the power of impression.

Since we'd exchanged plain gold bands on our wedding day, I had wanted a diamond ring. When I shared this desire with my mother, she replied in true Texas fashion, "Get a big one!" Over the years, Michael developed connections all over the world, including with a diamond merchant in Antwerp. As a surprise, he bought me a gorgeous ring, in advance of an upcoming trip together to the Netherlands.

We arrived in Holland in the Challenger, and one of the wives of the men Michael was doing business with whisked me off on a bike ride through the famed tulip fields. While we were out biking through the beautiful countryside, Michael arranged for a courier to bring the ring to the hotel so he could have it for me when I returned.

Michael lived large in whatever he did and on the plane trip home, I wore the beautiful ring on my finger. To me, it was a symbol of how far we'd come together. I always wore the diamond ring with the small gold band he gave me on our wedding day, bringing then and now together.

Chapter Thirty-Three

For Michael, getting to take a breath and not be in the office or on the phone or thinking about the next deal was a welcome release. He was always happy to get home from a trip, stand over the kitchen sink and eat mangoes, letting the juice run down his face and his hands, a simple pleasure that delighted him.

Despite our painful first trip to Lubbock, Michael grew to love visiting my parents in their modest home. Whether in the backyard relaxing in a lawn chair under my dad's pecan tree or napping on a quilt in the sunshine, it was one of the few places where he was completely content. So much so, that he often suggested we rent an RV and make the 555 mile drive for a long weekend. No one needed to relax and recharge more than Michael, and he knew enough about himself to arrange activities that allowed him the badly needed downtime.

***

The A Bar A Ranch in Saratoga, Wyoming held great pleasure for Michael. He went there to hobnob and drink Wild Turkey with an association of top airline executives known as the Conquistadors. He enjoyed the dude ranch so much, he took us there for a family

PART VI

vacation. One year, we went in the DC-3 and landed on a short asphalt runway full of potholes. Michael had a tremendous time treating any guest who was interested to a flight over the dude ranch. The ranch was also great fun for Jimmy and Olivia, who spent their days riding, fly fishing and hanging out at the kids' corral making friends. Jennifer and I spent the day hiking, horseback riding, and being together. Everyone but Michael enjoyed the amenities. Without other airline industry people in attendance and no cell phone signal he was a little lost. While everyone else relaxed and had fun, Michael spent the day in the ranch's makeshift "business center," a room the size of a closet but with a land line. His hours on the phone equaled ours having fun. Chad, like Michael, spent the days working on his laptop. He also had this dream job, but it came with never-ending demands.

The A Bar A had a gourmet dining room complete with excellent wines. The evening hours were Michael's favorites.

***

Early on, in the leaner days, we took a trip with the Dessels in the infamous Vanagon to Aspen. More memorable than the tight quarters was the bouillabaisse we made in the tiny kitchenette. The delicious meal made a huge mess that splattered all over the kitchen area of the vehicle and had to be cleaned. That duty fell to me, and, as a result, there was no more bouillabaisse prepared in the small bus!

***

Michael, David, and Gene had fun wherever they went. Even though they'd become accustomed to staying in the best hotels, they still enjoyed sharing simple pleasures like taking the Vanagon to go fishing in Eagle, Colorado. Dave didn't want to sleep inside because Gene snored too loudly and Michael tossed and turned, both of them shaking the vehicle with their noise and movement. David decided to sleep outside on an old beach chair. They laughed when he woke up covered in snow.

They ended up on a Vanagon trip again following a business trip to London, during which Michael asked if they wanted to go fishing in Scotland.

David and Gene enthusiastically said yes, and the next thing they knew, Michael had spoken to a travel agent and they were on their way to Edinburgh.

While they all had a bucolic Scottish stream in mind, the travel agent had arranged for them to fish in a hatchery which featured a series of numbered ponds. They laughed about how ridiculous the place turned out to be and made the best of things, but Michael was disappointed. To make up for it, he arranged a re-do trip in Eagle, Colorado where David's niece managed a huge ranch. They went to a dilapidated camping cabin that had the exact, fish-filled streams they were hoping to find in Scotland.

On another fishing trip, David didn't want to buy any food because he planned to live off what he caught. He didn't catch anything. Michael and Gene, were, of course, amply supplied. After much in the way of jests and jokes, they finally relented and invited him for a sumptuous meal.

PART VI

Michael and company went fly fishing in Montana, to the San Juan River in New Mexico, and up to Alaska where Michael brought along a contingent of Boeing executives. Michael flew the gang in his latest plane, a retrofitted, renovated DC-3. Once there, Michael rented RVs and they toured the glaciers, and, of course, fished for cod, halibut, and salmon.

Shorter trips were usually made in the DC-3, while the Challenger took everyone on the lengthier flights.

***

After Atlas went public, Michael became somewhat restless. He was proud of everything he'd built and accomplished but was a pioneer at heart. His entrepreneurial wanderlust seemed to translate into a need for adventure. When Michael went away on hunting and fishing trips with his buddies and (often) Jimmy, he was able to let go of the numerous demands on him and the constant tug of what would come next.

Michael loved to take Jimmy hunting. He gave his son a shotgun when he was ten years old, made sure he received his gun safety certificate, and taught him to hunt birds. He made a point of teaching our son that everything they hunted, they ate.

Jimmy loved the time he spent with his father. He enjoyed the usual father/son activities but was the happiest when they were on an outdoor adventure together. They would trek for hours in South Dakota, Nebraska, Wyoming, and Florida. They even tried to go hunting in the Dominican Republic, which, inevitably, didn't turn out particularly well. One winter, Michael and Jimmy tracked elk outside of Vail, Colorado. It was freezing and unsuccessful, but Jimmy vividly remembers Michael taking him outside of the tent to look up at the stars.

Olivia and I went along on bird hunting trips to Kiowa at a club east of Denver, where Michael belonged. Our dogs, Sunny and Rocky, would go too. We focused on the labradors, considering them the best part of the whole day. These bird hunting adventures were some of my favorites. A bright Colorado fall day of working the dogs, while Michael shot birds, flooded me with gratitude, peace, and happiness.

An especially memorable bird hunt took place in a big hunting lodge in upstate New York. We flew into White Plains and took a limo up the Hudson Valley. It was a particularly cold and snowy winter. It was a gorgeous drive because the sky was blue, but so frigid the snow wasn't melting. We arrived and had lunch with a group of business people. After lunch, everyone got into their hunting clothes, loaded up the dogs and the guns, and went out into a field for an afternoon of bird hunting.

That evening we had an opulent duck supper.

***

"Let's get a boat." Michael would often say when he was on a trip. "Let's go fishing."

He took his family and friends fishing all over the world. Olivia recalls a particularly rainy trip in Canada to a place called the Totem Lodge. Their guides were Ojibwa Indians who spoke to each other over the radios in their native tongue and knew all the best spots for pike and walleye. After they'd catch the fish, they would go straight to shore, batter, and eat them right there for what they called a shore lunch.

***

Michael made arrangements to take family and friends rafting, ballooning, skiing and on more than one occasion, his favorite, bird hunting. He brought six bottles of very expensive wine on one of our duck hunting adventures but didn't have a corkscrew or any glasses. We ended up hunting for bars so we could get a bartender to give him a corkscrew. We spent an evening drinking wine out of the top of two thermos lids.

***

On another trip, Michael hired a guide in Oregon who guaranteed they were going to bag any one of a number of different birds. They took rented Ford Explorers into some serious backcountry but didn't get a single shot the whole trip.

Michael was frustrated. He didn't have the patience or the time to stay on a hunting trip for a week, so he would choose hunting guides that guaranteed a kill. A day in, if nothing had happened, he'd say, "Let's move on."

Gene would joke that for a certain price he could pay him to strap something to a tree. He wouldn't tell anyone and Michael could shoot it.

It wasn't all that far-fetched. Michael relished the opportunity to make a kill. At one point, during an especially frigid winter, Virginia ended up with a frozen elk hind leg in the back of the Toyota truck she was driving, because the tags were not reconciled correctly and Michael didn't want it to thaw before he got it processed.

It finally thawed anyway, and, of course, it fell to Virginia to disposing of it.

Michael thought it was hilarious and was already planning his next adventure...

Chapter Thirty-Four

"Why are we even here?" Michael continually asked Vicki Foster through dinner at the 1999 Ernst and Young Entrepreneur of the Year dinner in Palm Springs, California.

"Michael," she said shaking her head. "We're here because you are a nominee for Entrepreneur of the Year."

He'd received other awards and accolades including a 1998 induction into the International Air Cargo Association Hall of Fame. This was different, however. Along with Michael and his entourage were 1000 captains of industry in formal attire, including the founder of eBay, and featured entertainment including a performance by Riverdance.

Still, from the moment they boarded the BBJ, he kept asking the same question. "Why do we need to go?"

The answer was simple, the organizers had called Vicki to tell her Michael had been nominated and said, "You really want to be there."

Michael's focus was elsewhere, but Vicki not only insisted he attend, but that he buy a table and bring along some of the top executives from the company.

Everyone had a grand time during the flight from Denver. Champagne flowed for the adults. Olivia and Jimmy enjoyed a fun trip with all of us, including the chance to "hang out" like big kids with Tina on the BBJ while everyone attended the gala.

Michael was jittery and on edge throughout dinner and kept asking, "Why did we bring all these people?"

Vicki was nervous too, but hopeful, if not confident, he was going to win. If he did, which she kept telling herself he would, she knew the award would be a fitting way to showcase his accomplishments. As he grew more and more restless however, she began to worry. What if he didn't win? Had she made a huge mistake by dragging the top executives in the company out to Palm Springs for a long dinner and a short show?

The awards ceremony started.

The emcee announced the name and a video of each of the finalists in the category of Entrepreneur of the Year in the Commercial Transportation Services.

Vicki's heart pounded as Michael's video appeared on the giant screen, but she didn't dare look over at him as the emcee paused.

"And the winner is, Michael Chowdry."

As everyone began to congratulate Michael, Vicki allowed herself to breathe, but her relief didn't start to sink in until he got up from the table and reached the podium to accept his award and give what turned out to be a warm, heartfelt speech. He spoke of being a boy in Pakistan who dreamed of flying and seeing his American dream fulfilled.

At the end, he pumped his fist and said, "God Bless America!"

As we celebrated all the way back to Denver, Michael said, "Why didn't we bring more people?"

It was a proud and joyful moment for me to see my hard-working husband of many years honored for the difference he had made in the airline industry. I remembered his words from long ago in the Air Link offices when he said he wanted to make a difference. His dream had become a reality.

Chapter Thirty-Five

By mid 1999, Atlas had executive offices in Golden, Colorado, Operations at JFK Airport, offices in White Plains, and a secondary hub in Miami. It was decided that Atlas would function more smoothly if the various satellites office were centralized. A building was leased in upstate, Purchase, New York. Michael continued to travel back and forth and had started bringing me along to shop for houses, knowing he couldn't put off relocating from Colorado for too much longer.

He had juggled balls pretty much his whole career and thrived on it. Now Atlas was a mature operating company and behaved as such. Because he had a board of directors, Michael wasn't as free to operate as he wanted and he'd begun to grow disenchanted and a little bored. He didn't want to move to upstate New York. He longed for the chaos of how things were at Aeronautics Leasing, and when Atlas was a fledgling company dependent on him to survive. The day-to-day realities and obligations of serving as CEO and chairman of the board began to weigh heavily on him.

While some people equate workaholism with a fear of failure, Michael worked because he genuinely loved what he did. Atlas Air continued to thrive. Profits were good and everything was leased, but he saw an industry-wide slowdown on the horizon. The airline business was highly volatile and he saw it as his obligation to remain ahead of the market as much as possible. As such, he'd started to think about selling off his shares and was quietly considering the idea of negotiating a takeover by another leasing company.

He was also starting to think about what was next. Michael was an entrepreneur who had accomplished what he'd set out to do. In fact, he'd told me, "If I die tomorrow, I die a happy man. I have a good family, I have built my company, and have made peace with God."

A statement like that caught my attention, but I brushed it aside.

His passions had started to shift. Because his Uncle Salim had owned movie houses back in Pakistan, Michael always had a fascination with the movies. He was attracted to fame and famous people. He had invested in the Broadway play "Chicago" and made money. He was ready, at least in his mind, to pursue a goal he'd always talked about—produce Bollywood movies. As farfetched as it sounded, he was serious. And when Michael wanted to make something happen, it seemed destined to become a reality.

I wasn't as convinced. *You don't know anything about the movie industry*, I thought to myself. *We're going to lose our shirts.*

Of course, I never said anything to dash his dreams. He was one of the most successful Pakistani men in the country and he enjoyed the notoriety, but the money never gave him lasting security. He was always looking at the next dream, and how he could use the money he'd made to start afresh.

That was Michael Chowdry, gambler, visionary, and true entrepreneur.

PART VII
THE CRASH

Chapter Thirty-Six

The week of January 20, 2001 was whirlwind, even for us. On Friday morning, January 19, Michael and I climbed aboard the BBJ and headed to Washington D.C. for the swearing in of the forty-third president, George W. Bush. Michael never got into the political debate but leaned toward being a Republican. As Atlas continued to grow, he felt it would be valuable to have some political pull and had given $100,000 to George W. Bush's first campaign. As a result, we were invited to the Inauguration and a number of the accompanying parties. While this would be a once in a lifetime experience for most people, Michael thought of the galas and events as a black-tie blip in an already jam-packed week.

Michael did enjoy the opportunity to take the BBJ to such an auspicious event and made arrangements with U.S. Airways to service the plane when we arrived in Washington D.C.

Michael and I flew in and disembarked at Dulles. An ice storm was predicted for the next day, so Michael insisted the BBJ be stored in a hangar in order to protect the plane and its custom paint. The pilot was directed toward a hangar that had been designed for older 737s. Unaware that the tail on the new generation BBJ was higher than a standard 737, the U.S. Air ground handling crew banged the tail of the airplane as they towed the aircraft into

PART VII

the building, bending the tail itself, part of the frame, and pulling out electronics.

Because of the severity of the damage, the plane couldn't be flown to Boeing in Seattle for repairs. Engineers had to fly to D.C. and the plane was out of commission for nearly two weeks. Although Michael understood it was an honest mistake, he was angry and frustrated.

Olivia, who was nine at the time, answered the phone when I called home and told her about the incident. She knew that despite a weekend filled with events, parties, and Washington hobnobbing, her father couldn't be happy. At that time, she only flown in our private planes.

"Oh no," she said entirely innocently to Virginia, who was looking after her and Jimmy, "They're flying home commercial!"

Chapter Thirty-Seven

We arrived home in Denver on Sunday evening. Michael went straight to Taiwan on Monday, January 22 for a short meeting, left immediately after, and was in Seattle by Tuesday afternoon, January 23 for a five-hour negotiation with Boeing over a multi-plane 747 deal.

In addition to discussing Atlas 747-400 purchases, one purpose of the meeting with Boeing was to gauge their interest in developing a larger passenger and freighter aircraft. Always looking ahead to the next step in Atlas development, Michael had discussed with Airbus the possibility of Atlas being the launch customer for the A380 freighter. At the time, Boeing was skeptical of the marketability of a larger passenger aircraft to compete with the A380. In later years, Airbus declined to offer a freighter version of the A380, but Atlas went on to operate the larger 747-8F aircraft that Boeing developed.

Following the meeting in Seattle and a same day turnaround, Michael arrived home in Denver well after midnight.

The kids were eating breakfast before school on Wednesday, January 24 when Michael, having heard they were awake, came out of his bedroom in the oversized, terrycloth, yellow hooded bathrobe he often wore around the house. He picked Olivia up under the arms and swung her in a circle.

"Do you know how much I love you?" he asked.

They giggled together, he put her down, and he did the same thing with Jimmy.

Michael then went back into the bedroom to dress for the day. When he returned to the kitchen, I had come upstairs from my morning workout.

"You're up early," I said, knowing how late he'd arrived home and realizing how little he'd slept.

"Huge day today," he said. "I have that interview with the Wall Street Journal."

He was up bright and early for the moment he'd been looking forward to, not only all week, but for years. More important to Michael than the Bush inauguration or his meeting at Boeing, was his morning interview with the aviation editor for the Wall Street Journal.

His excitement was palpable as he sat down to the fruit salad, hard boiled eggs, and Assam tea Virginia had prepared for him.

"Where are you meeting the reporter?" I asked.

"Front Range Airport," he said.

"You're taking him flying?"

"The man writes about aviation for the Wall Street Journal." Michael grinned broadly. "Of course I'm taking him flying."

Given the fatigue inherent in the breakneck pace of the past week, I wondered if it was a good idea. I was even less sure when he added:

"I'm taking him up in the L-39."

"You're taking him up in the military jet trainer?"

"Definitely," Michael said.

"You can't take the reporter up in the DC-3 or one of the other planes?" I asked, more than over his penchant for pushing the envelope.

"No way."

"Are you even current in that plane?"

"I am. Vicki is bringing my certificate to the airport," he said, confident of his abilities and excited to show off his plane.

"I swear, you're going to kill yourself in that thing."

"You'll be a rich widow," he said, not taking me seriously.

"I don't want to be a rich widow raising two kids," I said. "I want you around."

"You worry too much," he said, and kissed me goodbye.

"I love you," I said. "If you kill yourself in that plane and are in heaven, know I'll be mad as hell."

"I love you," he said, gave me another kiss, and headed on his way.

***

To say Vicki Foster was excited about that morning's interview with the Wall Street Journal was a huge understatement. She'd been working for the better part of eight years to score a feature of this magnitude about Michael Chowdry and his accomplishments. She'd gotten up extra early and made sure she was at the airport ahead of either Michael or the reporter.

While she waited at the Front Range airport, Vicki reveled in the beauty of the foothills and the crisp dry air. She'd just flown in

PART VII

the evening before from upstate New York where Atlas, and everyone who worked there, had moved six months earlier. Everyone in the company but Michael and the top executive team, that was.

She wondered how she'd allowed Michael to talk her into selling her house, having her husband give up his job, and move away.

By the time Michael arrived for the interview, she was feeling homesick and a little cranky.

"You're never going to move to New York," she said instead of hello.

"Vicki, we're looking at houses now."

"What time did you get in last night?" she asked, noting he looked fatigued, particularly around the eyes.

"Three a.m," he said. "But I'm fine."

"No doubt," she said, not liking his dismissive tone. "Are you sure you want to go up in the L-39?"

"You sound like my wife," he said. "There's no way I'm taking the aviation reporter for the Wall Street Journal up in anything but the L-39."

Michael was a pilot who was qualified to fly a number of aircraft, so Vicki was confident in his abilities, and she had the current flight certificate.

"Ready to run through my flight plan with me?" he asked.

Vicki was only too happy to go down the safety list necessary to fly the L-39 that morning. Together, they went through every item, Michael saying, "Got it," over and over until he'd checked off everything. She watched him fold the flight plan and put it in his jacket. While he followed up with a visual check of the aircraft itself, Vicki went to greet Jeff Cole, the Wall Street Journal reporter.

As she escorted him over to meet Michael, she found herself steering their esteemed guest toward the DC-3.

"The DC-3 is a great plane," she said. "I think you should go up in that."

Michael spotted them and waved from in front of the L-39.

The reporter looked as excited as twelve-year-old Jimmy when he heard they were going to take the jet trainer for a spin.

Vicki knew her idea had fallen on deaf ears.

She watched them prepare, Michael providing Jeff Cole with a flight suit, helmet, and everything else he would need. Before they climbed into the cockpit, Michael detailed various information, including important instructions about the canopy lockdown and release system. Michael then helped his passenger into the rear seat, clipped him in, climbed into the pilot's seat, gave the thumbs up, and closed the canopy.

Vicki gave them a friendly wave.

A Cessna 401 pilot watched the L-39 pull up nearby on the run up pad and observed Michael following a full-blown, in-cockpit checklist including several "high engine" run-ups over a five-to-seven minute period.

Michael and his passenger took off at 11:26 a.m.

All of the pilot witnesses but one said they could not recall hearing any radio transmissions from the jet while taxiing. One pilot, who was on final approach in a Piper Comanche before the jet took off, reported he'd heard Michael say on Unicom, "Departing Runway 26."

Witnesses reported that the airplane never reached more than 400 feet and appeared slow for a jet. It was oscillating, made a steep

PART VII

left bank, straightened out, and then slammed into the ground less than a minute later.

The plane, full of fuel, caught fire on impact.

Jeff Cole was 45.

My husband, and the love of my life, Michael Chowdry, was 46.

Chapter Thirty-Eight

"I'm about to go up," Michael had said to Tina Ferry on a phone call just before he'd taken off.

The next call she got was from Rudy, Michael's chief pilot on the BBJ at the time.

"Michael crashed," Rudy said. "He's dead."

"That isn't funny," Tina said, angry at what she assumed was a crass joke. "Not in the slightest."

"I'm not joking," Rudy said.

***

Vicki had been on the phone with her husband when she saw the smoke from Michael's plane. She mumbled something incoherent, hung up, and jumped in the car with one of the employees. As they neared the fiery crash site and spotted the smoking debris of the plane, she knew there was no way either of the men she'd just spoken to ten minutes earlier had survived.

Numb with shock, she called Tina and they went immediately into problem solving mode. They knew how fast bad news spread and understood the breadth of Michael's influence across the globe. The horrifying reality was going to affect Atlas Air and well beyond.

PART VII

Vicki, from the airfield, and Tina, from the Golden office, quickly delegated all business-related concerns: the receptionist would take calls and reroute them, someone else would start working on a press release, another would break the news to the employees, etc., while the two women moved into a far more crucial role. Michael had always been there for them in times of need. He had always cared about them as people and treated them like family, and now they wanted to be there for me and the kids.

With broken hearts, they compartmentalized, and took on the most difficult of challenges.

***

I had just walked out of a Barnes and Noble with a book for an upcoming computer class. As I was getting into my car, my cell phone rang.

"Linda, there's been a crash," Vicki simply said.

My first thought was that I was thankful to be sitting there parked instead of driving.

"You mean Michael crashed?" I finally managed to ask.

"Yes," Vicki said.

"Is he alive?" I heard myself ask, but I already knew the answer before Vicki could utter the dreaded word.

No hung in the air between us.

"Don't try to drive," Vicki said. "Just sit where you are. Tina is coming to get you."

I remember little more than sitting in my car hyperventilating as I watched a man pull into the open parking space next to me.

Unable to process what had happened, I fought the urge to roll down my window and say, "My husband just died in a plane crash."

Instead, I sat waiting for Tina to arrive and bring me home.

***

Virginia Kiely entered our home from doing errands to a ringing phone.

"Is it true Michael Chowdry is dead?" the person on the other end of the line asked.

Virginia thought it was a prank and hung up.

The phone rang again.

When she picked up a second time, she was asked the same question.

Virginia hung up again confused, angry, and wondering why she was getting such a bizarre prank call. Michael had left the house not two hours earlier. Why would someone call and say such a horrid thing? She thought about phoning me but couldn't figure out how she would even phrase such a question. Instead, she called the office still not knowing what to say but needing clarification from someone.

The receptionist answered in a tone that sounded entirely business as usual.

"This is Ginny at the house," Virginia said, allowing herself to feel ever so slightly relieved. "I'm sure this is going to sound weird, but someone just called here and asked me if Michael was dead, so I just wanted to confirm that it was a cruel prank or…"

The silence on the other end of the line was deafening.

"Hello?" Virginia finally asked.

PART VII

"Yes," the receptionist whispered.

"Yes, what?"

"Yes. It's true. Michael was just killed in a plane crash."

***

Tina arrived at the house with me where Vicki was waiting.

Virginia met us at the door.

I enveloped Virginia in a big hug and whispered. "Now, you are in my life to teach me how to be a widow and a single mother. I'm blessed."

As Virginia, who'd also lost her husband, prayed for the strength to do a good job, I went into triage mode. "Colorado Academy plays the news in the classroom and I don't want Jimmy and Olivia finding out about their father that way. We have to get them out of school." As Virginia called to let the administration know they were coming, I turned to Tina. "You have to go pick up the kids because Virginia will just cry. She won't be able to make it home without falling apart."

Tina did as she was told and I called Shazad so he could be at the house when they got home. David Brictson, who'd heard the news from Vicki, sent his wife, Jan, straight to our house. He arrived soon after. John Blue was at the office and came over right away. As other shocked, grieving friends and family began to gather at the house, I proceeded to call my daughters.

Jennifer was a schoolteacher in Seattle and it was the middle of the school day, so I tracked Chad down in his office at Microsoft instead. With the news, he felt his legs go weak and slumped onto the floor. He says he remembers me saying, "You need to go tell Jennifer at school, but don't drive. Make sure you don't drive."

Jennifer was in the middle of a lesson when Chad walked in along with another staff member. She knew something was up because her husband had never shown up to her school while she was teaching.

"I'm going to take over," the staff person said. "You talk to Chad."

They walked out of the school together and he told her.

They headed directly to the airport to be with me and the kids.

***

Regan was in Hawaii living on the Big Island when I called. Her son, Suka, was four at the time and she'd had little if any contact with me or Michael since his birth. She had finally found some peace and happiness in her life living far away from the rest of us. Our lives were so totally different that she saw no way our paths could cross again.

"Michael died in a plane crash," I said to my estranged daughter. "I have lost my husband, and I need to regain my daughter and my grandson."

Thankfully, Regan and Suka made their way back home to their family.

***

It was just after lunch in Olivia's third grade classroom during the quiet period of the day known as DEAR (Drop Everything and

PART VII

Read). The overhead lights were off and the whole class was immersed in their books. The school nurse, Mrs. McKnight, came into the classroom and conferred with Olivia's teacher, Miss Sadie. Olivia was told Tina was there to pick her and Jimmy up a little early. Olivia knew something was off and remembers being concerned that Sunny, the family labrador, had died. Tina assured her the dog was fine as she drove toward the house with the kids.

It was January 24, and Tina hadn't seen Olivia or Jimmy since before the holidays. Jimmy, ever his father's polite, caring son, inquired about her Christmas vacation. Tina did her best to say as little as possible, but Jimmy had heard that her husband's grandmother had died while they were back east visiting family.

"You know," he said, innocently consoling her, "it's really hard when people leave us, but in some ways, it means they're no longer in pain."

It was all Tina could do to keep from breaking down in front of soulful, sweet, twelve- year-old Jimmy and darling nine-year-old Olivia. She prayed silently, *Lord, Jesus, help me keep my act together* and diverted the conversation until they pulled off I-70 and wound their way up the curvy Genesee roads toward the house.

Olivia noticed all the cars in the driveway and asked again what was happening.

Tina pulled into the driveway and turned off the engine. She paused in silence before opening the door. "Whatever happens," she said, as she escorted them up the big stone steps leading to their house, "remember I love you."

Both kids found it odd that their Uncle Shazad was waiting for them. Even more unusual was that I took Olivia by the hand while

Shazad did the same with Jimmy and sat them down in the formal living room we rarely used.

Telling the children what had happened was the hardest thing I had ever done or would ever do. I remember not knowing how to say the words and simply blurted them out.

Jimmy let out a horrific scream that echoed throughout the house.

My heart was in a million pieces.

Olivia heard me say that her dad was in an accident and had died. She vividly remembers hearing her brother scream and begin to sob hysterically. Shazad comforted Jimmy while I comforted Olivia the best I could. The pastor from our church was there for everyone. So were the Brictsons, John Blue, and other people from the office. Jan Wilkins, Olivia's best friend Ellie's mom was there too. Olivia recalls her talking about how her husband Ross enjoyed hunting with Michael and how sad he was going to be. From that point on, Olivia remembers only confusion and people walking around the house crying and speaking in hushed tones.

Later that afternoon, Jan had to run down to the school bus stop to pick up Ellie and asked Olivia if she wanted to come along. Olivia joined her, not saying anything to Ellie in the car about her father. They drove back as though everything was normal. When they got to the house, she brought Ellie into her room and told her there. In Olivia's mind, nothing she'd heard felt real. Her dad was often away on business trips for weeks at a time. It was simply easier to pretend he was on a really long trip. In shock and denial, she had Ellie spend the night at our house and went to school the next day. She was met at school by her teacher Miss Sadie and was

PART VII

able to escape the sadness at home. After school, she went straight to the horse barn. Those beautiful creatures carried Olivia through the darkest days, forever sealing her relationship with horses.

***

Jim Matheny had travelled to Seattle from Denver with Michael. After returning to Denver, Jim got on a commercial flight back to New York. When he landed, his secretary was on the line with the news about Michael.

Jim was stunned and knowing his fellow employees at Atlas viewed Michael as more a family member than a boss, he proceeded to the New York offices to do the best he could to help alleviate the pain everyone felt from suffering such a personal loss.

***

Sheila had met with Michael the day before in Seattle. She was shocked and horrified to get a call from Van Rex at noon on the 24th. Van Rex had flown in the L-39 with Michael a few months earlier and was that much more rattled.

***

Larry Gibbons had just left the Purchase, New York offices and was headed down to Dulles airport in Washington D.C. to catch a plane to Europe with Gene. He was in a taxi going to the Westchester County airport when his secretary, Maria Shay, called sobbing.

"What's wrong?"

"I just don't know how to tell you this," Maria said, "but your friend is gone."

"What are you talking about?" he asked.

"Michael was killed in a plane accident."

***

Gene Dessel landed in Washington at Dulles and turned on his cellphone. There were three urgent messages on his voicemail.

He was on the next plane to Denver.

***

John Dietrich received the news while on the road. He hurried back to Denver struggling to comprehend that Michael was gone. John, who'd only been with the company for a year and a half, was just gaining the seniority that allowed him to work with Michael on a regular basis. The loss was huge for him, the company as a whole, and for each and every person working there.

***

Becky Stolhammer Porter and her husband Eldon were living in Bolivia. Eldon had traveled out of the country and happened to pick up a Wall Street Journal in a U.S. airport. In it was a small article about Ejaz's death. After Becky learned about the crash, she called her parents to let them know that the young man whose eyes were always on the sky had died far too soon. She took solace only in knowing he was doing exactly what he loved most.

Chapter Thirty-Nine

The morning after the crash, there was a picture of the burning aircraft on the front page of the Rocky Mountain News. I saw it briefly and simply turned away. I was devastated but still far too deeply in shock to react or even cry. Michael was the center of my universe and I simply couldn't grasp that he was gone.

Shazad, a doctor, kept an eye on me, giving me medication to help me sleep as the funeral was scheduled and arranged for that Saturday. As flowers continued to fill the house, Tina and Vicki went to work, pulling together a PowerPoint tribute for the memorial and the reception afterwards.

Olivia, who had invited her friend Ellie to spend that first night with her, woke up early in the morning and went upstairs to my room to find Jennifer had arrived.

Regan arrived the next day.

The day of the funeral was frigid and snowy. Our favorite limo driver arrived to chauffeur me to the church. People flew in from all over the country to attend Michael's standing-room-only memorial at the Lookout Mountain Community Church.

I was amazed watching the event come together and surprised and comforted by the number of people who'd dropped everything and traveled long distances at a moment's notice to honor Michael.

I remember little more than reciting a tribute I'd written to my husband of twenty years, starting with an opening remark that heaven was rejoicing that day and closing by saying that Jimmy and Olivia and I would carry on as Michael would have wished.

As befitting my husband, there was a huge reception afterward with big tables overflowing with food. Along with an abundance of tears over a far too early demise, everyone truly celebrated Michael and a life lived to its absolute fullest.

***

In aviation, they say a person who has passed away has *flown west*. Upon learning that Michael Chowdry had been killed, the Experimental Aviation Association sent Carl Williams to attend the funeral on behalf of the organization.

Michael's friends like to believe he flew west and is now with all the aviators who came before him. He died doing what he loved and it is every pilot's hope upon his passing to be reunited with aviation friends and share tales of their flight experiences. They feel sure Michael is looking down with a smile thinking about all he accomplished and saying, "Man, wait until you get up here and see the incredible view!"

Chapter Forty

Soon after the crash, a crew from the National Transportation Safety Board (NTSB), various Atlas employees, my younger brother who'd come up from Texas, and even Chad who'd accompanied Jennifer back home to Denver, were out in the field searching for debris.

Chad located a piece of the windshield—cut his hand on it—as he gave it to one of the inspectors. In his continuing state of shock, he didn't even realize he was bleeding.

Both the NTSB and an Atlas team led by Gene, conducted separate investigations into the crash. Early on, there were a number of different theories as to the potential cause. The most likely centered around the throttle which appeared to be in the idle position when the plane crashed, and a theory that the Wall Street Journal reporter may have accidentally released the clear, Plexiglas cockpit cover, changing the aerodynamics of the plane.

It would be months before the NTSB sorted out the discrepancies and details and issued what they determined to be the probable causes and related factors. Articles about the crash appeared in the Wall Street Journal, New York Times, and numerous aviation publications. The following article appeared in the Denver Post on February 3, 2001 by staff writer Jeffrey Leib:

PART VII

PASSENGER MAY HAVE SPARKED PRIVATE JET CRASH

The passenger on Atlas Air Chairman Michael Chowdry's fatal plane flight may have accidentally released the clear, plexiglass cockpit cover from the plane only seconds before the crash, aviation experts said Friday.

Chowdry, the 46-year-old founder and chairman of air cargo giant Atlas Air, and his passenger, Jeff Cole, 45, a Wall Street Journal aviation reporter, were killed Jan. 24, shortly after the Czechmade L-39 jet took off from Front Range Airport.

John McAvoy, who runs a company called Czech Jets Inc. that performs maintenance on L-39s around the country, said it is all too easy for a flier unfamiliar with the jet to inadvertently grab the canopy-release handle in flight.

McAvoy, based in Milpitas, Calif., was in Denver this week to offer technical assistance to the National Transportation Safety Board, which is investigating the Chowdry crash.

In examining the plane's wreckage, McAvoy said he found the rear seat's canopy release handle in the open position, while the comparable handle for the front seat was in a closed position. Cole was sitting in the rear seat and Chowdry was piloting in front.

Don Dewey, maintenance coordinator for Chowdry's fleet of airplanes, said he heard the Atlas chairman give Cole instructions about the canopy lockdown and release system before they took off.

"Michael was very safety-conscious," Dewey said.

George Cambron, a United Parcel Service 767 captain who flies L-39s in air shows and instructs others in flying the Czech jet, said the loss of the rear canopy with the jet going more than 200 miles an hour could have been very distracting to the pilot in the seconds before the crash.

The tremendous noise and rush of air could have led Chowdry to think he was going faster than he really was, and to reflexively reduce power by pulling back on the plane's throttle, said Cambron, who flew for the U.S. Marine Corps for 12 years before joining UPS.

Chief NTSB investigator Jim Struhsaker said the investigation appears to show the throttle was in the idle position when the plane crashed, but cautioned it's still too early to identify the cause of the accident.

Struhsaker would not say when an official report on the accident would be available.

The force of the accident also may have caused the throttle to return to idle, McAvoy said.

But if Chowdry accidentally pulled the throttle to idle, he might not have had time to apply power again and keep the plane aloft, Cambron said. Jet engines like the one on the L-39 can take nine to 12 seconds to "spool up" and regain power.

Gordon Gilbert from AirOnline.com filed a similar report but implicated Michael in the crash:

The NTSB's recently released factual report of the crash on January 24 last year of a privately owned Aero Vodochody L-39 former Czech Republic military jet trainer that killed Wall Street Journal aerospace editor Jeff Cole riding as a passenger and pilot Michael Chowdry, founder and CEO of cargo carrier Atlas Air, draws attention to the pilot's skill, experience and attitude, as well as a possible severe and sudden change in the airplane's handling characteristics when it lost the aft canopy during takeoff from Colorado's Front Range Airport.

Chowdry became one of the first customers to own and fly a Boeing Business Jet, and he worked with Boeing to publicize the BBJ. Chowdry received an ATP certificate in August 1999 and he was a CFI. He also had a type rating in the BBJ. On his last FAA physical in July 2000, he reported that he had 5,100 hr of flight experience, with 250 hr during the last six months. On his last insurance policy, Chowdry stated he had completed a biennial flight review and instrument competency check in August 2000. But the sum of his flying experience is not clear because he reportedly never kept a logbook. In addition, former BBJ pilots who flew with Chowdry do not paint a flattering picture of him as an aviator.

Chowdry reported in that August 2000 insurance application that he had 150 hr in the L-39, but his flight instructor estimated he had between 40 and 50 hr, and maintenance logs suggested that Chowdry had 38.6 hr of L-39 experience, 6.6 of which were in the 18 months preceding the accident.

Chowdry made his first flight in the airplane in October 1997, then purchased it and registered it as N602MC in December. In March and April 1998, he received 13 hr of ground school and 11 hr of flight training in the airplane. On April 17, 1998, the FAA issued a letter of authorization (LOA) to Chowdry that was valid through April 30, 2000. The LOA required him to make at least three takeoffs and landings in the L-39 within the preceding six calendar months, or the LOA would be rescinded. In July 2000 he received an estimated two hours of ground instruction and two flights in the airplane with an instructor for a total of 2.3 hr. The FAA issued Chowdry a new LOA that was good through the end of last month.

The NTSB investigation will consider the possibility of pilot fatigue as a factor in the accident. According to the Safety Board, an employee of Chowdry said he flew to Washington in his BBJ for the Presidential inauguration and associated events on January 20 last year. On January 21 and 22 he flew (with three other crewmembers) to Europe and on to Shanghai, China, with stops at several locations for business meetings. On January 23 he was in Seattle, Wash. for a five-hour meeting, and then flew home to Denver that evening.

At about 11:26 the next morning he took off in the L-39 and crashed less than a minute later. Witnesses reported the airplane never reached more than 300 or 400 ft agl, appeared slow for a jet, was oscillating and, just before the crash, made a medium to steep left bank before straightening out. The FAA estimated the speed of the airplane was 200 kt when it crashed.

Was C.G. Change a Contributing Factor?
Witness statements and maintenance records indicate that Chowdry had nearly all of his L-39 flight experience with his

airplane's empty weight c.g. between 34 and 35 percent MAC. In October 1999, during its annual inspection, about 200 lb of weight was placed in the airplane to produce an empty weight c.g. of 27.6 percent MAC. Maintenance records and a flight-tracking sheet suggest that the pilot had 6.1 hr of flight experience with the airplane at this c.g. moment.

In October 2000, during its next annual, the 200 lb of weight was removed from the airplane to create a c.g. of about 34.98 percent MAC. Witness statements and maintenance records indicate that the accident flight takeoff was Chowdry's first since the c.g. had been adjusted back to the 34- to 35-percent MAC range.

The Safety Board will also try to determine if the c.g. of the airplane shifted considerably aft. An experienced L-39 pilot told the NTSB that the flight controls become "very sensitive" in an aft, out-of-c.g. condition. An L-39 instructor pilot told of an owner who had lost his rear canopy while on climbout, without a passenger in the seat. That owner reported that when he was trimming the nose down, the rear canopy suddenly separated from the airplane. The airplane immediately "nosed up in a dramatic fashion" and that "aggressive nose-down trim and forward stick movements were required to restabilize the airplane."

Another experienced L-39 pilot said that an aft c.g. would cause the airplane to oscillate. "At a given oscillation amplitude, the airstream will get under the airplane's nose to produce a violent pitch up." L-39s are "very pitch sensitive" and the trim works "very fast," according to this L-39 pilot. L-39s have a "tendency to oscillate" right after takeoff. The airplane is "very easy to over-control, particularly if the pilot is startled," said another L-39 pilot. "You've got to be well trained and current to fly the airplane."

A pilot witness to the accident said the airplane was "moving up and down very quickly, in a real quick jerky manner." He said the up and down movements were so fast that there was no apparent altitude change.

History of Canopy Problems
An employee pilot of Chowdry, who had LOAs in MiG fighters, said he flew with Chowdry in the back seat of the L-39 on Nov. 18, 2000, about three months before the crash. He said that while in flight, during high-g maneuvers, he could hear and feel the rear canopy chatter loudly. This abnormality, along with a persistent intermittent canopy ajar light, persuaded him to end the flight after approximately 30 to 35 min in the air. This was the last flight before the accident.

Another L-39 pilot said that on two occasions he has had passengers inadvertently move the blue seal depressurization knob (deactivating the rear canopy seals) while getting into the back seat. He said that for low-altitude flights, the front-seat pilot probably would not be aware of it.

During an L-39 flight in March with Chowdry at the controls, a non-pilot passenger said they flew around the airport at approximately

100 ft "and the airplane seemed to be wallowing around." After an uneventful landing and taxi to the hangar, the engine was shut down. "When Chowdry opened his canopy, it swung all the way over" and fell to the ground, said the passenger. It was also discovered that one of the engine air intake covers had been left in place and had made its way "some distance inside the engine air intake duct."

Following the crash, an examination of the damage to the rear canopy and the aircraft's structure by the Life Science Laboratory in San Antonio led investigators to believe both the front and rear canopy locks were not properly secured. Pieces of the failed acrylic transparency of the aft canopy were also sent to the U.S. Air Force Research Laboratory in Ohio. Its representative stated that the back canopy transparency failed because of acrylic "embrittlement" (chemical contamination to the acrylic substrate). He said this could be a result of "aggressive cleaning fluids getting into the canopy frame and staying there during thermal and structural loading."

Although the accident airplane was a 1996 model, the canopy design comes from the 1950s, and there are no channels in the canopy frame to allow fluids to dissipate.

Former Atlas Pilots Comment on Chowdry
A former pilot for Chowdry's BBJ said he never saw him "keep any sort of logbook–a perennial problem with our insurance carrier." Another former BBJ pilot who worked for Chowdry told NTSB

investigators he "didn't like to follow the rules, had weak situational awareness skills, had aviation-oriented attention deficiencies, panicked easily and had spontaneous incapacitations." Chowdry had "weak crew communication skills, poor utilization of checklists and weak procedural skills," according to another former Atlas BBJ pilot. (Atlas sold the BBJ shortly after Chowdry's death.)

Yet a Cessna 401 pilot who watched the accident L-39 as it pulled up next to the Cessna on the runup pad before its last flight said "it appeared [Chowdry] was following a full-blown checklist." There were several "high engine" runups over a five- to seven-minute period.

All the pilot witnesses but one said they could not recall hearing any radio transmissions from the jet, in flight or while taxiing. But one pilot witness in a Piper Comanche on final before the jet took off said Chowdry reported on Unicom that he was "departing Runway 26."

It will be several months before the NTSB sorts out all the discrepancies and details of this tragic accident and issues the probable causes and related factors.

***

Gene, a veteran of crash investigations, did his own independent evaluation for Atlas alongside the NTSB. While pilot error is the default ruling in most crashes, he believed and continues to believe the accident was not Michael's fault.

PART VII

Fighter planes are very unstable. They are designed that way for maneuverability purposes. At low altitude, a pilot can't make any mistakes. The L-39 was a trainer that could be used as a fighter plane, but the particular version Michael had was never armed. It did have ejection seats, but they were disarmed as well. The aircraft was converted or reduced, to some extent, to a civilian use. It was single engine, it was high performance, but it was subsonic.

Michael had owned the L-39 for a few years and was a capable pilot. In addition, Atlas had a maintenance person who did the actual work on the aircraft while Gene, who held the airframe and power plant license in charge of maintenance with the FAA, was the designated director of all maintenance.

Prior to the time of the fatal flight, Gene was aware of some recent, minor issues with the L-39 but all had been addressed. Michael had taken Atlas's CFO up in the L-39. Prior to the flight, he'd asked the CFO to take out the intake plugs, but didn't check to see that he had only removed the plugs from one side. Michael took off and managed to get the airplane off the ground, but couldn't develop any power. As a result, Gene had to go back and borescope the engine and make sure it hadn't been over temped. The L-39 had also been taken up to Oshkosh, so it had some hours on it and had been surrounded by people who were photographing, admiring, and potentially touching components of the aircraft. Gene determined that neither of these factors had any impact on the fatal incident. Following the crash, Gene had the engine cut open and checked to confirm that it was functioning perfectly at the time of the crash. It was.

The plane went through its annual inspections and checked out. The mechanic assigned to the plane was capable and competent.

The engines were fine and there were no malfunctions with flight controls. He readied the aircraft properly that day and brought it out for Michael and his guest. Michael noted that one of the lock lights was flickering intermittently but dismissed it as an issue.

Front Range Airport is east of Denver International Airport so pilots cannot take off to the west or they run into DIA airspace. To remedy this, they typically take off and make a left turn. Gene believes that Michael took off properly, but that during the left turn, the F canopy fractured due to a poorly adjusted left latch.

Because the canopy was constructed of reflective glass, it fractured into small pieces and a large section of the rear canopy departed. The frame was still there, but not the Plexiglas. The L-39 appears as if it has one homogenous canopy, but there are actually two. Gene assumes that Michael wouldn't have been aware that the rear canopy had departed other than maybe hearing something or noting a slight difference in pressurization. There is a circumferential seal that goes across and also a bridge portion which is nitrogen filled and fairly high pressure.

It is also possible that the flickering light was inconsequential, just as Michael believed, but that the reporter, nervous and stuck in the claustrophobic cockpit of a fighter jet with a man he was meeting for the first time, may have inadvertently grabbed the wrong handle during take-off. On the L-39, a red canopy jettison handle is positioned on the right side of the frame. A normal canopy lock/unlock handle is also red and is located on the left side. The fact that both handles are red, and that both are located at approximately the same height and depth, can lead to accidental canopy jettison by an untrained person reaching for the wrong handle.

PART VII

Both handles are in a location where they could act as hand holds, another cause for inadvertent canopy jettison.

In addition, both cockpits have full controls, so the aircraft could be flown from the forward cockpit or the rear cockpit. In the L-39, the person in back is not merely a passenger, but has the ability to take full control of the aircraft. Clearly, the reporter wouldn't have tried to take over, but if the canopy shattered in back, he may have panicked from the wild wind and kicked the right rudder pedal which would have caused the plane to turn and then nose up. If his foot remained on the pedal, the aircraft would have rotated longitudinally and the rudder would have become an elevator.

Witnesses say that as soon as they took off, the plane was in the turn. It nosed up a little bit and then it was under control at all times, except that it lost altitude. Gene believes the only mistake Michael probably made was to pull back on the thrust lever a little bit, but he didn't orb in. The plane was under control and he was flying the airplane. He knows this was the case because Michael crashed flat.

The plane, which was full of fuel, caught fire and burned when it hit the ground. It did not blow up. It also barely disturbed the surrounding grass. Michael and the reporter were strapped into their seats which left the plane on impact. The reporter lost his hat and his headset in the wind after the Plexiglas shattered. Michael was just forward of the right wing and the reporter's seat had been catapulted ahead of him.

Both died instantly on impact.

Michael was a very good pilot. He flew a variety of different aircraft including a DC-3 and was fully certificated as a captain on a 737. In Gene's opinion, the crash was purely a matter of losing altitude. There was a takeoff, an incident in the air, and then a crash.

Michael was just trying to figure out what was going on in a split second and hit the ground at an oblique angle.

***

The following is the National Transportation Safety Board's factual report of the crash:

On January 24, 2001, at 11:27 mountain standard time, an Aero Vodochody L-39CT, N602MC, was destroyed when it impacted terrain while on departure from Front Range Airport, Watkins, Colorado. The airline transport pilot and his passenger were fatally injured. MAC Flightlease, Inc., of Portland, Oregon, was operating the airplane under Title 14 CFR Part 91. Visual meteorological conditions prevailed for the local flight that was originating at the time of the accident. No flight plan had been filed.

According to airport personnel, on the morning of the accident, the airplane was topped off with 135 gallons of jet fuel. The tip tanks were not fueled, and an employee of the pilot said that the pilot always flew with them empty. Several witnesses observed the airplane taxi to runway 26 for departure (a tail wind departure). A pilot, in his airplane on the run up pad for runway 26, observed the accident airplane begin its takeoff roll while there was a Cessna 172 (possibly a 182) over the numbers on the departure end of the runway.

A pilot in a Cessna 182, who was on 3/4 to 1 mile final when the accident airplane took the active runway, said she was surprised to see the jet on the runway in front of her. She didn't hear any radio calls from him to indicate that he was taking the active runway for departure. She said that she had to slow down and do a couple of "S" turns to allow for spacing. Another witness said that the accident airplane lifted off after a ground roll about 3,800 to 4,000 feet, but appeared to be flying really slow. Several witnesses observed the airplane make a sharp left turn, at approximately 100 to 300 feet above the ground, just past the end of the runway. Another pilot observed the accident airplane taking off and thought it was "very low" and then observed it make a sharp left turn (estimated to be 70 to 90 degrees of bank). He said he could see the whole top of the airplane in the turn. Another pilot said that the Cessna in front of the jet was flying its crosswind leg when the accident airplane began its turn over the departure end of runway 26. One pilot said that she heard no radio transmissions from the accident airplane through his entire departure sequence from Front Range Airport.

Federal Aviation Administration (FAA) radar data indicates that at 1126:19, the airplane crossed the departure end of runway 26 at approximately 173 knots. At 1126:33, the airplane was turning southbound, and had lost an estimated 15 knots of airspeed. No altitude information could be retrieved from the radar data because the airplane's transponder was not emanating any signals. Approximately 2 nautical miles (nm) south of runway 26, the last raw radar return was recorded at 1126:56; the accident airplane's airspeed was estimated to be 200 knots.

A witness, driving south on Imboden Road, reported seeing a cloud of debris depart aft of the airplane, and flutter in the sunlight to the ground. She said it looked like the airplane was discharging trash. She said the airplane suddenly nosed down and headed straight for the ground. A pilot driving north on Imboden Road said he saw the airplane fly nearly straight at him at approximately 300 feet. He said the airplane rolled left, and went straight down. A retired airline mechanic also driving north on Imboden Road said he estimated that the airplane was 400 feet above the ground and flying straight at him. He said that it was moving up and down "very quickly, in a real quick jerky manner [short frequent longitudinal oscillations]."

A pilot flying approximately 1.5 nm behind the accident airplane said that she observed the jet to enter a very slight left bank, and climb slightly. Suddenly, she saw the jet's nose "go straight vertical," as if entering an aerobatic maneuver. The pilot then observed the jet nose-over to the right (west) and impact the ground. A witness standing outside of his home said he saw the airplane's right wing suddenly drop, and the airplane nosed down approximately 45 degrees. He said that there was never any discernible change in its engine noise. The witness said the airplane appeared to be flattening its dive and may have rotated slightly clockwise before disappearing from sight.

The first police and fire/rescue personnel arrived on the scene at approximately 1140.

PART VII

PERSONNEL INFORMATION

According to FAA records, the pilot received his airline transport pilot certificate on August 30, 1999; he was also a certificated flight instructor and ground instructor. On his last FAA flight medical application dated July 26, 2000, he reported that he had 5,100 hours of flight experience with 250 hours during the previous 6 months. The pilot reported on his last insurance application, dated August 27, 2000, that he had successfully completed a flight review and instrument competency check on August 15, 2000.

The pilot flew his first demonstration flight in the airplane on October 21, 1997, then purchased it and registered it with the FAA on December 16, 1997. During the months of March and April of 1998, he received 13 hours of ground school and 11 hours of flight training in the airplane. On April 17, 1998, a Letter of Authorization (LOA) was issued to the pilot by the FAA; it was good through April 30, 2000. The only flight limitation of his LOA was that he could not fly in formation with another airplane. The letter also required the pilot to make at least three takeoffs and landings in this model airplane within the preceding 6 calendar months, or the privileges of the LOA were rescinded. On July 15 and 16, 2000, the pilot received an estimated 2 hours of ground instruction and two flights in the airplane with an instructor for a total of 2.3 hours. The FAA issued the pilot a new LOA which was good through July 31, 2002.

A pilot flight logbook, documenting the pilot's L-39 flight time could not be found. The pilot reported on the airplane's insurance application, dated August 2000, that he had 150 hours in L-39s. His L-39 flight instructor estimated that the pilot had between 40 to 50 hours of L-39 flight experience. Maintenance logbooks, an aircraft flight log tracking sheet, and statements from other L-39 pilots suggest that the pilot had a total 38.6 hours of L-39 flight experience and 6.6 hours during the last 18 months.

An employee of the pilot said the pilot flew to Washington D.C. in his Boeing Business Jet (BBJ) for the Presidential inauguration and associated events on January 20, 2001. On January 21 and 22, he flew (with three other crew members) to Europe and on to Shang hai, China, with stops at several locations for business meetings. On January 23, he was in Seattle, Washington, for a 5 hour meeting, and then flew home to Denver that evening. The next morning he flew the accident flight with the L-39.

AIRCRAFT INFORMATION
The airplane was a Czech Republic military single engine, turbofan (jet) trainer, two seat tandem airplane (39.8 feet in length; 31 feet total wing span), which was manufactured by the Aero Vodochody Company in 1991 (approximately 3,000 were built). It was never delivered to the original buyer, and was refurbished and recertified in 1996. It was powered by an AI-25TL turbofan engine which had two shafts, by-pass flow, 12-stages of compressor, annular combustion chamber, three stages of gas turbine, which had a maximum sea level static thrust of 3,790 pounds. One pilot, who flew the airplane, said that at 25,000 feet, the airplane easily cruised at a true airspeed of 320 knots; the airplane's flight manual states that

the airplane's maximum airspeed, without wing tanks or external stores, was 490 knots.

The airplane was certified for a maximum takeoff weight of 10,600 pounds, and a maximum landing weight of 10,582 pounds. The fuselage fuel tank held 289 gallons (1,936 pounds), and two 58 gallon wing tanks held an additional 104 gallons of usable fuel (704 pounds). The engine had an estimated 180 to 200 gallon per hour fuel burn rate. The maintenance records indicated that the last annual inspection was performed in Oklahoma City, Oklahoma, between August 14, 2000, and October 28, 2000. The previous annual was performed in Gadson, Alabama, between September 27, 1999, and October 19, 1999.

The airplane's empty weight when it left the factory in the Czech Republic, was 7,362 pounds; its center of gravity (CG) was 27.8 percent of mean aerodynamic cord (MAC). The manufacturer's manuals state that the airplane's CG, in its empty weight condition, must be 27.7 percent, plus or minus 0.5 percent of MAC. The manuals further state that a standard aircraft load (with two occupants and main fuel tank full) should have an approximate flight CG of 23 percent, not to exceed 25.5 percent, for the airplane's self-dampening characteristics to be effective. That is, if a sharp, spontaneous elevator movement is made by the pilot, the plane is designed to self-dampen long period longitudinal and short period longitudinal oscillations, if the CG is in the 23 percent to 25.5 percent envelope. As the CG moves aft of this envelope, aircraft control becomes progressively more sensitive, and the flight regime of negative static stability (divergent stability) increases.

The accident airplane was last weighed in Oklahoma on November 17, 2000; its empty weight was 7,349 pounds and maintenance personnel calculated its CG to be 34.42 percent of MAC. A representative from the airplane's manufacturer, using the November 17, 2000 weight figures, computed the airplane's CG to be 34.98 percent of MAC. He further stated that with two pilots and main fuel tank full the CG would be 29.58 percent of MAC. The CG flight envelope, according to manufacturer's specification, is 21 to 26 percent MAC. Calculations by an L-39 maintenance consultant indicate that the loss of the rear seat's canopy transparency would move the CG aft an additional .25 percent of MAC. The airplane's manufacturer's representative said that an L-39 had been flown by a very experienced, factory test pilot with the whole canopy and the ejection seat missing, and had an estimated 34 percent to 35 percent of MAC.

Witness statements and maintenance records indicate that the pilot had nearly all of his L-39 flight experience with his airplane's empty weight CG between 34 percent and 35 percent MAC. In October, 1999, during its annual inspection in Gadson, Alabama, approximately 200 pounds of weight was placed in the airplane to produce an empty weight CG of 27.6 percent MAC. Maintenance records and a flight tracking sheet suggest that the pilot had 6.1 hours of flight experience with the airplane at this CG. On October 17, 2000, during its next annual, the 200 pounds of weight was removed from the airplane to create a CG of 34.42 percent [recalculated to be 34.98 percent] MAC. Witness statements and maintenance records indicate that the accident flight takeoff was the pilot's first takeoff since the CG had been adjusted back to the 34 percent to 35 percent MAC range.

An experienced L-39 pilot reported that L-39s require approximately 4,000 feet of runway to get airborne. He said that he departed a runway in Colorado once, and he used approximately 2.5 nm to accelerate to a recommended maneuvering speed of 220 knots. He also said that L-39s stall in clean configuration at approximately 98 knots. When they do stall, he said, they give an "aero rumble," nose down 3 to 5 degrees, and fall at about 2,000 feet per minute. The airplane's ground training guide states that during a stall "all control devices remain effective."

An employee of the pilot, who performed the airplane's preflight inspection with the pilot, said that the airplane's flight hour meter read 118.1 hours. He further stated that the ejection seats on the accident airplane were not armed.

METEOROLOGICAL INFORMATION

At 1053, the weather conditions at the Denver International Airport (elevation 5,431 feet), 315 degrees 7 nm from the accident site, were as follows: wind 050 degrees at 5 knots; visibility 10 statute miles; cloud condition 3,500 feet agl few, 22,000 feet agl broken; temperature 34 degrees Fahrenheit; dew point 24 degrees Fahrenheit; altimeter setting 30.35 inches. The density altitude was calculated to be 4,792 feet.

The sun was approximately 30 degrees above the horizon on an approximate 166 degree heading from the accident site.

AERODROME INFORMATION
The Front Range Airport (FTG; elevation 5,512 feet), Watkins, Colorado, is not serviced by a control tower. Two runways are available, 26-08, and 35-17. The airport lies under Denver International Airport's Class B airspace, which has a floor of 7,000 feet over Front Range Airport. The eastern edge (to the ground) of DIA's class B airspace is located 5,200 feet west of the departure end of runway 26. When aircraft use runway 26, a southbound turn is required so as not to enter Denver's class B airspace; the boundary is designated by Imboden Road (north-south).

WRECKAGE AND IMPACT INFORMATION
The airplane was found on a rolling grass covered field (elevation 5,546 feet, N39 degrees 45.75', W104 degrees 34.75') approximately 2 nm southwest of the Front Range Airport. The main debris path was oriented 168 degrees; the impact point ground scar suggested that the longitudinal axis of the airplane, at impact, was heading 225 to 230 degrees. The impact ground scar (including appropriately identified red and green navigation light lenses) and identifiable wreckage, suggested that the airplane impacted the ground relatively wings level and in a flat orientation.

All of the airplane's major components were accounted for at the accident site. Flight control continuity could not be established due to impact damage and postimpact fire. The instrument panel and flight controls were destroyed and/or separated from the fuselage. The fuselage was found approximately 250 feet from the impact point and the pilot was found associated with it. The passenger was located approximately 315 feet from the impact point.

Postaccident examination of the engine revealed no evidence of an in-flight fire, uncontainment, or case rupture. The turbine blades and vanes did not have any metallization on them. The fan blades were bent opposite the direction of rotation and the vanes were bent towards the direction of rotation.

The rear ejection seat was firmly attached to the ejection seat rails. An acrylic transparency (Plexi glass) fragment field (approximately 300 feet long by 150 feet wide), containing the back seat passenger's hat and head set, was found approximately 1,000 feet north of the main impact site (150 feet east of Imboden Road).

MEDICAL AND PATHOLOGICAL INFORMATION

An autopsy was performed on the pilot by the Adams County Coroners Office, Brighton, Colorado, on January 25, 2001.

The FAA's Civil Aeromedical Institute (CAMI) in Oklahoma City, Oklahoma, performed toxicology tests on the pilot. According to CAMI's report (#200100020001), the pilot's muscle tissue sample was tested for drugs with negative results; carbon monoxide and cyanide tests were not performed. The following volatiles were found in lung and muscle samples: ethanol and acetaldehyde.

CAMI personnel reported that the ethanol and acetaldehyde (an ethanol intermediate product; either production of or metabolite of) found in this case may potentially be from postmortem formation.

TESTS AND RESEARCH

The L-39CT's canopy acrylic transparencies were manufactured by Aerospace Composite Technologies located in Luton, England. The 3/8 inch thick acrylic transparencies were installed in their respective canopy frames at the airplane's factory in the Czech Republic in 1996. Pieces of the failed acrylic transparency were submitted to the Department of the Air Force, Air Force Research Laboratory, Wright-Patterson Air Force Base, Ohio, for analysis. Their representative stated that the back canopy transparency failed because of acrylic embrittlement (chemical contamination to the acrylic substrate). He said this could be a result of aggressive cleaning fluids getting into the canopy frame and staying there during thermal and structural loading. He said the canopy system design comes from the 1950's, and there are no channels in the canopy frame to allow fluids to dissipate. Surplus inappropriate cleaning chemicals can build up and soak into the acrylic substrate. Subsequent thermal and/or mechanical stresses can fracture the acrylic. The research scientist, who determined that the back seat acrylic transparency was altered, said that destructive testing was not accomplished. She said that the test that was performed only showed polymer deterioration, which could be attributed to ultraviolet exposure, thermal exposure, chemical damage, or manufacturing defect.

PART VII

The Life Sciences Equipment Laboratory, Brooks Air Force Base, San Antonio, Texas, examined the airplane's back canopy frame. A representative of that facility said the following:

"The damage observed on the rear cockpit canopy structures indicate that the front and rear canopy locks were not properly secured to their respective latches at the time the damage occurred. It also indicates that the top of the canopy locks were in contact with canopy structures that were adjacent to both sides of the front and rear latches. It is considered improbable that the type of damage noted in this mishap was the result of a single motion such as aircraft impact with the terrain. Instead, it is considered much more likely that the damage observed was the result of multiple motions, such as flexing of the canopy frame while in-flight; resulting from rear canopy locks not being properly secured at some point during the flight prior to aircraft impact with the terrain."

The airplane manufacturer's maintenance manual indicates that the L-39CTs have rubber seals between the canopies and the aircraft's frame. When the canopies are lacked closed, these seals can be inflated pneumatically, which permits cabin pressurization, external noise reduction, and holds the canopies securely in place. The airplane's Pilot Ground Training Manual states that on the back seater's center console, there is a round blue knob (up and down actuation) which permits the back seater (normally the flight instructor) to deactivate the rear canopy seal only. This would permit the flight instructor to demonstrate a cabin depressurization while in flight.

An employee pilot of the accident pilot, who had LOAs in MIG fighter type aircraft, said that he flew with the pilot in the L-39CT on November 18, 2000. He said the pilot had asked him to fly the airplane, but the employee agreed to do so only if the pilot flew with him. The employee flew the airplane from the front seat, and the pilot rode in the back seat. The employee pilot said that while in flight, during high "G" maneuvers, he could hear and feel the rear canopy to chatter loudly. This abnormality, along with persistent intermittent canopy ajar light, persuaded him to terminate the flight early. He landed the airplane after approximately 30 to 35 minutes of flight. This was the last flight before the accident.

Another L-39 pilot said that on two occasions, he has had passengers inadvertently move the blue seal depressurization knob (deactivating the rear canopy seals), while getting into the back seat. He said that for lower altitude flights, the front seat pilot probably would not be aware of it.

ADDITIONAL DATA
The airplane, including all components and logbooks, was released to the owner's insurance representative on March 21, 2002.

***

Chowdry was a bold, excellent pilot, an aviation engineer, and an entrepreneur the likes of which has rarely been seen. To this day, I wonder what, if anything, I could have done to keep him from

PART VII

going, but I know that when Michael made up his mind to do something, there was no stopping him. I have peace in my heart because he died doing that which he was born to do.

PART VIII
LIFE AFTER MICHAEL CHOWDRY

Chapter Forty-One

Just before Michael died, we had decided we needed to make the move to the East Coast and were looking at houses in the New York City area. After the crash, both kids pleaded with me to stay in Denver.

Olivia was determined to move forward, but Jimmy didn't go back to school for ten days. When he did, he continued to grieve and struggle. Even though I inherited all of Michael's stock, making me Atlas's majority shareholder and the official chair of the board, I decided it was best for the kids to remain in their home amongst familiar people and surroundings.

We were all grieving, but I was obligated to travel back and forth to Purchase to sit in on board meetings. I was out of my depth as chair of the board of a company on the New York Stock Exchange and had to deal with various members calling to influence me in one way or another. Political jockeying was a role I didn't want and wouldn't have embraced in the best of times. When I'd walked through Atlas's offices in the past, I'd been with Michael. Now I was expected to, in effect, *be* Michael.

I took great comfort during this time in the amazing support I had from David, Gene, and John, who helped me navigate business and financial concerns. At home, I had the help of numerous

PART VIII

people who stuck by us and took on a number of administrative duties for me while we adjusted to life without Michael.

Tina, who had worked at Atlas for two years, stayed on to help during this transition, but, after a few months, took a break. Six months later, she and I got in contact, realized how much we missed seeing each other, and scheduled lunch. By the end of the meal, Tina had agreed to be my personal assistant. She would work for our family in some capacity for a total of fourteen years.

Above all, we had Virginia who didn't take a day off during the year after Michael died. She not only slept at the house, but spent many nights on the floor of Olivia's room. She stayed at home during the day with Jimmy who struggled to attend school. When Virginia's daughter, Bridget, was on break from college she'd come over as well. Bridget developed a close relationship with Jimmy and Olivia.

Virginia helped me to be resilient and strong during this unbearably sad, painful time. I was hurting but soldiered on, putting on a good face as I flew back and forth to New York for meetings and to give speeches, sometimes to the whole company.

Always gracious, Virginia says she felt privileged to be at our home with the kids during that year. She felt that God put her where he needed her, helping us transition from our devastating loss. Virginia's glass-half-full attitude helped everyone make the best of the aftermath of Michael's passing. She took on whatever tasks needed to be done—driving, cooking, cleaning, and even volunteering at the kids' school.

Over time, Virginia started to talk to the kids about how Bridget had dealt with the loss of her own father. She also comforted them with happy reminders like, "Your dad's looking down from heaven and smiling," or, "Your dad would be so proud of you for doing this."

To this day, the kids still view Virginia as the most positive person they've ever known.

I see her as a true lifesaver.

Chapter Forty-Two

From Money Magazine, January 30, 2001:
Wall Street reacted cautiously to the death of Atlas Air founder, chief executive and majority shareholder Michael Chowdry. The US cargo carrier's share price fell after news that 46-year-old Chowdry and passenger, *Wall Street Journal* aerospace reporter, Jeff Cole, had died on January 24 when Chowdry's ex-military Aero Vodochody L-39 Albatross jet trainer, piloted by Chowdry, crashed soon after take-off from Front Range airport outside Denver, Colorado.

The price recovered when it became clear that a strong management team remained in place at Atlas, with the firm's executive vice-president, Richard Shuyler, becoming chief executive, and executive vice-president Jim Matheny becoming president and COO and continuing in his post as head of airline operations.

Nevertheless there is some concern for the future of the carrier as Chowdry, who founded Atlas in 1992 and retained a 47.3% stake after last year's initial public offer, was a "hands-on" chief executive, personally negotiating many of the airline's wet-lease deals.

PART VIII

The carrier operates 37 Boeing 747 freighters, 12 of which are -400s, with orders for four more of the type. Chowdry had been negotiating purchases for Atlas with Airbus and Boeing, including new widebody twinjet freighters and a 150t payload freighter fleet: an Airbus A380 or Boeing 747X.

Atlas has grown rapidly by operating freighters for other carriers under so-called ACMI (aircraft, crew, maintenance and insurance) contracts. Although the cargo market is growing there is increasing overcapacity as more widebody freighters enter service. Pakistan-born Chowdry learned to fly in a crop duster, says Shuyler, eventually buying the company he worked for. He was qualified to fly aircraft up to the Boeing 737, and bought the Czech-built L-39 jet trainer around two years ago.

The L-39 is popular with warbird enthusiasts, and is flown in the USA under experimental category rules for private use only. Two L-39 accidents have occurred in the USA, both in 1998, says the National Transportation Safety Board, which is investigating the Chowdry crash. In one, two died, after the aircraft went missing over Lake Michigan.

***

Businesswise, everyone understood that Michael's untimely passing was a tremendous loss, particularly on the sales and marketing side of Atlas. At the same time, he'd done a terrific job of surrounding himself with very capable, seasoned veterans in the industry who were able to take on the responsibilities and keep the business running.

David Brictson was close to retirement age but committed to staying on as secretary of the board, accompanying me to New York for meetings. Gene Dessel, Tom Scott, Stan Ray, Jim Matheny, and Larry Gibbons all agreed to stay, at least temporarily, while the CFO of the company moved into the CEO position.

Grieving for my husband, and with all eyes upon me, I found myself as majority shareholder and chair of the board as a woman in a room full of men. Despite the retention of all of Atlas's high profile executives, there was a significant, nearly insurmountable void. Michael, like many CEOs and entrepreneurs, was passionate and thrived on growing the business. In addition to being the leader of the company, he was also the lead salesman.

Unfortunately, Michael's passing was the start of what turned into a perfect storm for the company. By mid 2001, a recession hit. The terrorist attacks on September 11, 2001 further impacted the aviation industry and the market in general. The company had expanded too much, many of the aircraft were heavily financed. Others were difficult to refinance. Atlas, heavily leveraged and facing labor challenges, searched for efficiencies and was forced to downsize. Atlas Air shares started to lose their value.

Most believed that had Michael lived, he'd have found a way to put all of Atlas's assets to good use, and while the company may not have been as profitable as they'd been in the past, he would have found a way to navigate through the difficulties they faced. Just like he'd done with ING, he'd have convinced financial institutions they were going to be in a worse position without him than sticking by his side. In the airline and financial communities however, the perception was that without Michael, the rainmaker, the airline could not survive.

Despite a unique understanding of my late husband's mindset, people in the airline industry had done business with him, not me. There was no stepping into his shoes.

The stock dropped and continued to do so. I could not legally sell my shares so I had to watch them do a slow glide from $36 all the way to zero. There was talk of taking the company private, bond holders taking over, and eliminating the shareholders because they didn't have any value with Michael gone. As the company headed toward Chapter 11, I faced the unenviable task of firing the replacement CEO.

On January 30, 2004, Atlas Air Worldwide entered Chapter 11 bankruptcy.

Atlas didn't face a liquidation but did require a financial restructuring. Led by Steve Green, Joe Stewart, and the board of directors, ownership of the airline was transferred from the shareholders to the bond holders in a pre-negotiated bankruptcy that was completed in a record time of six months. The venture capitalists came in, purchased the bonds, and took over within two years. Through it all, there were enough remaining contracts so that the airline was never totally grounded. Atlas continued to fly.

One of the main things that kept Atlas going were their new 747-400s. Some of the older and more expensive equipment was ultimately phased out, but the 747-400s on which Michael had made a big bet, ultimately allowed Atlas to stay aloft.

Jeff Erickson, the CEO, and other members of the management team would face particular business challenges during that period of time by asking, "What would Michael do in this situation?"

It was a question that would resurface often in the years following his passing.

Atlas went to the lenders when it went bankrupt, but because Atlas never ceased operations, the company survived. In July 2004, the parent company completed its restructuring plan and emerged from Chapter 11 bankruptcy protection.

During that time, David Brictson retired. Jim Matheny left, and Larry Gibbons voluntarily resigned his position amidst cutbacks. Larry was lured back to a strong, thriving Atlas in 2005 by John Dietrich who now headed up Human Resources, and would continue to rise in the organization.

In 2006, Jeff Erickson elected to retire. The board did an external search and appointed Bill Flynn, a transportation industry veteran, to take over as CEO. Flynn, who embraced Michael's entrepreneurial spirit and vision, ushered Atlas into over a decade of successful expansion and diversification.

***

Ever since we'd married, I had left money matters up to Michael. John Blue knew all about our personal finances and stayed on as my advisor.

I was well aware of my husband's predilection for all or nothing deal making and spent a few sleepless nights watching Atlas's stock fall to zero. While Olivia and Jimmy had never known a different kind of life, I was from modest circumstances and would do whatever it took to provide for my family.

Thankfully, prior to the IPO, Michael established a family trust for estate planning purposes, funding it with a significant portion of his Atlas stock. At the time of the secondary issue, the family trust participated in selling much of this stock ensuring a significant amount of wealth existed outside of his holdings of Atlas Air.

***

Atlas remains firmly planted on the foundation built by Michael. Today, Atlas Air has over 100 airplanes. Larry Gibbons, now senior vice president of procurement and head of engineering and maintenance, remembers speaking with Michael when there were just over twenty planes in the fleet.

"This is going to go to at least seventy-five airplanes," Michael said predicting the growth of express delivery. "It's going to become much more prevalent to ship by air. We're just going to grow."

As Michael predicted, shipping via air has grown ever more in demand, especially with the rise of Amazon and online shopping. As a result, Atlas has not only survived but thrived. There have been two public offerings of common stock and two public offerings of convertible notes since those ill-fated years in the early 2000s and the company is on very solid footing.

The Atlas Air website reports the following:
In March 2010, Atlas Air was awarded a contract for the operation

of the Boeing 747 Large Cargo Freighter (LCF) 'Dreamlifter' for transporting aircraft parts to Boeing from suppliers around the world. It commenced operation in July 2010 under a CMI (Crew, Maintenance and Insurance) contact.

In 2011, Atlas Air took the first North American delivery of the Boeing 747-8 Freighter (Boeing 747-8F).

In September 2012, Atlas Air renewed a training contract with the United States Air Force to continue to provide training for the pilots of Air Force One. The contract also provides training for the Presidential Airlift Group.

On April 7, 2016, Atlas Air Worldwide Holdings purchased Southern Air for $110 million in an all-cash deal. The transaction included Worldwide Air Logistics Group, Inc. and its two operating subsidiaries, Southern Air Inc. and Florida West International Airways Inc.

On May 5, 2016, Amazon.com and Atlas Air announced a deal for Amazon.com to lease 20 Boeing 767s in order to fuel growth to their new Amazon air freight service, branded as Amazon Air. The deal also warrants Amazon the ability to buy up to 30% stake in the company over the next 7 years. Under the agreement, Atlas Air, Inc. will lease the aircraft to Amazon for 10 years and will provide CMI service for 7 years. This move comes after Amazon's similar deal with Air Transport International for 20 aircraft, also to be branded under Amazon Air.

PART VIII

In February 2001, Atlas Air Worldwide formed its current holding company structure with Atlas Air as a wholly owned subsidiary. Atlas has now been in business for over twenty-five years. Since the financial restructuring, the company has enjoyed a steady tailwind.

Other subsidiaries include:
- Polar Air Cargo Worldwide, Inc., 49 percent-owned by DHL Express, express and cargo service for DHL and Polar's other customers
- Titan Aviation, dry leasing
- Southern Air, intercontinental and domestic ACMI and CMI services

Atlas bought Polar Air Cargo in November 2001, which they transformed into a profitable business. Atlas was historically a 747 operator, but has now diversified into 767 cargo operations, 777 cargo operations, and 737 cargo operation through their acquisition of Southern Air. The company operates a fleet of 11 passenger aircraft and does extensive charter flying for the military. While their primary business is moving troops on a charter basis, they also fly sports teams and entertainment outfits. Between mid-2010 and mid-2017, they offered a unique three-times a week service from Houston to Angola, Africa called the Houston Express where they flew oil executives and rig workers back and forth to the United States.

Atlas Air Worldwide is the leading global provider of outsourced aircraft and aviation operating services. They are the world's largest operator of Boeing 747 freighter aircraft and the only outsource provider of Boeing's 747-8F. They provide customers 747, 777, 767 and 737 freighter and passenger aircraft for domestic, regional, and international ACMI, CMI, charter and dry lease applications.

Today, Atlas is a somewhat different business given the focus on process and the regulatory oversight that comes with public companies, but the family-oriented, big little company environment is still intrinsic to the office culture. From the start, Michael drew upon the industry by bringing in a number of subject matter experts and then treated them so well these employees and executives stayed with the company for their careers. Even though it is a public company operating in a global environment, Atlas continues to maintain a small management team that strives to be agile rather than bogged down in bureaucracy.

On July 2, 2019, after thirteen successful years at the helm, Bill Flynn announced his retirement and John Dietrich, who started as assistant in-house counsel in 1999 and rose through the ranks, was named as incoming CEO.

John was only at the company for a year and a half before Michael's tragic death. One of his biggest regrets, particularly now that he will be guiding Atlas into the future, is that he didn't have the opportunity to get to know Michael Chowdry better on a personal basis. As a businessman, however, he spent enough time working under Michael to know the secret to Atlas's long term growth and success is to always be looking for ways to add value for the customer and to always know *what's happening in this world.*

In Their Own Words

Jennifer

I have a recurring dream about Michael where we are all in the present, living our lives as things are now, and somehow, he comes back. It is always unclear where he has been.

In my dream I am asking, "What does this mean for all of us? Does life go back to how it was before or have things changed so much that they can't possibly go back?"

In my awake life, when I reflect back on my time with Michael Chowdry, it does seem like a dream. Life with Michael wasn't without pain and hurt, but life with him was also fun, joyful, unpredictable, and enriching. I cannot deny that I am who I am today in part because of his influence. I look back on those years as bittersweet. I know Michael was like the rest of us; seeking relationships, wanting to belong, to be understood, to be loved, and to be relevant. He, like all of us, was a complex person navigating his own history, mix of cultures, family life and an intense professional life. Now that I am older and have my own family, I can appreciate some of his personal battles and have more compassion and appreciation for him. He is often described as a man who was larger than life, but for me he was an enigma. Like in my dream, when I think of Michael, I am often left with more questions than answers.

PART VIII

Jennifer, Chad, and their kids live in the San Juan Islands off the coast of Washington.

Having been there during the good times and the bad, Jennifer is close with me and values our good relationship.

Regan

Jennifer and I sometimes felt a sense of servitude as younger girls, but when I got old enough to work outside of the home, I began to appreciate the skills I'd learned from Michael. I'd been trained to talk to people, to entertain business guests, and interact with adults. I'd learned to be hospitable and available. I was also capable of many different jobs which served me well.

Even though I was hurt and suffered greatly due to my relationship with Michael, I came to understand, and even appreciate, that he was not squandering his chance in the land of opportunity. I admired and learned from his determination to find a way to achieve his goals and appreciated that he brought that awareness to my life.

Today, Regan is married to a very kind and wonderful man and they live on a beautiful organic farm in Oregon. She has teenage daughter and her son, Suka, is in his twenties. She rides horses, plants gardens, and opens her heart and home to young girls who have come from difficult family circumstances. We are very close. After Michael's death, we spent extensive time ironing out all the difficulties in our relationship. Although always the lone wolf, she stays close to and builds relationships with her siblings. She's taught both of her kids *to be able to sleep on the floor as well as sleep on the bed.*

Jimmy

My dad was my best friend growing up. I got so much from him despite his hectic schedule. We were always welcome in his office, unless there were closed door meetings. It never felt like Atlas or his career were separate from home. If anything, I think maybe my early education suffered in some ways because he always wanted us to travel with him around the world.

A lot of people at his level had massive pedigrees and went to Wharton, Harvard, or Stanford, but he came out of aviation school in Minnesota and became one of the top competitors in his industry. I'm sure he experienced discrimination, but I think a lot of his motivation was to elevate himself to the point that he became so big, it didn't matter where he came from. How he made that happen wasn't necessarily calm, cool, and collected, but it was amazing to watch.

His success was fueled by his courage and faith in making things work. He may have been creative in how he got there and his thinking was outside of the box, but he was always one step ahead. If he was going to make a mistake, he already had a solution for how to fix it.

As a kid, I never remember being bored for any reason. There was always some level of excitement going on. My mom did the majority of the cooking, but if he was home, he was in the kitchen working on something elaborate, amazing, scientific, and delicious he wanted me to understand and help him create.

There's a Pakistani word, gupshup, which essentially means chill time. When it is chill time in Pakistan, people congregate, eat, drink lots of tea and spend hours on the couch talking. It's all meant to be very communal. Gupshup was very important to my father.

I know that my father was really big and important, but I also knew that I was equally, if not, more important to him. He treated everyone who worked for him that way too.

The human component, being able to relate to people, was the most important thing to him and became the most apparent and important to me too.

I am proud to be his son.

Jimmy moved to California in 2008 to attend Whittier College. He stayed in Southern California after graduation and worked with different artist management groups. He also did some marketing. After a trip to San Francisco, he enrolled in California College of the Arts and earned his MBA in Design Strategy. He still resides in San Francisco and works at a non-profit which focuses on socially responsible investing.

He has been able to travel to Pakistan and see where Michael was from, where he went to school, and to smell onions, garlic and garam masala just like his dad used to make. Losing his father so young, he believes gave him a greater understanding of the fragility of life.

Olivia

One of my dreams was to eat a mango with my father in Pakistan. After dinner on any normal night, Dad and I would eat mangos. No fork. No knife. We would just stand over the sink, the juice from the sweet fruit dripping down our wrists.

    I miss him. Sometimes more than I think I should given how much time has passed.

What I remember most about my dad was his boundless energy.

Even though business was always on his mind, he still wanted to know what was going on in our lives. I used to come home and sit in his lap in one of the really big chairs at our house in Genesee, and we would discuss the day.

My dad also liked to eat, drink, and entertain. He took great pleasure in friends, family and time together, and he passed that joy onto me. I love having people in my house and the warm energy and light of laughter, close friends, and food. My passion for cooking also came from him.

In so many ways, my father was larger than life. He knew how to think outside the box and regularly accomplished what others might say "couldn't be done." He was persistent, ambitious, and always present. Dad owned every room he entered. He had a way of convincing people to do things his way. I don't think he was pushy or mean—just firm in his convictions, and very convincing.

My father was young when he died. Some people wait their whole lives for their big break, but my dad didn't let anything stop him until he reached the top—an immigrant from Pakistan who conquered corporate America.

I'd give anything to have ten minutes to just talk to my dad again, to be able to ask him questions about life and business.

He made a big impact and left a wonderful legacy. A dad-shaped hole in my heart. Give a squeeze and hold on tight to the people in your life. Tell them how much you love them. Time is priceless and grief is simply the price of love.

The ambition Olivia inherited from her dad has manifested in her passion as a competitive equestrian. She was raised with a very strong sense of social justice and giving back to others outside of her close connected community. She is often referred to as a hard-wired optimist and lives with an attitude of looking at challenges as opportunities not obstacles. Her parents both instilled a deep sense that with resources comes responsibility and with options comes accountability. She suspects she will eventually focus on an entrepreneurial pursuit that centers around a sustainable impact focus. For now, she is competing at a high level with her horses and engaging in an educational opportunity in social impact investing and sustainability in the developing world. Spending time over shared meals with her loved ones remains of great importance.

My Thoughts

A major theme running throughout scripture is "speak truth in love." This principle was my guidepost as I worked on this book. Writing the story has been a joy, as I learned more about my husband through the eyes of others who knew Michael. I relived those magical twenty years. In the process, I learned we can never truly capture another's life story. There is always more to tell. I did hitch my wagon to a star and took off on an unforgettable ride with a larger than life character. Who would have thought a girl from a west Texas farm town could have such a story to share?

After living in Denver for another fifteen plus years after Michael's death, I've recently moved to the San Juan Islands in Washington. It is so very beautiful, and I am closer to family.

I experienced some difficult times mentally, but there have been more good times than bad. I'm on steady footing now, and I count my blessings every day, and remember the man who stands out as one of my greatest gifts. It's been a privilege to share his story.

CPSIA information can be obtained
at www.ICGtesting.com
Printed in the USA
FSHW012329270721
83459FS